TRANSFORMERS

THE THERAPISTS OF THE FUTURE

Personal Transformation:
The Way Through

By

JACQUELYN SMALL

DeVorss & Company, Publisher
Box 550 - Marina del Rey - California 90294-0550

Second Printing, 1984

ISBN: 0-87516-529-X

Printed in the United States of America

In Appreciation . . .

of the great world teachers whose inspiration created this synthesis. . . . Hermes, Pythagoras, Solomon, Plato, St. Francis, Sri Aurobindo, Gurdjieff, Hermann Hesse, Carl Jung, Roberto Assagioli, Abraham Maslow, and the unsurpassable Jesus, the Christ.

And, more tangibly, the persons whose hard work and dedication brought this book into concrete form: Brenda Shea, my daughter and business partner, who has earned the title "co-author" for putting as much time and energy into this production as I have. Catherine Lee, Hedda Lark and Betty West, whose creative editing spared all of you the task of reading a scrambled mess!

And of my husband Mark, and Tommy, Brett and Yala, our other children, for their patience and understanding for all those endless hours of preoccupation that kept me away.

Contents

BOOK TWO: THE PRACTICAL WORK OF THE TRANSFORMER

A Dedication

To all of you in the people-helping professions who have shared so deeply with me in the workshops and seminars we've experienced together . . .

This book is an outpouring of the knowledge, experience and endorsement I have gained from my work with each of you. On many levels, you are its author.

A Message

While reflecting on writing this book, I asked my Higher Self to guide me, by telling me whom the book is to reach. I then closed my eyes and waited quietly, and here is the symbolic message I received:

> An expansive blue ocean came into view. And then, as though descending from the sky, a majestic, snow white ship floated down and silently perched on the water. The ship was made of porcelain, brilliantly white, with an indigo blue deck. On its side were written two words: "Mother Ship."
>
> Once the ship landed, it dropped over the side a rope ladder made of hemp, small and unimpressive, but quite sturdy. The ladder had six rungs, barely reaching the surface of the water.
>
> Then I noticed there were people swimming in the ocean, hundreds of them. Most were swimming away from the ship, some playfully, some dreamily, others frantically. There were others further away, hundreds more, it seemed, who were drowned, or drowning. Then, closer in there were several swimming toward the ship, obviously excited about its arrival, and enthusiastically moving in its direction. Three or four had actually grabbed onto the rope ladder and were struggling to pull themselves up by their own weight (since no rungs were underneath the water, which would have made it much easier to climb).
>
> I was puzzled for a minute when I realized there were only six rungs, since I wanted to write about seven levels of consciousness. But as I watched the first swimmer climb the ladder, I realized it took seven steps to get to the top and over the side. At the seventh step the traveller disappeared onto the rich blue deck, as though entering another dimension.

For those of you interested in this particular journey . . . welcome aboard!

Prologue

Some of you don't fit in too well with your usual groups anymore. And you find you are really interested in only one thing: your own journey into personal transformation, and sharing this journey with others.... not because you know where it will take you, but simply because that's all that preoccupies you these days!

And suddenly you are aware of a gnawing dissatisfaction with what you see around you, and you find you are quietly (or not so quietly) seeking a setting where you can express your own meaning and purpose in life... a place or a role through which you can "sound your own note."

People, especially authority figures in your life, just don't understand you anymore. They seem boring to you, and they tend to make judgments that you know are really a complete misunderstanding about what's going on. With a rather quiet desperation, you are searching for "the new," expanding beyond your ordinary reference points, seeking a voice or a written word that resonates. And you cannot rest until you find "it."

Well??? Hello.... You are awakening. And you're not alone after all. You are becoming part of the conscious circle of humanity.

Just before Abraham Maslow's death he wrote that he had discovered there were two types of self-actualizers: non-transcenders and transcenders, "those who were clearly healthy, but with little or no experiences of transcendence, and those in whom transcendent experiencing was important and even crucial." One type of person seemed "practical, realistic, mundane, capable and secular" while the other was motivated more by a unity consciousness and a sense of destiny, having had "illuminations or insights or cognitions which changed their view of the world and of themselves."[1]

In 1975, Robert Ornstein popularized the research on the split-brain experiments which pointed to the two dominant modes of thinking we now call "right-brain/left-brain," the Western scientific analogy of the ancient Chinese Yin/Yang, the feminine and masculine principles that creatively polarize the creative/intuitive and the logical/analytical modes of consciousness.[2]

Five years later, Marilyn Ferguson reported a research study indicating there is a certain group of people who are quietly but powerfully bringing about a social transformation.[3] These people have no titles, no organizations, no outstanding identity, but instead they are held together by a unity consciousness and a common vision. They recognize each other and need no words to communicate their coherent understanding of "The New Paradigm" that is, among other things, synthesizing the left brain and the right, the science of the West with the perennial wisdom of the East.

They merge within themselves, through the process of personal transformation, the practical and the mystical view of reality, transcending the dichotomy between these alleged opposites. They see value in *all* of life's experiences, and are more concerned with process and patterns than with content and specific events. She calls them "conspirators."

While studying with Fritjof Capra, outstanding physicist and author of two acclaimed books,[4] I became convinced that we are indeed undergoing the most dramatic paradigm shift in consciousness that we've experienced on this planet for ages. In Jean Houston's terms: "It is so far-reaching in its implications that one might call it evolution consciously entering into time, the evolutionary potential asserting itself. It needed a certain critical mass, a certain merging of complexity, crisis, and consciousness to awaken. Now it is happening."[5]

This paradigm shift will affect our work in the health/mental health field in every possible way. The conditions of health, rather than the symptoms of disease, will be stressed; and process, pattern, vision, symbolism, paradox, and flow will replace the outworn emphasis upon specific events, outward form, and modification of the parts. Wholistic healing, intuition, warmth, love, and a focus on spirit will replace diagnostics, labeling, testing and prescribing.

In the words of an American doctor observing a Tibetan physician while visiting an American hospital: "I know that I, who have palpated a hundred thousand pulses, have not truly felt a single one."[6]

Only Transformers can bring about the manifestation of this new vision in health care, for they carry the consciousness that gently, but confidently invites others to risk being themselves. Transformers have undergone the personal transformation that must be experienced to be understood. Reformers cannot do this work: they are holding their own selves away from the journey into Self that teaches one the new paradigm; consequently, all they can do is judge it from the outside, offering criticisms that are based on an outmoded mechanistic model of reality. Don't expect a reformer to understand; they cannot get hold of it intellectually. *"It" can only be experienced.*

Just to outline for you in more detail some of the differences we will be seeing as the new paradigm comes in, here are some points of reference:

"Non-invasive intervention techniques, such as diet, psychotechnologies, meditation/contemplation, Self study, communing with nature, and exercise, will replace the current over-emphasis on drugs and surgery." The "body as machine" will become "the body as a dynamic energy system flowing in relationship within larger patterns." The professional as authority will become the professional as therapeutic partner. Mind will become the primary or coequal factor in *all* illness. Primary reliance on quantitative diagnostics, tests and charts taken by the physician will be replaced by qualitative information such as the patient's own subjective experience, the physician's intuition, etc. And most important of all, the body/mind continuum will replace focus on the disease of fragmented "parts" of the person experiencing ill health.

Fritjof Capra is being described as the scientist at the "top of the pyramid" in his ability to communicate the current scientific revolution. He views the paradigm shift as a merging of East and West, a rise in the feminine principle (after 2000 years of a patriarchial society), the end of the fossil fuel age, and a move away from the mechanistic world view of Descartes and Newton to "a globally interconnected world in which biological, psychological, social and environmental phenomena are all interdependent."

Capra feels that the current major crises in our country are all facets of the same problem: being stuck in the materialistic world view begun by the once relevant but now outgrown Cartesian-Newtonian assumptions, seeing what is considered "normal" from this old paradigm-bound viewpoint that no longer explains reality. Our emerging, scientifically-explored "reality" has not only outgrown this viewpoint, it is completely inconsistent with it! When relativistic/quantum physics began studying the basis of life in the subatomic structures, scientists discovered what the ancients have always known:

that matter, indeed, *all form simply does not exist as anything solid:* Life is relationship, fluctuation and dynamic flow.

Consciousness (denied by the Cartesian-Newtonian physics) may be the connector in life's events that creates "real-ness." We are paradoxical creatures, not just biological machines, but also unlimited fields of consciousness.

The mechanistic world view cannot make us healthy because it misses the point of who we are: conscious beings passing through an evolutionary process, creative and fluctuating in nature, and able to transcend to new levels anytime we fall into entropy—never victims of our past, but instead, capable of being in the past, present and future all at once, in charge of our own destiny. If we continue to focus on "the objects" in our lives as "truth" (events, labels, other people, problems, and mind-sets we adhere to are all examples of this), we will miss the point entirely.

For us this means moving from such ordered, analytical therapies to the more intuitive and synthesizing ones, drawing more on the feminine principle that is receptive, creative, expansive and spontaneous. Movement, music, integrative bodywork, meditation/yoga, prayer, the mystical traditions, Taoism, Gestalt therapy, Sufism, Christian mysticism, the Gurdjieff system, Psychosynthesis and all of the transpersonal therapies fit with the new.

Approaches that label and diagnose from the viewpoint of "the professional," behavior modification, and Freudian analysis are fading away. The truth of the client is to be drawn from the client's own inner self, with guidance if needed. Therapists become guides and must be able to *tolerate* where their clients are, which can only happen if the therapist has worked through these places in himself or herself. Counselor training in the new age will focus on "work-on-oneself" to elevate level of Being, as opposed to memorizing and practicing labeling systems and techniques, which elevate knowledge level only.

Those of you who carry the Transformer consciousness need to remember: You are standing right at the entrance of the new era—and you are its Seedbearer. You who see the vision as it unfolds, and accept the challenge, are the catalysts ushering in this dramatic shift where science and mysticism are coming together in the form of synthesis. The once and future psychology is emerging.

As the old analytical and building-block model of reality shudders and resists its inevitable demise, you who are Transformers will often be the target of disdain. But that's okay. It has always, throughout history, been the case. We are in a time of "abnormal science," meaning the majority are still clinging to a scientific view that does not explain reality. It is natural that your new efforts will be mistrusted. So hold the larger picture in your mind and stay focused on what your part of the plan is.... and stay in touch with us. You will discover that you are in the process of your own re-birth and re-membrance of what it all means, and you will feel exhilarated by this awareness. But it might get painful: anything within you that cannot be contained within the light of the new *must* be transformed. And I promise you, it will! Since personal transformation interacts with institutional transformation, it follows that some of us must undergo this dramatic "shake up" of our consciousness in order to seed the larger shift.

Be content and do not resist your personal challenges. The Spirit will guide you, for it's all in the flow, and your time has come.

Introduction

Ever since the 17th Century philosophers Descartes and Newton infiltrated our thinking, Western civilization has operated under a false notion that there is a material world that exists independent and apart from human consciousness, and that the human mind can know this material world "objectively" and can therefore control it. Humanity *against* Nature, rather than humanity participating in harmony with its nature, has been the result. And this mechanistic, deterministic world view based on Cartesian-Newtonian physics pervades every aspect of our lives today.... an attitude we've learned to label "the American Way"—technology and materialism.

Our technological advances over the past 300 years have brought such dramatic improvements in our outer world that we have tended to accept this materialistic, concrete model of reality as the only reality, completely forgetting sometimes that it is our inner experience of our world that truly determines how we feel and act most of the time. Our psychological states and spiritual yearnings are much closer to the "truth" about us than the comforts and discomforts of the furnishings with which we surround ourselves.

In the words of physicist/photographer Jane English, "Over the past 300 years changes in consciousness have lagged far behind the theoretical and technical changes. For example, we are using the powerful tools of atomic physics with a consciousness rooted in Newtonian physics.... Great effort was made to remove the 'contamination' of subjective experience from scientific work. Scientists lost touch with the mystical aspect of their work and instead came to value the ability to predict and control the material world. Analytical and separative thinking is ideal for this pursuit and has deeply affected how most of us see reality, people as well as things."[7]

The material world does indeed exist. But it is just one-half of reality.... the *created* side. It is the part that has manifested in a concrete, physical form. The more subtle realms of reality, however, where our psyche resides, is the spirit of humankind.... our essence.... and much more the "determiners" of our experience than the external conditions studied by science.

The two functions of our spiritual nature, *the power to create* and *the power to experience meaning* are what provide us with a reason to live. This is our human consciousness which can be defined as "the bestower of meaning and light upon the darkness of the material and psychic worlds."[8]

As we learn more and more about the basis of life from the "new paradigm" emerging from the marriage of science and spirituality, we are re-discovering that healing is not something bestowed upon us "from without." It originates from deep within the psyche, gradually pushing its positive, life-giving energies toward the surface of our lives to manifest in our outer appearance as a final result.

Materialism is not an untruth, but a half-truth.... unfortunately permeating all areas of life in the United States, even our scientific efforts, almost to the exclusion of the deeper side of truth we actually experience; i.e., human qualities such as love, courage, hope, wisdom, beauty, and a yearning to merge with something greater than ourselves—self-transcendence. And these intrinsic qualities, according to Abraham Maslow[9] turn out to be *the most species-like* for the human being. No other portion of the life chain carries these traits, neither the minerals, the plants, nor the animals.

We can, therefore, conclude that science has not been able to study the *core* of human nature.... the characteristics that literally make us human! Why? Because scientific methodology cannot harness these qualities in an experimental laboratory. By its own definition, science must stick to what it can observe through the senses: i.e., see, smell, taste, touch and feel.

Psychology, which has fought long and hard to become a science, with its emphasis on defining the Self materialistically, has also missed the point. Viewing the Self as merely a personality (persona: mask) seeking constant ego gratification, is failing to provide answers to the deeper questions we have about the meaning and purpose of our lives. When these deeper questions continue to go unanswered, we get scared and sicken, and often an addiction will become the method of relief.

For this reason, the study of human consciousness and the process of addiction are intrinsically related. The anxieties and sometimes *terrors* of experiencing the expansion of our consciousness to include more and more of the unknown will nearly always take us into addictions that block our awareness and temporarily provide a pseudo "ease" as the old gives way to ever-increasing newness. This is, simply put, the human predicament, something we all must face if we are to grow.

A redefinition of Self is currently being explored by theories at "the growing edge" of the human sciences—theories that go beyond personality (the home of the ego) into the essence of the individual. The study of Essence has been relatively ignored by science because our Essence is our *Soul.* And the Soul belongs only to the realm of the softer, unprovable stuff of religion and metaphysics, a scientist would say.

This Essence that is being so underplayed, however, turns out to be the authentic *unifying center* behind our personality. It is the knowing Self, residing in a realm beyond concrete reality, which bases its choices on the *essentials* about us.... our unique mission and purpose in life. Essence is the seat of our vision, our hope, creativity, intuition, spiritual yearnings and purpose, love, wisdom, and all the other qualities that really give our lives meaning.

Essence puts us in touch with the true powers of being human. All the human virtues lie within the realm of this amazing superconscious energy field, a place where all of humanity merges. Learning to elicit a response from this incredible knowing Self is vital in letting go of self-defeating, mechanical addictions and meaningless habits that occur on the personality level in our daily lives. Understanding Essence puts us in touch with our power. *Experiencing* Essence obviates addiction.

This book is about the process of Self-creation that is the inner work we do on ourselves that teaches us the crucial difference between personality and Essence. This process leads us, step by step, to a realization of our Higher Self. Our temporal, fragmented little ego "selves with many faces" that function as our personality—the image we show the world—fade in importance as we come to understand them. And gradually, we become Essence-dominated—more unified, more constant in the midst of all our varied experiences. But even though Essence is sitting there awaiting our notice, we have the responsibility of creating a realization of it. It won't happen automatically: we must commit to the work of manifesting Essence, for it is our very *being.*

In all fairness, we must credit Western psychology for its expertise in studying the mechanical self, the personality, our masks that behave like predictable "rolebots".... the deficient self. But psychology has lacked knowledge and understanding about Essence, the Self that is our blueprint, awaiting its creation in the here-and-now world of experience.

It is paradoxical to note that Western psychology as a group lacks interest in the psyche (Soul), the very unit of analysis they have professed to study by their own definition! They focus instead on the *vehicle* of the psyche, the outer covering, our personality.

Sri Aurobindo has perhaps said it most eloquently:

> "I find it difficult to take these Western (psychologists) at all seriously.... yet perhaps one ought to, for half-knowledge is a powerful thing and can be a great obstacle to the Truth.... They look from down up and explain the higher lights by the lower obscurities; but the foundation of these things is above and not below.... The significance of the lotus is not to be found by analyzing the secrets of the mud from which it grows; its secret is to be found in the heavenly archetype of the lotus that blooms forever in the Light above."[10]

We are so ingrained with this philosophy of density, we will have to undergo a radical change in consciousness before we can break through this veil of partial truths. Until we can comprehend this difference between personality and Essence (the Soul), we cannot begin to know the Self.

This book offers to you this expanded version of the addiction process and the road one travels during recovery, and on to *discovery* of the True Self that needs no addictions.... beyond materialism into an understanding of the process of Self-creation. It is written for you who are seeking a deeper understanding of the human process than you've been able to find in the education and treatment areas existing in our current programs.

The philosophy underpinning this work is based on the assumption that *controlling* one's addiction is only a beginning. Once we enter into the exploration of Essence, we find that an addiction can be *transformed,* and its host can proceed toward never-before-dreamed-of natural highs!

A further assumption is that each of us is evolving according to a unique plan, with everything that happens to us in life having a useful purpose, even our addictions! We travel in *two* worlds, not one.... the outer, materialized world, and an inner, invisible one; and we must understand *both* before any of the journey begins to make sense. Without an understanding of the inner world, our outer experiences can appear meaningless and unconnected.

Another important assumption underlying this work is that humanity is now entering a new stage of evolution where the task is to shift the focus of consciousness from the outer world to the inner one.... from the material life to a more spiritual, purposeful existence. Work in addiction comes to the forefront in this monumental shift, because chemical addiction is an obvious, exaggerated case of outer focus, of attaching one's personality.... for its very life.... to something residing outside the Self — often in a bottle.

As we begin to work with these two worlds, the outer and the inner, the first thing we discover is the Self stands somewhere between the visible and the invisible realities, relating to one through the senses and to the other through inner states of being. "I" stands in the middle, attempting to align these two worlds with each other so it can feel comfort.

We are learning, often quite painfully, that the outer life does not satisfy the inner longings. And this pain, quite naturally, is a seedbed for chemical addiction.* This very dissatisfaction becomes the motivating force behind this inward shift of consciousness. And as we enter more into the inner worlds, we discover that the next step in our evolutionary process contains a very large and exciting truth: *OUR INNER STATE OF MIND DETERMINES OUR OUTER LIFE, NOT THE OTHER WAY AROUND!* Switching our focus from the Outer Life of Experience to the Inner World of Wisdom is the transformation process known as Self-creation.

The work of Self-creation frees us from the bondage of addiction. Self-creation is our inherent birthright. The human organism naturally strives toward growth, just as a flower reaches for the sun. Surely, we all realize that we get off the mark easily, for the journey is fraught with pitfalls. But even though our Essence can become buried under myriad false selves — roles, habits, unexamined belief systems —*it refuses to be denied!* And it will continue its not-so-gentle nudging until we attend to its urgings.

What is needed at this stage in our evolution — what is crucial — are persons who naturally carry transformation energy to take the

*Over 57,000,000 prescriptions for valium were dispensed in 1977 alone!

lead in the health-related fields. *Transformers,* not reformers, so beautifully described by Alexis on page 12. Counselors bent on changing, remolding and scolding are not able to endorse a client's delicate inner nature striving to emerge; they only increase the energy in self-hatred or in developing more and more of the mask, the outer personality that later must be transcended.

A Transformer is a catalyst for one's natural unfolding, i.e., Self-creation, the acceptance of what *IS,* and the ability to lift this *IS*ness to its highest possible level. Self-creation is spawned from a base of self-love and conscious awareness. Transformers know this and do not deny any portion of our humanness as we seek the expression of our genuine Selfhood.

Transformers do not work merely from logic, which is our outer-world mode of thinking our way through linear time, but mainly from a higher intellect called the intuition — a type of knowing that comprehends *whole* truths rather than fragments of truth. Intuitive knowledge is a combination of logic and inner knowing based on experience, a synthesis of the left brain and the right.[11]

Transformers know that there is nothing new under the sun, that all truth must be *re*discovered individually, as the quest that gives each of our lives meaning. They know that we don't *have* to evolve, but if we choose growth, no one can do it for us! We are self-evolving organisms. Consequently, Transformers are not so concerned with the outer self; they focus on the inner.

Somewhere I heard that Truth can never really be taught, but It *can be caught!* This fits with my experience as a trainer/teacher. When one is ready to hear something, it is as though a match has been thrown into a pile of dry wood, bursting forth upon contact. The very same truth might have been given out the day before, but it simply passed on by unnoticed.

It is the inner nature, the Essence, that catches Truth, based on a reminder of previous experiences that have now become a part of our very being. The outer self (personality), tied to the external world, only memorizes facts based on data from the Outer World of Experience which turn out to be fragments that often add up to nothing significant, or worse, an erroneous interpretation of a portion of life.

In the West, we have emphasized reformer consciousness, striving to master the outer world. Consequently, we know a lot about personality and its director, the ego.

In this book, this personality self that connects with the outer world is called the Lower Self and is depicted as a triangle pointing downward (an upside-down pyramid).

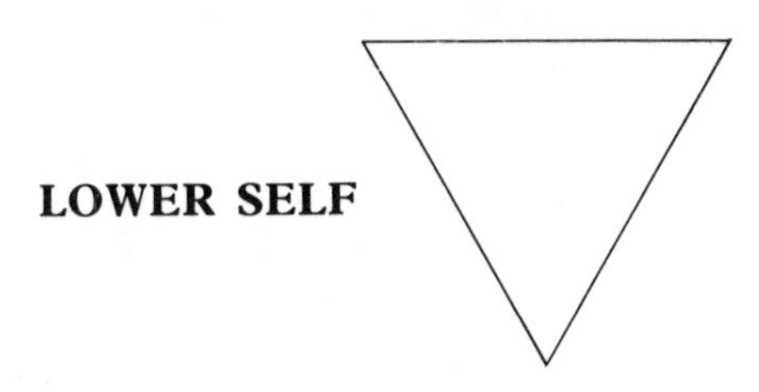

In the East, emphasis has always been on the advancement of the Soul of man, the inner Self, which draws its knowledge from the Inner World of Wisdom based on data received subjectively from within. The Self is viewed as Reality and the outer world as Maya (illusion). Maya is only the setting we create with our mind from whence the Self enacts Its predicaments designed to teach It life's lessons. In this book, a triangle pointing upward (a pyramid) represents the home of the Higher Self.

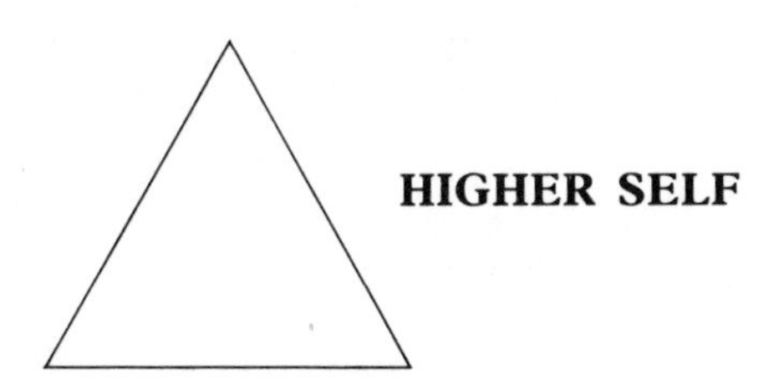

The West is dominated by the left brain, the East by the right. And we will learn that *one without the other is never sufficient.* The Lower Self, without the aid of the Higher Self, becomes too identified with the mundane nitty-gritty in life — its predicaments become its reality, and it gets stuck with its feet in the mud.

The Higher Self without the use of the Lower Self, however, is just as unproductive. It is like a puff of wind with nowhere to land. It is formless and meaningless, for it cannot express itself without its concrete form, the Lower Self.

★ ★ ★ ★

I cannot say how this book will aid you in your work with clients, or in your own life. As Transformers, *you* will determine its usefulness. I offer it to you as a part of myself and invite you to participate in its reading on whatever level feels right for you. I honor your ability to recognize Truth when it is offered.... and to weed out the parts that don't compute. Trust your intuition, for it is your Higher Self! It is the voice of your Soul!

Transformers: The Therapists of the Future offers a glimpse of the therapeutic attitude for the coming age. Transformers are the artists of Self-creation, the guides for the process of personal evolution. In the addictions field, they serve as the pathfinders for the journey beyond abstinence. Working from a new paradigm of human nature that sees value in *all* of our experiences, these loving, diligent "conspirators" are spreading the seeds of transformation *in every major cultural system throughout the world....* each and every one single-mindedly dedicated to the evolutionary purpose of ushering in the New Age.[12]

A Story that Happened in the Mind

When it became time for Abraham Maslow to receive his doctoral diploma, he discovered that he felt extremely ridiculous standing in an academic procession in an awkward-looking cap and gown. But as he stood there, he suddenly became aware he was perceiving himself differently — as a symbol of "The Student" existing in eternity rather than a bored, irritated individual in a specific place at a specific time. He envisioned the eternal academic procession, stretching forward endlessly toward the future, from 'way back into the past, with Socrates at its head.... that many scholars and students had come before him, and many would follow. In his mind he became the successor to all the ones who had come before in the world of the intellect. He thrilled at being in such a procession, feeling connected to such a dignified and meaningful procedure. He was no longer an individual, but instead he had become the Platonic Essence of "The Teacher".... transformed! He began to feel personal and affectionate toward the world's greatest minds — Spinoza, William James, Plato, and others. Personally he was now connected with these energies, as if they still were alive as ever.[13]

Transcending the limitations of our little personal ego leads to transformation! And it happens in the mind.

BOOK ONE

THE WORLD VIEW OF THE TRANSFORMER

We bring so much energy and enthusiasm to everything we do. But it is our own energy, our own enthusiasm, of which the supply is limited. Why not, instead, draw upon universal energy, which is limitless, allowing it to flow through us, while we remain the channels, the transformers, for this energy? Let us allow this energy to transform us as it flows through us, and through us to transform our world. Why not become transformers of mankind, rather than self-depleting reformers who criticize and seek to correct? A transformer creates the new through that which already is, a reformer seeks to destroy that which is in hopes that something better will take its place. The reformer's work is ceaseless, never ending, never satisfied. The work of the transformer is always complete and perfect within itself; it is always at peace as the energy streams through it out into the world to heal, transform, energize and uplift. Allow yourself to be the transformer — which you truly are.[14]

—Alexis Edwards

Transformers: The Artists of Self-Creation

The distinguishing characteristic of Transformers, the therapists of the future, is their de-emphasis of Personality, demoting it to the role of a mere instrument for the more important, synthesizing aspect of our nature we call Essence, or the True Self. These therapists are the alchemists of addiction, possessing an intuitive understanding of how to transmute the energy constricted in a negative habit pattern into its true nature, a pure, refined quality of the Soul.... literally "changing lead into gold."

Therapists of the past have stressed development and modification of Personality extensively and exclusively, thereby dwelling on the negative patterns of the Lower Self, with little or no knowledge of the Higher Self and its function in relation to human personality. Many of them even deny the existence of this deeper, less definable Essence their research instruments could not discern. Personality was considered to be "human nature" in its totality. And until the humanistic period of the '50's and '60's, human nature was considered basically naughty or downright evil. Consequently, many of our therapists are reformers, attempting to correct or remake a bad person.

Today, as our knowledge and consciousness expand, we are moving beyond Personality, beyond "the mask," and beginning to focus more on our deepest, most unified nature.... a core Self we experience as "I" that remains constant in the midst of all our varied experiences.... that part of us which is never fooled. This Self doesn't even balk at death, recognizing that it too, is just another experience.

Transformers, working from the highest levels of consciousness, will teach us to be less identified with the Personality, our little, temporal, fragmented "selves with many faces," and more centered in the awareness of this Essence, or Soul, moving from ego-dominance to Essence-dominance. In the future, with the aid of Transformers, we will search out ways to recognize our Soul's purpose, which will flood our life with meaning. We will find a language with which to describe the Soul. And eventually, we will operationally define the Soul. We will learn the techniques for aligning our "instrument," the Personality, with our Soul's purpose so that we no longer experience an uncomfortable split between who we are and what we are doing.... that familiar feeling of being "off the mark." This work of alignment is the process of Self-creation.

It is a misunderstanding to say that Personality is unimportant, however. To read this into what is being written would be to miss the point entirely. It is, after all, through the development of a strong ego that we grow into our fullness as human beings, and it is the vehicle of the Personality through which our essential wholeness takes form. Personality is our unique expression in the world.... an individuation of Spirit in action. We are, indeed, a fascinating, mind-boggling invention!

Personality, as we have seen, is an instrument, a machine, if you will, consisting of three distinct "bodies" or realities:

1) A physical form that naturally moves and acts on instinct and on orders from our mind. This physical form has its own set of laws that govern it. For instance, it lives in time and space. And also, it has to be acted *upon;* it is not capable of thinking. (Remove my foot, and it will not walk off!) Even our human brains, which we tend to confuse with "mind," cannot manufacture thought without the use of an inspirited body. We can assume, then, that our bodies are not the Cause of us, for they must be acted upon in order to function. And anything that must be acted upon is an *effect,* caused by something else. This "something else" the Transformer studies is Essence, the center of our being.

2) An emotional "body," operating from laws similar to hydrodynamics. If our emotions become blocked, we are like a river whose flow is dammed up, building up untold pressure until some release occurs; or we go dead inside and stagnate, diseased and toxic to ourselves and others. Transformers know that pent-up emotions are to be released and understood so that this constricted energy can be expressed for the purpose of manifesting our authenticity in the world.

3) A mental life, our unique world of personal thoughts, that is creative by nature and has no limits except those it chooses to construct for itself. Since we exist within a Universal Mind that is all-

knowing and limitless, we can know that limitation is not a universal law but only exists in the individual use we make of these universal laws.

So we can conclude that Personality exists in time and space, it senses and feels, and it thinks — creatively or destructively, whichever the case may be, for it has free will *within* the laws of nature that govern it. It is grounded in the material world and at the very same time can also transcend itself and expand outward — back into the past, ahead into the future — wherever it chooses to go — through the use of its mental processes. Amazing! Certainly we must value it immensely, and learn to care for it intricately.

But Personality is NOT who we are. It is something we HAVE.

And this distinction, Transformers believe, is the key to our evolution!

> I *have* a body, but I am not my body. I *have* emotions, but I am not my emotions. And I *have* thoughts, but I am not my thoughts. I am something much larger and grander than all of these. I am the master of the vehicle. I am pure Essence which has taken a form in order to experience a life in time and space. I am Spirit, both visible and invisible, with individuality, unique meaning and a special purpose.[15]

The purpose of our life is to dis-identify from out false selves and to remember our true nature. As we learn to express our Self authentically in the world, we fulfill our part in the grand scheme of things. Unless I am my True Self, manifesting Truth through me, I really do not exist. Therefore, I am here to shed — oftentimes painfully — the many "not selves" I have created in forming my personality, discovering as I go along which "parts" belong to me and which do not.

When I get stuck and think I *am* my body, my emotions or my ideas, I am consumed with ego, seeking to arrogate unto itself through one of its sub-vehicles all the power of my being. And my ego can take me into some very illusory places. But I must also remember that this little ego has formed over a long period of time and has built up a tremendous amount of energy. I cannot stomp it out, viciously attacking it, because a wounded ego is exceedingly dangerous and only builds itself a stronger fort from whence to get its now multiplied needs met. So I must learn to respect its power, working through its energy, but gradually withdrawing its authority until it learns to be submissive to a more integrated me, my True Self. In other words, I do not wish to kill my ego; I want to tame it and allow it to become a dutiful servant to the master self, my Soul.

Therapists of the new age are learning to understand this process of becoming Essence-dominated. And they are doing it by choosing to become conscious themselves.

In order to become conscious beings, we must die to the dominance of our ego. Christianity and other major religions recognize this truth. Alcoholics Anonymous understands. And so do the more integrated therapies and philosophies that have taken a long look at human nature. We are talking about the process of surrender. "Lose your life so you may find it." "I have to let go and let God." "I am ready to serve only one Master." "I had to die in order to become reborn." All of these are speaking to this process.

Becoming centered in Essence is not merely becoming a better self; it is becoming a *different* self. The Lower Self has to quit guiding us before the Higher Self can get through. Turning our lives over to this Higher Self is not giving away our power. Quite the reverse is true: It is reclaiming our power, co-creating with the Power that creates *all* life, the energy behind creation.... opting for choices based on Truth and Goodness.

The Transformer realizes that the process of addiction to anything outside ourselves is *ego attachment*. It is thinking that we cannot live without this object (including people), and believing our ultimate security resides in adding this "thing" unto ourself. But this is false, of course. And so addiction never works. It only takes us off track, looking in the wrong direction for something that can only come from within.

Addiction *can* serve as our teacher, however. And Transformers realize this as well: Our addictions can lead us to a Truth by allowing us to experience enough pain and disillusionment to get the point. Transformers, for this reason, do not attempt to remove pain from clients too readily. For one thing, they know they can't anyway: the client will suffer until he decides to seek another way. The Transformer is never an enabler. Having suffered enough himself, he knows the nature of suffering — its secrets and its power. He relieves *unnecessary* suffering, when possible, but knows intuitively when someone needs his experience, negative and self-defeating as it may be.

The energy we have invested in building a strong ego becomes constricted energy as we grow and evolve toward a relaxed perspective. Like an old garment, too small and worn out to feel good anymore, the ego needs begin to feel like imprisonment. As our awareness increases, we realize the ego is designed now for another purpose — to actually begin the process of destroying itself for a higher calling. Like the tough acorn that has built itself protectively around the little seed of the oak, ego lets go and becomes absorbed in the act of being Essence Realized — the True Self. The protective covering has burst open and expanded beyond all recognition when this Self-transformation process occurs. Reformers cannot do the work of transformation: They try to make us into better and better acorns! Reformers work with what is *not* and usually do not recognize what *is*. They adopt the image of some external ideal and attempt to mold, reshape or tear us down, trying to make us into something "other." Sometimes there may be a place for reforming, but it should never become *the governing principle* for the whole process. Growth occurs by becoming more and more of who we *are,* not by trying to be someone we are *not,* as the Law of Transcendence will teach us further along in this book.

Transformers work with what *is* about us, not what "ought to be" by someone else's standards. And by their positive acceptance of us — their total endorsement of our being — they serve as catalysts for lifting us to our highest, most integrated level. They work from above, downward — from the perspective of perfection, they weed out the *im*perfection, focusing on clearing the way for more and more of the authentic masterpiece to shine through.

Transformers look right through you, with a gentle humor, and ask disconcerting questions before which facades and falsehoods crumble.... questions like "Who are you?" "What are you doing here?" "Where did you come from?" and "Where are you going?" They love you freely, but are not attached to your current melodrama. And above all, there is a fire, or magnetism that emanates from them that gives off a solid sense of their spiritual certainty.

When you are in the presence of a Transformer, you sense that he is who we all can be: rooted in the never-changing, guiding himself from direct perception of Truth rather than others' dogma, fearing nothing and evading no responsibility he considers rightfully his.

He is tangible proof of the intangible operating in and on the world. He gives us a perspective that adds dignity to our human strivings.

Transformers are with us now. They are growing in number, like a quiet conspiracy steadily working toward humanity's reawakening. We have been hypnotized too long.... losing touch with ourselves, getting caught up in the journey, as though the journey is who we are. Transformers are here to re-mind us of our Essence.... the Self we were intended to be before we lost our way.

The Mind As Creator

"What I see without is a reflection of what I have first seen within my own mind. I always project into the world the thoughts, feelings and attitudes which preoccupy me. I can see the world differently by changing my mind about what I want to see."[16]

— GERALD JAMPOLSKY

We live in a world that is infinitely responsive to what we make it. Without our input, the world is neutral, meaningless.... a blank canvas. You and I paint the canvas according to the image in our mind, colored by our feelings. *We* give it its meaning. This is why two people can have exactly the same experience and respond to it so differently. We are creators! And creators *act*. We are *not* robots, who can only *react*. Unless, of course, we are operating in the world like sleepwalkers, in which case we will be robots, and we will not be creative.

As you will see later, all unconscious actions turn out to be robot-like reactions to life, perfectly predictable, following our program by rote.

Addictions are predictable.... mechanistic, unconscious acts, programmed from habit, founded on a stress reaction that happened in the past. At some point in our development, an inner "alarm" went off, warning us that something could not be handled. And in response, we turned to something predictable.... a bottle of alcohol or a prescription for Valium, to give us our solution. Now perhaps several years later, we've forgotten what the original danger was; we are simply unconsciously following our habit like a basset hound follows his nose.

But creators are artists. And artists create originals! When I am creating, my canvas will respond accurately to whatever I choose to put on it. And I can constantly continue to choose, moment by moment, what I want to put into my world. If I opt for a negative experience, I *descend* into a universe that says "Okay, a negative experience it will be." And instantly, the negative forces surrounding this particular event become my reality. My consciousness, for this moment in time, is residing in a world that I created, where all negativity about this particular subject hangs out! Until I choose to shift out of this "place," this negativity builds upon itself, attracting more just like it, and I can become overwhelmed. If I opt for a positive experience, I *ascend* into another universe that immediately cooperates, and instantly, forces begin moving to manifest a positive result. And as the positive gains momentum, I find myself feeling wonderful, delighted by the beautiful world about me.

On a more abstract level, this same principle holds: Choosing to know myself or not is also a choice that I have. The work of Self-knowledge is a very high work: Socrates saw it as the three most important words in the human language: *Man, know thyself.* If I choose not to know myself, perceiving my life as meaningless and turning my back on the search for Truth, I begin to die. *My Self does not evolve.* The universe will immediately cooperate and help me die. Everything I experience will indeed lack meaning — become death-like. On the other hand, if I choose to know myself and am willing to struggle to find this very special kind of knowledge, I am given more help than I could have dreamed possible. Self-knowledge is suddenly everywhere I look! And my world becomes transformed. I find that I have stumbled onto the path that leads to enlightenment. My teachers appear to guide me, and I feel exhilarated and compelled to follow!

When we choose this path of Self-knowledge, we begin to discover we are in an inner state of harmony where our actions begin corresponding to a deeper truth within us. It is as though everything flows naturally and easily. Even what had seemed "impossible" before fades into non-existence and a new possibility takes its place. And we know we are on The Path.... our path.

When the inner state is disharmonious, we emit a certain vibration which automatically reverberates in our outer world, connecting up with other vibrations of the same type. This produces a general jamming, which disturbs everything in the outer life, making it all seem wrong. We know we are off our path. Or, we could be resisting something we need to grow through that is on our path and painful to look at.

There is a rigorous correlation between our inner state of being and our outer circumstances. It is through Self-knowledge that we realize our life does not unwind from the outside inward, as we had always thought, but from the inside outward. When we make this transition in our thinking, our world becomes a miracle! For the first time we *feel* what it is to create.... even if only for a moment.... and this is exhilarating to the Self.

This transformation is *the first step in the act of Self-creation,* and it begins with powerful thoughts.... ideas that are bigger than we are.... seed thoughts that become planted in our consciousness, take root and grow, drawing to themselves everything they require to be sustained. They move us on past the little self we were before. A SEED THOUGHT IS AN IDEA WHOSE TIME HAS COME THAT TAKES HOLD AND CHANGES OUR REALITY.

When we opt for the choice of knowing ourselves, we become an individual. We leave the masses who are choosing non-growth for the sake of safety. And we will be condemned by many. It takes a great deal of courage to become a Self. Most people are content to be one of the "99 who did not go astray!" If we choose to leave the crowd, we will find ourselves beyond the clear-cut bounds of society, where all the laws are man-made, created for "the sheep." When we start thinking for ourselves, developing an individuality, we become lonely, for we don't fit in anymore. We have no choice but to move into the "wilderness," the vastness beyond the boundaries of the masses. Now we know *we* are the creators of our life, not society, not the outer world. Now we must become fearless! Our thinking has changed, and we are different. TRANSFORMATION DOES NOT OCCUR FROM CHANGES IN THE WORLD OUTSIDE US; *WE* CREATE THE MIRACLE.... FROM WITHIN!

Even so noble an act as turning our lives over to a Higher Power will be a meaningless gesture unless we connect this dynamic energy force to something *within ourselves.* "I surrender" is an inner act of letting go, a *willed action* of getting out of the way so that Truth can come in. The "me" who surrenders is a little ego-dominated me who thought she had to run the show. Now the "I" who manifests my God-nature in the world, my True Self, can take over. She follows the dictates of the Higher Self, who receives its power directly from The Higher Power, the Source where all Truth resides.

For a clearer understanding of the process, see the diagram on the following page.

As my True Self emerges and takes charge, I discover this is my Essence — the one I lost touch with during my process of ego development. I realize that I no longer have to be caught in the web of mechanical addiction because now I have experienced a higher possibility. Using ideas that are bigger than "me," my mind has become the creator that has led me to the Truth of my being. I realize my connection with the Source of all knowledge, the Higher Power. As long as I thought I needed something outside myself to be complete *my world complied with this belief and made addiction my truth.* Now I know better! The Creator is not just outside me, but inside as well! This Energy is a dynamic, transforming power *within me,* not just a remote God-out-there-somewhere —the static picture of belief I'd been taught

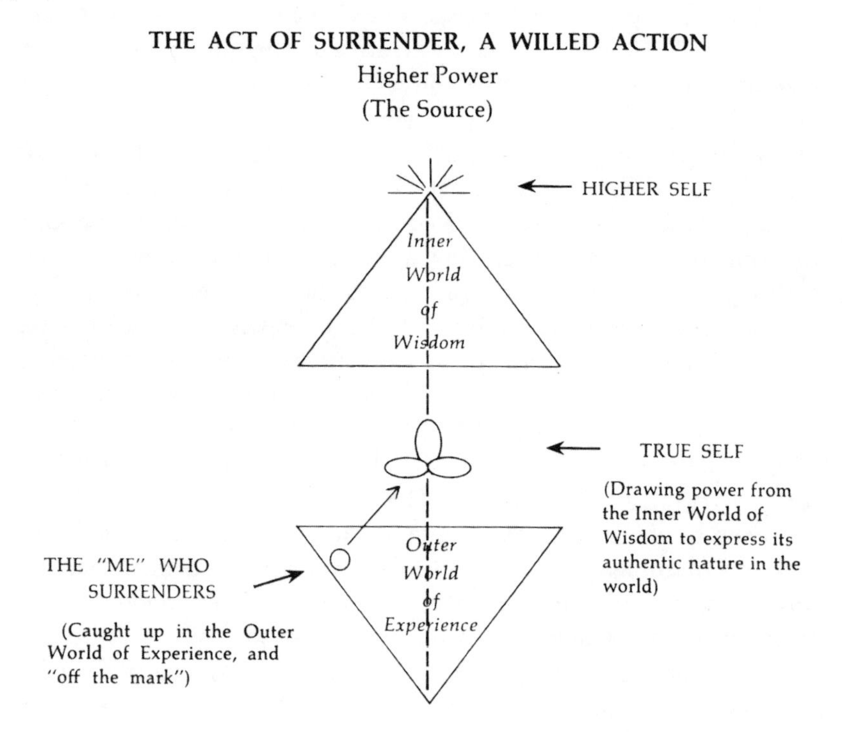

as a child! And in cooperation with this high Energy, I co-create my life. My act of surrender was doing my part. And *when I do my part,* based on the Truth, the Higher Power co-pilots my life!

The Higher Power can reach my True Self. It will not heed the "little me" that was caught up in the crowd of society, for it is *off the mark.* There is no alignment with Truth there. When I have the courage to be my True Self, I can surrender, and then the Divine can take over. Addiction to something outside myself is no longer my truth. My addiction is gone for it has lost its power. I am no longer allowing it to be my god.

As these new seeds of transformation take root in my mind, to say I must *control* an addiction, becomes an irrelevant concept! If I no longer live in a place where the addiction exists, what is to be controlled? Controlling implies pushing something away from me, conquering it, holding on. Controlling connotes a struggle.... incessant exertion! The addiction still has power over me because I am still having to concentrate on it, feeding it energy. I am saying yes, you still matter to me greatly! You are still my master.

When the True Self takes its rightful command, addictions can be let go of, simply dropped and walked away from. We will turn and focus our attention in another direction, on another way of being.... literally moving to another place. The same energy that was used in holding myself away from a powerful addiction is now freed up to be directed to its rightful place: *discovering the nature of the real need the addiction was masking.*

As I begin to Self-create, I realize that something very natural to my being was sitting there all along, awaiting expression, pushing to emerge. This is an important key — that this natural something was there all along — a little spark of my True Self ready to learn about itself through expression in the outer world.... ready to actualize. We are never *adding* new qualities to ourselves if they are part of our True Self; they are merely awaiting their turn to be made real. But because I blocked the emergence of this part of my Self, out of fear, I got stuck in an addiction instead. And then I thought addiction was my *truth!* Can you see how this works? If I *think* it is my truth, it will *become* my truth.

WHEN WE DECIDE TO LET GO OF THE ADDICTION, BY THE ACT OF SURRENDER TO THE HIGHER POWER — AN ACTION WILLED BY THE TRUE SELF — WE DRAW FROM WITHIN OURSELVES THAT QUALITY OF THE TRUE SELF THAT THE ADDICTION WAS MASKING. NOW WE ARE READY TO MANIFEST IT.

What aspect of my Self was trying to emerge when life seemed so painful that I chose an addiction instead of the natural process of becoming? When was that moment? Was I afraid to think? To feel? To *be*? And if so, what? At some point it happened. And I deluded myself into believing that something "out there" could give me what I needed. I turned outward instead of inward.... and lost touch with my Self in the process.

When transformation occurs, the energy vector swings from the outer world (the addiction) to the inner world (the quality in me seeking expression). I discover my addiction was my teacher, designed to show me what was trying to emerge. Maybe I thought I needed pills to calm my nerves. I learn instead that I'm only nervous when I'm not myself, trying to be someone I'm not! As my True Self, I can calm my nerves by becoming centered in realistic thoughts and positive actions, a good diet and healthy coping skills. And the more I practice these positive things, the calmer I get! I have courage! I can handle stress!

Or, as a woman, maybe I thought I needed a man to define me. So I drank to cure my loneliness and sense of rejection. I learn instead that my beautiful feminine True Self was sitting there all along awaiting the chance just to be.

Maybe I thought I had to be defined by society as "important." And so I became addicted to busy-ness to cover my sense of failure. I learn instead that I am inherently important, uniquely designed to do my own thing so perfectly that no one else in the world can do it like me. And "society" does not exist, *except as I define it!* Now I can see the answers are inside myself. And my strength comes from a larger Source, that Higher Power of which I am a valuable, irreplaceable part. And the universe says YES!!! It is so! TRANSFORMATION IS NOT TRYING TO BE ANOTHER WAY, PUSHING FOR THE ANSWER.... IT IS *BEING* THE ANSWER. BE *NOW* WHO YOU WANT TO BE.... EVEN IF "YOU" THINK YOU CAN'T!

This is the secret.... the key so many have missed.

As Yoda said to Luke Skywalker:
"Try, no! We do or we don't do. There is no try."

1

The Principles of Self-Creation

"You must know the whole before you can know the part and the highest before you can truly understand the lowest. That is the promise of the greater psychology awaiting its hour before which these poor gropings will disappear and come to nothing."

— *SRI AUROBINDO*

THE UNIVERSALITY OF TRUTH

We are microcosmic images of a macrocosmic Truth, creative in the same way as our Maker — only to a lesser degree. Therefore, whatever is true of the Whole will be true of each of us, scaled down to our individual level. Every tiny raindrop mirrors perfectly the entire scene that it reflects. Each droplet is a hologram of this immense Universe, and this analogy symbolizes man as well. Everything is following a plan based on the nature of the Creative Force. We do not live in a chaotic Universe. We can count on it! And whether we like it or not, there are laws governing this creation that are affecting us — that, in fact, *determine* our existence. When we abide by these laws, we become their master and they work for us. When we disregard them, we discover (often with great surprise) that our life has become a mess.

The road to Self-creation is the discovery of these laws in action, and the recognition of our ignorance that has caused the suffering we've created in violation of natural law. Our Creator never intended us to suffer. ALL SUFFERING IS A RESULT OF INFRINGEMENT OF UNIVERSAL PRINCIPLES. This idea may be upsetting to some at first glance. But if we will realize that the Universe is *for* us and not against us, *if only we get in tune with it,* we may find this a message of consolation, for it opens up the possibility of hope that there really is a purpose and there really is a plan in everything.

> "There is a reason, there is a rhyme.
> There is a season, there is a time.
> There is a purpose, there is a plan.
> And one day together we'll heal in
> the wisdom and we'll understand."[17]
>
> — *BOBBY BRIDGER*

Nowhere in the process of creation is there a necessity for addiction! We were never intended to become hooked on *anything* but the process of our own creation! *The antidote for addiction is Self-creation.* Nothing else is necessary. Discovering the Self brings with it an understanding of the Laws that create it. And our search for this Universal Truth of who we really are *is* our deepest urge.

Sri Aurobindo once said "Life does not die because it gets worn out; it dies because it has not found itself." Most addicts are keenly aware of this constant inner discomfort.... this search for the elusive "something" they are missing, but never quite find, is the basis for their addictions. They are looking for their life! Few are worn out! Most of them are filled with boundless energy.... so much so, they don't know what to do with it. The addict is going *toward* something, not *away* from it. He is not always motivated by fears from the past; more often, he is searching for his meaning, his purpose.... his definition! And when he finds this, the past, no matter how tumultuous, becomes redefined and diminishes to its proper size.... simply the tests he needed to get where he is.

Transformers work with this *pro*active view of man, rather than a *re*active one.... guiding clients toward their unrealized potential, their proper place in life, not seeking answers from the past so much as discoveries from the "future." They work with the future NOW.

Within this framework of living within the Law, which is immutable, and with Love, which is spontaneous, the Transformer needs only one definition of addiction:

ADDICTION = ATTACHMENT = NON-GROWTH

In this chapter we will discuss the Laws of the Self and the Laws of the process of Self-creation that have evolved from Transformers' direct experience of working with people needing help.

If the therapist will work with these Laws, she will discover that she is, indeed, a guiding light for the dynamic work of Self-creation.

THE LAWS OF THE SELF

We, as human beings, are inherently designed to merge the "angel" and the "fallen angel" within, the primordial conflict that has plagued humankind since the beginning of Time.

It is human nature to crave the experience of fading back into that undifferentiated "empty fullness" of the ineffable Eternal Parent who wraps her cloak of comforting wholeness around us in a state of non-dualistic, infinite Bliss. Paradoxically, it is also our nature to discriminate, to separate off from the masses and enter fully into a process of individuation, seeking our own creative expression. To get beyond duality and avoid feeling pulled apart by these opposing drives, we can learn to be in both "places" at once — unified *and* unique. This skill of "expanded focus" requires a penetrating understanding of the Self and its world.

When we study the meaning of the words "individuate" and "differentiate" we are provided with a clue to the paradox: *To individuate* means to exist as an indivisible whole, to be undivided! *To differentiate* means to divide, to be recognized as different. Some aspects of life serve to unite us, while others divide. And both types of experience seem to be necessary for our advancement.

Transformers, who work with the superconscious mind as well as the subconscious, have found that it is the *Soul* which individuates, concerned with our process of Self-creation, knowing we must each develop "one small measure" of the God expression, yet never losing sight of each one's indivisibleness. And it is the *ego* that differentiates, concerned with building something "special" to be noticed and rewarded by the societal world. Within the concept of individuation resides the reality of an enfolding/unfolding universe — one where events are drawn up from the undifferentiated whole into explicated occurrences. When our ego completes an event, absorbing its lesson and integrating another fragment of itself, the event fades back into the wholeness of life as something now completed and made known. Once a thing has been explicated by any one of us, the next time is easier for someone else.

> "By thy stumblings, the world is perfected."
>
> ...Sri Aurobindo

Transformation of the psyche (individuation) involves the resolution of opposites. Emerging from a womb-like state of undifferentiated potential, we first "fall" into the polarity of being/non-being, and ultimately descend on into our daily existence with duality arranging itself into numerous pairs of opposites that require our eventual and essential resolution — such splits as life/death, good/evil, effective/ineffective, conformist/non-conformist, desire/desirelessness, active/passive, and so on.

Transformers pay homage to a person's journey into Self, for they know that the experience of the human psyche *IS* the Truth that we seek — that Truth does not reside "out there" in bookstores, in gurus, in programs of self-control, or even in spiritual paths. They also know that this experience of the Self can never be known through societal mass-produced dogmas or concepts (even these). Rules for the masses have their place in group living for the unthinking populace, but not in the transformation of the individual psyche, whose integrity is internally consistent with what is good for the whole. Transformers know "from the heart" that we can never mistake formula for wisdom.

In understanding the process of individuation more deeply, two thoughts prevail:

1) *Life is never static.* (Least of all the inner life!) All of us are seekers, consciously or unawakened, forging our way through the densely-populated Unconscious masses of potential experiences, in the process of our eternal "becoming."

2) *To name is not to know; to experience is to know.* Because we are "ever becoming," the Transformer is leary of the "isms" and the "ics" of Western science. We must be willing to sacrifice at any moment our tightly-held beliefs based upon theories that peg and categorize from external world views. In the words of Goethe's *Faust:* "It is wisdom's final say that freedom and life belong to that man who must reconquer them each day." Psychology has substituted labels

for knowing; the Church has substituted faith for knowing. Either discipline can become a societal trap for the journeying Self.

Naming *from within our own process* as indicators of self-discovery *can* be helpful, so long as each label is viewed as not static, but emergent. For example, if my Observer Self (a part of my True Self) notices a pattern of behavior in me, stepping aside and objectifying it can free me from its control. "Oh, that's just my Mafia Mom self needing to over-react just now to feel her power with her children." Or "Southern Belle self just sent a manipulative thought through my brain to see if she could appear helpless and adorable." Getting distance from these "pseudo selves" frees me from their unconscious possession of my mouth, eyes, ears and actions, and I can choose to re-direct the energy. *The quality of each experience, as we explicate it from the mass of humanity's unexpressed potential, becomes the substance of our wisdom.*

Transformers deal constantly with the duality between Western psychology's need to label and pigeonhole the psyche's conditions and the formless flowing of the more Taoistic stance that life is happening in the intervals between the forms (words, concepts). A Transformer's experience with clients and other seekers has taught him or her that the therapeutic process one undergoes to become whole is always just beyond our conceptual grasp. Yet, there are certain axioms about the Self that have emerged from experience that we can utilize as guiding principles. Here are some significant ones:[18]

1) There is an indwelling spiritual component of the Self that is behind our body/mind that is also *an organic part of the human psyche.* This Self (*pneuma*) is experienced as the urge toward our wholeness, and has been left out of Western psychology until now with the advent of the Fourth Force Transpersonal component.

2) This *pneuma* carries on an active dialogue with our personality self, even though we have the free will to tune it out or distort its messages through our active, outer-directed left brain.

3) *Pneuma* has its way of speaking to us and it is through symbols. Its signatures are everywhere in our daily lives, actively participating in our unfoldment through dreams, visions, altered states of consciousness, and synchronistic events (those acausal "coincidences" alive with meaning if we will but stop and take note).

4) These spiritual dispatches reveal deep patterns and conditions that can be traced both forward and backward into Time as pointers to our true spiritual direction, keeping us "on the mark" as we travel through our conditions toward completion of our individualized purpose.

5) Prior to establishing conscious contact with *pneuma,* our lives are dictated by blind habits, beliefs and addictions, often leading to conflict or downright foolhardiness. Unaware of its roots in the Unconscious of humanity's collective history, the unaware self blindly sets out to re-create a semblance of its wholeness through unconscious, egoistic projections and falls into the familiar trap of thinking it alone is determining its events. It even further errs into believing the unconscious or deeper aspects of human motivation are "unreal" imaginations or fantasies, valuing the outer life to the exclusion of the inner. Our life is perceived as caused by external circumstances, when indeed, the causative levels remain hidden within the deeper strata of the Unconscious.

6) This alienation of the ego from its deeper Self, with its companion feelings of isolation, forlornness and homesickness must be fully experienced before it can be transformed. "Not out, but through!" becomes the psyche's wisened cry as it learns it must experience its own dramatic bout with darkness, the negative side of its nature, before it can complete itself. Why? Because if we just pursue the light, we become lopsided and lacking in substance, denying the "shadow" of our own nature and projecting upon others what we perceive as evil. Hatred, bigotry, war, and other forms of unacceptance have their psychodynamic roots in this phenomenon of projection. The negativity within us, being only one side of our nature, can hold its power only by remaining "in the dark." Once accepted, the compulsion to act from these incomplete dark elements within subsides and becomes balanced by each one's positive opposite quality. We return to our wholeness.

7) The goal of spiritual growth is an integrated *completion* of the Self, not a moralistic *perfection.* When completed, the Self resembles a being with qualities religion attributes to "God." Dualities such as love, wisdom, active intelligence, holiness (wholeness, health) all become manifested through us. "Ye are Gods" is not a statement of sacrilege but one of fact. This is not to say that *all* of God's work is

intrapsychically expressed through us; but it does give credence to the transcendental experiences of humankind that have been noted throughout the ages.

To make the Unconscious conscious is the real work of humanity .... its Divine Dance. And if we do it in the right spirit, we will neither be caught by the implicit or the explicit, but will instead hold each with a precious acknowledgement that ensues from maintaining an attitude of "expanded focus."

The process of individuation is the inherent tendency of the psyche to remain conscious and not give up its light of understanding by falling prematurely back into the undifferentiated void and dissolving into nothingness. The most important tool we have for this process of Self-creation is the controversial quality of *Desire.* Throughout history there has raged a battle between the "east" and the "west," wherein the one views desirelessness as the highest good, while the other appears caught up in a world of gratifications and achievement. When we attempt to resolve this dualism by spiritual dogma, we screech to a halt short of resolution — on the one hand feeling that desirelessness is phony and on the other, that desire is evil and unavoidable.

Carl Jung has provided a way to synthesize this apparent duality by defining desire as "a combination of pleasure and the urge to individuate." With this definition, desire translates into a commitment to the experience of the forces of life as it is, a path of consciously committed action — the "path of the heart." Dr. Jung warned that if we attempt to give up desire prematurely, we can perish from "psychic pernicious anemia" and become a "psychic corpse," lacking the motivation necessary to individuate.

Transformers view descending into the Earth's raw, transformative forces of vitality and tribulation as the link with Heaven's mission for us. Without the two coming together in an honored juxtaposition of acceptance, we will remain "unmade," irrelevant and in a great deal of confusion.

> "If you bring forth what is within you, what you bring forth will save you. If you do not bring forth what is within you, what you do not bring forth will destroy you."[19]
>
> ...The Gospel of St. Thomas: Logion 45

Now, with the Transformer's spirit, check this out with your own experience and you will know the Truth.

THE LAW OF TRANSCENDENCE
(Or the Paradox of Change)

Change does not occur when one tries to become someone he is *not*, but instead when he becomes more of who he *is*. This paradox has its roots in the Principle of Transcendence which says "I can move to a higher (more loving) level only when I have accepted fully where I am now." If we try to stop ourselves from being what we are now, the energy becomes super-charged into that very characteristic we are attempting to change. And since more and more energy is going into the undesired subject, we are only manifesting more of what we're trying to get rid of. Follow? If I am spending a lot of my here-and-now feeling that "I've just got to quit such and such" or "I simply must start doing so and so," that's *my* vital energy going into this particular aspect of myself I'm not liking, feeding it more and more; consequently, that energy is not free to go anywhere else. So, I am stuck in this particular behavior, spinning around in an addiction, putting more and more energy into this very concept of myself I so wish to be rid of. Now we can see why addictions cannot be controlled (as I grit my teeth and squeeze); they must be *transformed*, freeing up this constricted energy to flow in another direction. (Remember Yoda's words to Luke Skywalker).

If we examine this principle for a moment, we realize that statements we make to clients that are designed to reform them, trying to force them to be someone they aren't, do not work; they only contribute to the problem: "You'd better quit that behavior," or "Why don't you shape up and be more like your brother," are not helpful because they are based on a violation of the natural Law of Transcendence. They are confusing.... taking him further *away* from himself instead of more *into* himself.

Transformers use statements, instead, that sound more like this: "I'm aware this pain is happening in your life. What do you think could be the lesson in this for you?" Or "What new quality in you is trying to emerge?" Or "And, of course, the positive side to this is...." This kind of attitude accepts the person where he is and helps him discover the meaning in his suffering. It is an attitude that says we are all growing and we all get stuck in different places for different reasons, depending on where we are in our own process of growth. We do not grow at the same rate, nor do we grow evenly. I might be highly advanced in my ability to order my life, but very immature in matters concerning patience, while someone else might be patient and forgiving, while their life is in total disarray from a lack of order and precision. It is not for us to judge where someone else is growing or not growing.... but *Life* will show us, because we will receive the "tests" that we need in order to advance.

A Transformer just naturally feels it is okay for his client to be who he is, and is willing to be there to offer assistance if he wishes to open and become free of limitations. In other words, a Transformer is just naturally non-judgmental! And once a person feels this self-acceptance transferred from his counselor to himself, he is free to move on to the next level (more integration, more loving). Until this "miracle of self-love" happens, we are stuck right where we are. Transformers facilitate this beautiful act of Self-acceptance.

THE LAW OF POLARITY

We began in Oneness, because

God is Man
The Creator is The Created.

Like water and ice, which appear to us as opposites, the dualities we experience are really two phases of a single process. But once we became created, we hypnotized ourselves into seeing things according to man's laws (duality), rather than according to God's laws (Oneness). So, for every negative action, emotion or thought, there is its opposite of equal force that is positive, sitting quietly in the background for that moment *unexpressed.* And though we divide things into positive and negative in order to experience them, these polar opposites can never really be separated or they would lose their definition.

On this level of existence we tend to see everything as polar opposites: it is somehow important to us to split things into parts so we can work out our conflicts. How can I know pride if humility does not exist? How can I ever feel powerful if I have not known feelings of powerlessness? One will be "figure;" the other "background." And our tendency is to focus on the one that is currently figure. We still don't see the whole.

As we learn more about human growth, we discover this is natural, because we are progressing from partial truths to integrated wholes. But, in Truth, *all is working under the influence of One Purpose.* CONDITIONS THAT SEEM OPPOSED TO OUR HIGHEST GOOD ARE MERELY CHANCES TO TEST OUT THE TRUTH PRINCIPLE WE ARE CURRENTLY BEING EXPOSED TO IN ORDER TO EXPAND OUR CONSCIOUSNESS. While we are caught up in a fragment of reality, it is through experiencing opposites that we learn. But once the nature of the dualistic human factor, such as pride/humility, is understood, it becomes transcended into something entirely different (say, self-acceptance), living in a higher dimension, and the pride/humility split is no longer relevant for us; i.e., no longer draws on any of our energy. Work-on-ourselves often becomes just a matter of deciding which end of the continuum we are going to pay attention to.

Ancient Buddhist psychology (Abhidharma) worked with these wholesome/unwholesome mental qualities very pragmatically. Factors leading to mental illness were seen as having an opposite wholesome side of exactly the same strength. A Buddhist psychologist diagnoses people by whatever negative factor he sees in operation within the personality and prescribes as an antidote the positive, opposite factor. Building the positive side produces balance.... the tension goes out of the negative quality.

For example, if you have a client stuck in greed, help him acknowledge this element in himself.... become aware of it, see it in operation, and claim it *without judgment*.... then guide him toward its opposite characteristic, which would be non-attachment (not *having* to have something) or generosity. As he begins concentrating his energy on non-attachment or generosity, his "greed energy" becomes lessened, negative quality becomes transcended. In addiction counseling, some of the dichotomies we work with are these:

compulsivity	non-doing
false viewpoint	clarity of vision
powerlessness	will

greed	non-attachment
passion	compassion
envy	impartiality
agitation	composure
depression	expression
egoism	confidence
indecisiveness	direction
delusion	insight
extravagance	simplicity

Please note: delusion and insight cannot reside in the same space. Once clarity of vision is gained, false viewing is impossible. When impartiality (loving things equally) becomes your reality, envy is no longer an issue. Can you see how this works? Polar opposites are transcended to their original source, the point of Oneness from whence they came.

It will seem to us that we no longer contain energy in the particular "split" we felt about a certain thing. We will just *be* whatever it is we are when this split is no longer a reality. I won't have to *try* to be insightful, I just *am* insightful; I don't have to force myself to make decisions, I am a confident decision-maker, with a sense of direction in my life. No energy is expended battling this particular dualistic concept. Once we have risen above a certain difficulty in our nature, the "polarity" is no longer experienced, and we are functioning at a higher level of integration.

Our Two Natures. And the polarity continues outward, pervading our very sense of selfhood:

> "With the intuition comes a special joy.... a sort of recognition, as though we were always two, a brother of the light who lives in the light and a brother of shadows, ourself, who lives down below and repeats gropingly, in the shadow, knocking himself about everywhere, the gestures of the brother of the light, the movement, the knowledge, the great adventure of the brother of light, but it is all paltry down below, scraggy, clumsy; then suddenly there is a coincidence.... we are one. We are one in a point of light. For once there is no difference and this is joy.
>
> And when we shall be one at all points, this will be the Life Divine."
>
> — *SATPREM*

We feel drawn in both directions, by a lower nature and a higher one, toward an Outer World of Experience and an Inner World of Wisdom. Sometimes we are in one, sometimes the other, as though we are indeed living in two worlds, as two distinctly different natures. And then those rare moments occur when the outside matches the inside.... when it all comes together and we feel whole. So, who am I? Which nature actually represents my True Self? In seeking my identity, what do I look for? And how is my outside world supposed to fit with my inner sense of things? We are, indeed, a developing Self, seeking integration of the two worlds, the outer and the inner.... as though the Self is sitting in between the two, attempting to align the input from each reality.... a mixture of the energies from the lower nature and the higher one. The lower nature pulls us into the worldly life, while the higher nature urges us toward attainment of our highest, most integrated human qualities, such as goodness, truth and beauty.

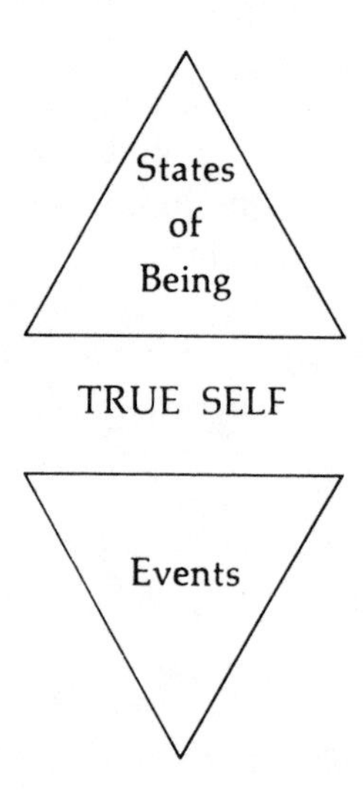

In the outer world, the personality experiences *events* designed to teach it how to live life consciously. In the inner world we experience *states of being*.... our psychological, mental and spiritual space. Here we attribute *meaning* to our outer experience, and this leads to wisdom.

In studying ourselves in depth, we discover that, in Truth, we are indeed one unified Self, but unfortunately, we do not often experience this unity. In the Outer World of Experience we actually function as many little partial selves, reacting this way and that to our environment. Sometimes these partial selves are even in conflict with one another.... my perfectionist self pulling me toward order and duty; my spontaneous self urging me to flow this way and that. Or, my quiet, meditative self nudging me toward inaction, while my frantic self drives me out of the house charging off in all directions. Without Self-knowledge, we are victims of these little selves, pulling us here and there, reacting to whatever comes into view. With Self-knowledge, we find we are on a path of discovery that is quite exciting!

We can formulate our life based on the truth of our experience! And this leads to integration. Or, if we fail to learn the truth from our experience, by computing our findings on a falsehood, we move, instead, toward disintegration. Or we stagnate. The most common way we misperceive our experience is by giving away our power to another who tells us how it *ought* to be. Until we reach a point in our development where we can observe what we are doing *as we are doing it,* we are hopelessly spinning around in a world we do not understand, repeating the same old patterns and tapes over and over again. This is non-growth (or neurosis). And when this becomes too painful, we often opt for an addiction.... we clutch at something "out there" to make us feel better.

This battle between Truth and untruth, the higher nature and the lower, is Life's game. It is the work of becoming conscious. It's a rough game.... especially when we don't know the rules! So learning about ourselves and our life, and the connection we have with Universal Truth is a life and death matter for all of us. And this matter of identity, this question of which me is in charge, turns out to be the cornerstone to Self-creation.

Fortunately, we have a helper within us for this process of becoming conscious. It is an umpire for the game of Life.... a "self" who can be impartial and point out what's happening in the process, to enable us to get a hold on it. It is an Observer Self, who gives us the option of acting rather than reacting. It is a portion of our True Self that is centered in Reality, for it is our Soul's agent in time and space. The Soul, living in the transpersonal dimension, cannot enjoy itself without some way to experience events. Consequently, it projects down into Life the Observer Self so that it can creatively manifest, in the image of its Maker, Spirit. Without an Observer, there can be no *experienced* experience.

Let's be clear, then, on the powerful significance of the Observer Self in our lives. It is the agent of our Soul! It is here to point out the Truth (Soul level) of each situation we encounter, talking in Soul language, doing its job of culling out the Soul events (separating the wheat from the chaff), or the *significant* Reality, of each situation we participate in. If we wish to evolve, we must listen to our Observer Self. It will keep us on our true course.

This Self is not caught up in melodramas and predicaments, but can see right through them and can choose to act consciously in any given situation. Our True Self is designed to actualize our perfection *in the world.* In order to transform addictions, we must learn to differentiate between the True Self and the little partial selves that are running around reacting to everything. The True Self draws its energy from the superconscious mind.... the Inner World of Wisdom.... our blueprint and our future. The little partial selves draw their energies from the subconscious mind, our past programming based on illusion and fear. We will learn more about these superconscious and subconscious energies later on.

It will be helpful at this point to refer to Appendix 1. "A Model of Human Nature," page 229. You will see here a model of the selves and how each one does its work in evolving our nature out of chaos toward integration.

The partial selves are the representatives of our lower nature. They are determined solely by a process of external cues and responses to life, like little robots. When one of these little selves takes over our organism and masquerades as The True Self, we are *stuck in mechanical reactions, not evolving,* as there is nothing unique about these responses that can develop individuality. They are merely carbon copies of pieces of many other people responding to the same cues in like manner in a particular set of cultural norms. "Aunt Sally always did it this way. That's why I do it." They operate solely in the Outer World of Experience, *without understanding.* They are concerned with getting their needs met, drawing from the subconscious, which is governed by the ego. When our needs are being met at any given moment, we feel contentment. But only until some other unmet need stirs.... and then we feel dissatisfied again.

These little partial selves are my Lower Self (a term I will use for convenience from now on to identify a partial self caught up in the Outer World of Experience). And here is what I'm like when my Lower Self takes over:

I get up in the morning and the sun is shining so I feel good. Or, it is gloomy and dark outside, so I feel bad. I go in to cook breakfast and discover we are out of eggs, so I feel bad. I wanted eggs! Then, in searching around, I discover some homemade muffins my daughter has made, so I feel good. Then my little boy comes in and says, "Mother, I'm mad at you 'cause you won't let me have company tonight." So I feel guilty and bad. Next, my older son comes in, kisses me on the cheek and says, "Hi, Mom, I love you." So I feel good. I think about my day and nothing excites me, so I feel bad. Then the phone rings, and it's a friend inviting me to lunch, so I feel good. I walk in and sit down at my desk and notice the huge utility bill for the previous month, and I feel depressed. Then I rebalance my checkbook and I discover I have more money than I thought I had, so I feel a lift. And on and on throughout my day.

And where, pray tell, am *I* in all this? *Who* am I? I am merely going through my day responding to whatever my outside world happens to drop in my lap. This is the robot me, my Lower Self, fragmented, filled with conflicting needs and preferences, living according to unexamined rules and dictates of my societal structure, in a world I do not yet comprehend. And since my society is based on contradictions, I have many of these little selves, part of me here, part of me there, one who can love being a certain way to please so and so, and another who can be its very opposite, to please such and such!

It is this sort of pain that finally leads us to a higher level of functioning where Self-knowledge begins to seep in, because, quite frankly, we just get worn out! As I grow and learn, and begin to seek this knowledge of my Self and my world, I discover I have another possibility, another me who can think for herself and escape the tortuous world of contradictions.... who can rise above it. This is my True Self that resides at the center of my personality, drawing its energy from a Higher Self who can know the Inner World of Wisdom. This True Self can direct my life creatively, gaining its perspective from its observing function, who stepped aside for awhile to get an objective picture of my reality. My True Self is becoming conscious! She is residing in the battleground between my two conflicting natures, my Higher Self and my Lower Self. And my True Self does get knocked out of the driver's seat from time to time, especially when my self-esteem is low, or I've experienced something painful and debilitating. She really has a hard time being heard sometimes, because she is often so utterly covered up by the web of externals and the noise of my Lower Self, babbling on and on ad infinitum.

But my True Self has an advantage: she receives energy from a very high place, at the center of my Selfhood.... She is the expression of my Soul! She is the integration of the knowledge and experience, both inner and outer, I've assimilated, equilibrated, and *completely* understood. She draws her energy from a Higher Power, "way above" my ordinary world of experiences.... a superconscious realm, the place where the Soul resides. She is a reflection of my Higher Self, my pure beingness. My True Self expresses my Soul's purpose *authentically* in the Outer World of Experience. Without her, my Higher Self would have no vehicle for expression in the world, no concrete form. Its energy would exist only in a world beyond the physical plane, where "experience" is an irrelevant concept.

> "I am from everlasting the seed of eternal life.
> I am the intelligence of the intelligent. I am
> the beauty of the beautiful...."
>
> — *THE BHAGAVAD GITA*

When I am operating from my True Self, I am the me that is unique, the one who has her own natural thoughts, feelings and ideas that come from being absolutely in touch with my own individuality. *No one else is exactly this, only me!* This is the me that is eternal, because this me is Truth. I am the intelligent of the Intelligence and the beautiful of the Beauty.... the authentic actions of Truth, eternally. But eternal life does not come about by chance, nor does it happen without tremendous effort. The eternal Self has to be nurtured into existence. In other words, if I don't do me, I don't get done! Self-creation is our human destiny.... really, the only purpose in life. We are here to re-cognize and real-ize our God nature. This is the earth experience (or as some say, the earth *experiment*). But we operate within a Law of Free Will. We do not have to evolve! We choose inaction, non-growth, ignorance, death.... addiction. We have the right, you know, for we are *not*, after all, puppets!

For those who choose to grow, however, we discover we are not alone. We are all here to assist each other in this incredible work of Self-creation.... even those who choose not to evolve are often our teachers. NO ONE COMES ONTO MY PATHWAY BY ACCIDENT. We come and go into each other's lives for a purpose. And the purpose is to point the way toward Truth. Consciously experiencing *untruth* can even lead to Truth!

We cannot always know what another's mission is, or where others are on their path; we do not have total understanding. But we can trust the process! We can become conscious of causes and effects that are operating in our lives, and we can begin to help ourselves and each other discover these patterns and consequences that are occurring by the choices or non-choices we are making. These causes, effects, talents, likes, dislikes, yearnings, aversions, all of it, lead us to Self-knowledge, to Self-creation. We are here as guides, students, teachers and companions for each other. Someone once said that Truth is God communicating with Himself. When I have the courage to allow my True Self to emerge, I am performing the work that is uniquely mine.... *being my Self.*

As we learn to observe the Law of Polarity operating in our lives, we begin to recognize an important fact: Our robot "selves" are also valuable little instruments for our advancement, working to produce order and comfort for us. It is good to keep these little selves well-oiled and polished, in excellent working order, because they are our way of connecting with our environment. My Lower Self is necessary. It reminds me of my needs and warns me when I'm overstepping my boundaries. It also cleans up the house, puts gas in the car, and fills the empty pantry. But it is *not* who I am! And it *will* meet my needs at whatever cost! So I must allow my True Self to guide these little selves, not the other way around. My Lower Self is ruled by ego. My True Self is the expressor for my Higher Self with two functions: observing fairly and choosing actions based on Truth. My Higher Self represents the whole, the archetype; my Lower Self, the fragments.

Higher Self is motivated by an urge toward our completion. For this transpersonal Self, manifested as the True Self, "It is the future which draws, not the past which pushes." (Sri Aurobindo) It takes the experiences from our past as grist for the mill, and applies meaning and purpose, love and understanding to these experiences, incorporates this meaning, and moves forward toward completion. It *never* hangs onto the past.

The True Self feels irresistibly drawn by its own destiny-in-the-making. For it is aligned with the Higher Self. It possesses the courage to act instead of react, even though it may be against popular opinion at times. It delights in authentic expression, realizing its creative powers as a portion of the larger energy source that powers all of creation.... the energy some call cosmic consciousness and some call God. Self-creation is a microcosmic action within the gigantic process of all creation. When we are Self-creating, we are aligned with The Higher Power. Addicts already know this. But perhaps they haven't had the words.

Beyond Polarity. In studying self-actualizing people, Abraham Maslow found that healthy people transcend dichotomies. They get beyond a world view that sees everything in opposites. Work and play merge; the most sexual person becomes the most spiritual; the most innocent, child-like person becomes the most mature, etc. No longer are they consumed with the conflict that expresses itself as "either.... or." Back in behind it all, they are in touch with the source, the Higher Self.... not of this world at all.... motivating us from a place beyond the personal. This is truly our permanent Self, the original Cause of our being.... the one that is with us always.

Even though our selves-in-the-world disappear when we sleep, are in coma or a faint, this Higher Self is always present to bring us back again to whatever reality we need to be in. From another dimension, it reaches down, making itself felt in our life. This Self is above our experiencing, and unaffected by it. It is not bothered by physical ailments, emotional swayings, or the busy flow of our mental life. The True Self is its "projection" in the field of personality. It is our synthesizing center. When we are centered, we are a pure reflection of this wondrous transpersonal Self.... like a lake that has no ripples —

> "Weapons cannot hurt the Self and fire can never burn him. Untouched is he by drenching waters, untouched is he by parching winds. Beyond the power of sword and fire, beyond the power of waters and winds, the Self is everlasting.... never changing.... ever One. *Know that he is,* and cease from sorrow."
>
> — *THE BHAGAVAD GITA*

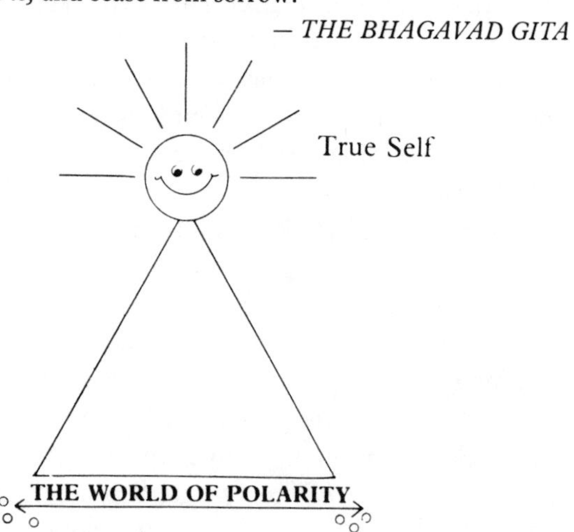

THE LAW OF LOVE

(Expansion or Contraction)

And now, the most important law of all, for it is the Law of God:

"You live that you may learn to love. You love that you may learn to live. No other lesson is required of Man."[20]

—*MIRDAD*

"All is Love, and All is Law" is another paradoxical ancient maxim. Love is Spirit expressing itself; Law (Truth) is the *way* Love is expressed. Love is spontaneous, ruled by the Law of Free Will: we can give it or withhold it — it's up to us. The Laws of the Universe are set and immutable. But only the spontaneous expression of these Laws, the *choice* to express them, can bring them into practical use in our everyday lives. Once we understand this, the Laws become ours to express, lovingly. Infinite Spirit (Love) is expressing through immutable Law. Love is spontaneous; Law is impersonal. This resolves the paradox about Life seeming to be made up of spontaneous actions on the one hand, but controlled and fixed on the other. Both statements are true: LOVE POINTS THE WAY FOR US TO EXPRESS OUR HUMAN NATURE; LAW MAKES THESE WAYS POSSIBLE.

But what *is* love? I cannot think of a word more often misused or misunderstood than the word "love." Everything from simple preferences to grand acts of passion become subsumed under its heading, when, in fact, love is not even a subject-object matter! Love is a state of being. Love is not a virtue, but a necessity.... more essential than food, light or air, for until we are love, we do not possess a Self. All love begins with love of Self, because the Self is God, and God is love. There is nothing but love.... but we have not discovered that yet. We are still bothered by love, pained by it. And as long as this is the case, we haven't found love, for we have not found our Self. In loving anyone, or anything, we are truly loving our Self. When we cannot love a person or a thing, we are not loving a part of our Self. Total Self love is Universal Love.... love of all.... where nothing is deprived of our lovingness.

Love clears the perception so that Truth is seen. Some have said that love is blind because it can see no fault in its beloved. Would we could always be that loving! For that is Truth: There *is* no fault in our beloved! Whatever fault we find in another is always just a fault of our own. We are to love all that is earthy, because all of the earth is in us. And we are to love heaven, too, because all of heaven is in us.

"Love is the only dimension that ever needs changing" writes Thaddeus Golas.[21] At any moment I have a gauge that tells me whether or not I am loving and to what degree. This knowledge is contained in my physical body. Contraction is the move I make toward unlove. Expansion, like space, is total openness, total love. Whenever I am in a state of expansion, I am permeable. I do not resist anything; therefore, I am able to flow absolutely, and everything and everyone can become a part of me and I a part of them. Contraction is fear. It is addiction. It is insecurity, anger, paranoia. I know when I feel it because it makes me very tired. Holding in like that is exhausting.... especially when I feel it is crucial to do so. Working on loving is a nice kind of work. It means as I go down the street, walk into a room, sit at my desk, whatever, I can ask myself how much am I loving right now? Why am I loving so much? What is making it possible for me to feel this way? Or, uh oh, I'm feeling contracted and unloving. I really cannot stand her! I wish she would go away! What's going on now? How am I stopping myself from being able to love this particular person at this particular moment? My work-on-myself becomes an exercise in awareness about the continuum of love, *my* continuum of love.

Love is a state of being, not a subject that needs an object to fulfill it. When I am loving, I love everything, and when I am unloving, I cannot love anything or anyone. This is how it works. *Love needs no subjects or objects.* Learning to love means learning to tap into that part of me that loves and can invite others into that space with me. Unlove means I leave others outside, and I am therefore isolated. Love is our natural state of being; unlove is an unnatural state. You can help your clients discover specifically what and how they love or do not love. What are the conditions that make love easy, and what are the conditions that seem to make it impossible? It's all all right. That is where you are just now. Just try to love yourself as much as you can from whatever state you find yourself in at the time. This is the beginning of love. Love yourself as much as you can.

This is always where you are to start.... *exactly where you are!* This is total honesty.... the Truth.... the only way you can be fully present and centered in the here and now. And you *must* begin with yourself. Why? Because you will only be able to love others to the extent that you can love yourself; there is no boundary line between you and others. In love, we are all one. In unlove, we are all separate. Love yourself as much as you can and you will see that you are loving others as much as you can. And love takes in everything else, even unlove. So, pretty soon you are loving even the unloving.

If your clients learn how to love, you will have done all that is necessary; they will not need you anymore. But learning to love is very difficult, because of all the obstacles we've constructed within our personality that get in its way. And in order to become loving, everything within our personality structure that is incompatible with love must be transformed. Because love and unlove cannot share the same space. This is the work-on-ourselves that takes a lifetime. And we never arrive, for we are always just beginning. There isn't even any place to go! It's all in the journey. Here it is.... right now.

SUMMARY

So here are the three major principles of Self-creation — Transcendence, Polarity and Love.

Whether you find yourself a seeker of help or one who is sought out by another, I hope the knowledge of these Laws will help you. Because it is all the same dance. It is merely a question of whether you are leading or following at any given moment. The truth is, all of us, all of the time, are doing both. I conceptualize it as a human chain like this....

There you are, leading others you're a little ahead of and being drawn by some who are ahead of you. This is the human chain of love which we become a part of as we begin following our true path, the way of Self-creation.

And now the ancient saying, "When the student is ready, the teacher appears" becomes a thundering reality to you. You will discover that everything and everyone on your path is a potential teacher, and always has been (if we had been awake to see it). But we can wake up now! Because it is never too late: we are always just beginning.

The Transformer facilitates this transformation from reacting to action.... from being tossed about by the "winds of fate" to living a life of meaning and direction. We help others feel their *own* potency (not ours) and discover their *own* unique purpose in life (not our idea of it).

When modern psychology began to study healthy people, much that had gone unnoticed about human nature came to light. One of the biggest discoveries has been that when man becomes passive, unhealth tends to feed upon itself. Creative energy, originating from the Higher Self, tends to be self-renewing, producing, its own chain of growth-producing events and patterns in a person's life. In the neurotic (or unhealthy) person, this creativity is perverted: energy goes into self-protective or self-defeating directions; or is stymied altogether, handling inner fears and imaginings; or attempts to assuage a passion or a desire. And these behaviors are not noticed because they are unconscious, therefore not available for critical analysis or reality-testing. Unless this perverted trend is reversed and a feeling of potency and intentionality awakens our creativity, a chain reaction of powerlessness, self-hatred and passivity sets in. This description of how unhealth develops is the story of addiction. WE CAN RECOGNIZE AN ADDICTION BY ITS LACK OF LIFE-GIVING QUALITIES. IT DRAINS US OF OUR PRIME ENERGY, THE ENERGY TO SELF-CREATE.

Addiction, therefore, is the block to Self-creation, because it is passivity. It is being stuck in the past! Going over and over the same old tape, even though it does not work. The key to growth, then, is reversing this passivity, this non-growth choice, into *intentionality* toward a creative act that utilizes one's creative energy pool. Moving toward something chosen and healthy! Like a muscle that atrophies when not used, creative energy goes slack and needs a big push to get back in shape if it hasn't been used for awhile.

Addiction, then can be viewed as THE INVERTED FORM OF OUR NATURAL HUMAN CREATIVITY.[22] The evolutionary drive toward health inherent in man cannot be ignored or violated, as it is our core human quality. So, in that sense, it is undeniable. Illuminating our individual way of Truth is the purpose of the Higher Self; *following* the way, is the work of the True Self, operating in the World of Outer Experience.

And now Aurobindo's statement "Life does not die because it gets worn out; it dies because it has not found itself," can be more fully realized. To be true people-helpers, we become Transformers, drawing people forth toward their potential Reality. We carry the vision of a life lived in active freedom, that fascinating, courageous, so-very-human act of Self-creation.... the *real* "turn on" most addicts will die for, or without.

A Human Being has

.... the spirit of god
.... the soul of a mortal
.... the body of an animal

"Of all the fables in the world, we ourselves are the most fantastic."
– *MANLY P. HALL*

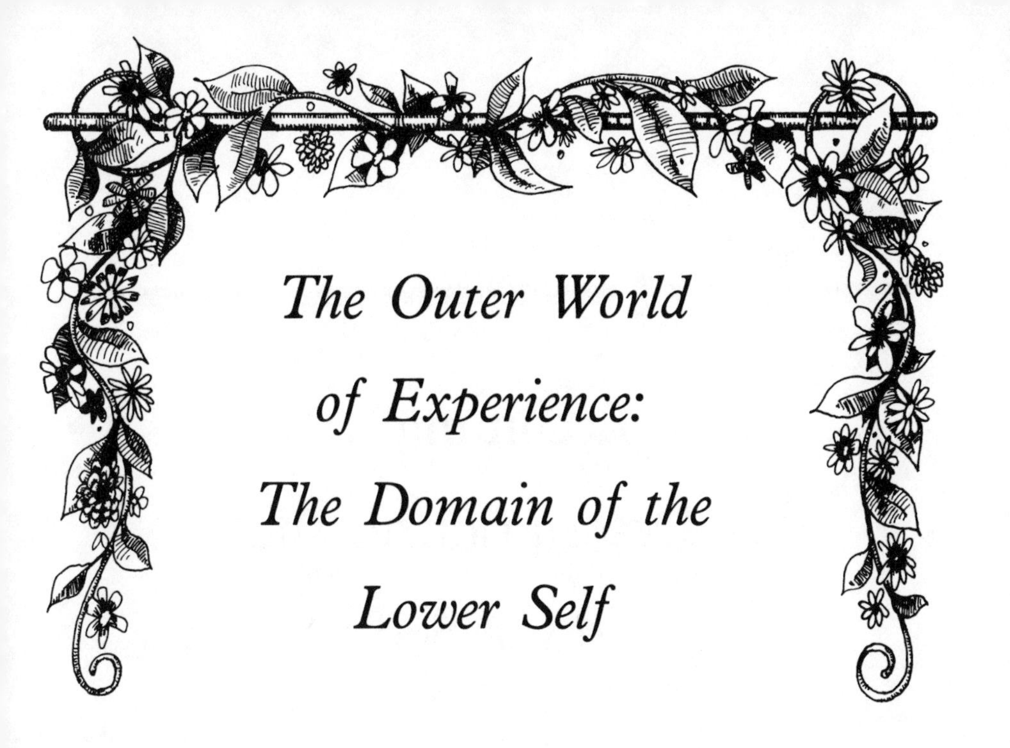

The Outer World of Experience: The Domain of the Lower Self

BECOMING

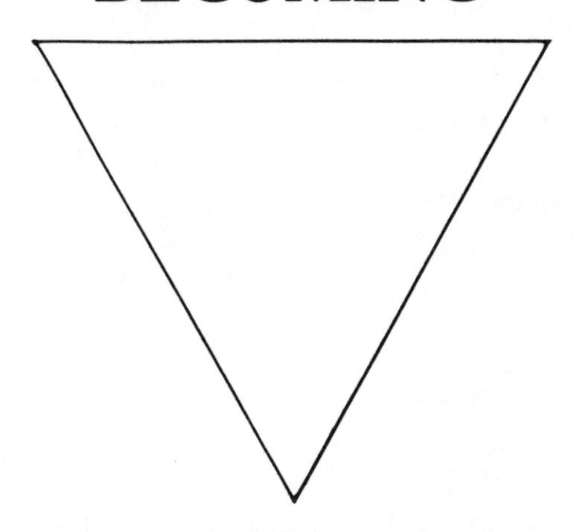

2

Becoming: A Description of the Lower Self

This multi-leveled human being in the process of self- evolution is indeed a complex creation! It is no wonder we stay so confused. Especially since most of us believe we are acting as one unified self! Until we can understand "our many selves" and the manner in which they function in the world, we are like a person standing on a plank while trying to lift it: we cannot get any distance from ourselves in order to see what's happening.

Consciously choosing to enter into the process of becoming *is* man's evolutionary task — his deepest existential urge. And this urge translates into our *felt* experience as *tension.* We are painfully aware of the gap between what we are now and what we know we can be. And we *know* no one can evolve for us! We must do it ourselves, and we fear that we cannot.

So let's take a deeper look now at what actually happens to the Self as we proceed through The Outer World of Experience — Life — toward integration of the personality, the cornerstone of Self-creation.

By our very nature, we are a mixture of the many aspects of the Self, each with its own way of assisting us toward Self-creation. We are here to express ourselves in the world *where we live....* not in some never-never land of Nirvana or Paradise. We have been given a concrete, actual form of expression (our bodies) that need not be denied.

Remember the Law of Transcendence: We don't get to "heaven" by trying to be something we are not, but by accepting *fully* who we are.

Our physical, material self is our instrument for bringing the higher energies into direct manifestation in the world of relationship. This is our Lower Self who experiences, without which we would be formless and ineffective, like a puff of wind with no substance. Even if it is pain I am experiencing — I am learning to understand it more completely, and as I do, a great wave of love and appreciation sweeps over me.... to *realize* for even a moment the absolute beauty and perfection of this physical being in which I am encased!

And further, I realize that my ego is a very loyal friend! Its sole desire is to take care of me. But now that I am understanding the nature of the many selves that I am — my partial selves, my True Self, and a Higher Self — I see that my ego must be guided from energies higher than my personal reality; for, unchecked, it is liable to do *anything* to get my needs met, including self-defeating, neurotic or addicted behaviors! IN PERSONALITY WE ARE MANY; IN ESSENCE WE ARE ONE.

When in doubt about what my ego is doing to/for me, I can always go higher, within, to that place of wholeness that knows Truth. The ego gets caught in fragments of my reality, seeing the particular portion it is caught up in as "the whole truth;" consequently, my ego can deceive me greatly about my total reality. For example, my daughter may get angry with me and move out of the house. I might interpret this action through the lens of hurt feelings and conclude that she doesn't love me anymore. When seen from a more comprehensive level of reality, in the entire context within which this event is occurring, it becomes apparent that she needed this anger to gain the momentum to break her dependency on a mother she was too identified with. In order to achieve the natural developmental task of individuation, she utilized anger for a higher purpose. The experience of an angry interchange was a temporary state, a fragment of reality; the process of individuation was the Truth. If we become identified with the anger, we might sever a relationship; if we remain steady and identify with the Truth, the relationship flows on gracefully to the next stage.

Ego, the master of my personality's needs in the Outer World of Experience, that which we call Life, operates along three planes of reality; a physical/instinctual plane, a sensual/emotional plane, and a mental plane. This is the Lower Self functioning in the everyday materialized world, and there are principles operating at each level that determine its natural course. The physical plane is driven by a FEAR principle —to motivate us to achieve the basic needs of self-preservation. This energy transmutes into self-mastery, or Right Action, when the needs are appropriately met, manifesting as an ordered life. The emotional level is driven by PASSION, the motivating force that gets our needs for sensual gratification met, and this energy is how we naturally experience pleasure and devotion which transmute to compassion when properly dealt with — Right Feeling. The mental plane is driven by the IDENTITY principle, which motivates us to meet our needs for self-definition. This energy, properly used, is analysis and comparison and transmutes into Self-knowledge, or Right Thought.

The three types of energy converge upon each other, building in a hierarchical manner so that each greatly affects the other two. This evolutionary process is how the personality structure becomes *human.* Without its monarch, the mind, which develops at Level Three, this hierarchical construct has passions, but no reason; emotion but no intellect; desires but no will. In other words, this Lower Self can act as a dangerous animal if not constrained by a responsible intellect capable of recalling the past and being cognizant of a future.... the function which distinguishes the human from the animal.

This personality construction is best expressed by a triangle — the only pattern where three lines converge.

LOWER SELF

PERSONALITY, PERSONA, MASK

(Potentially, the vehicle for the True Self)

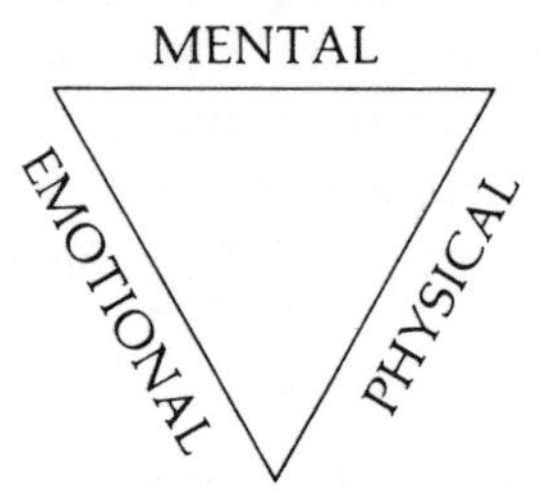

As we evolve, our physical/instinctual and sensual/emotional experiences form our mental life, so that these become a hierarchy from the densest to the most spacious (unformed) types of energy:

LOWER SELF
(BECOMING)

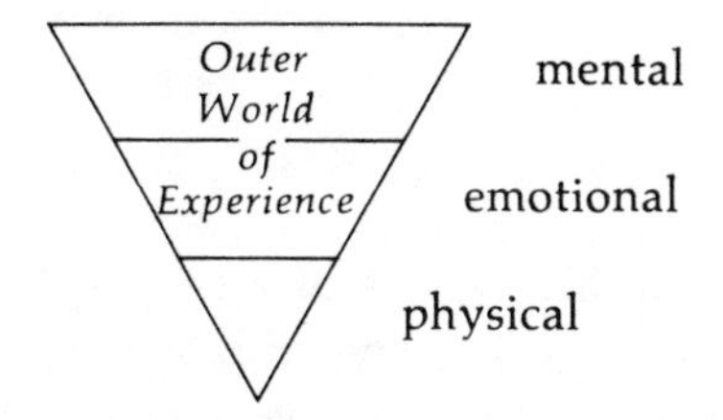

Later, we will see how during the process of Self-creation, the Higher Self (manifested as the True Self) drawing energy from the Inner World of Wisdom, utilizes these same three planes or levels (physical, emotional and mental) within a formless dimension. Since we are built "in the image of God" and the materialized self is a microcosm of the greater macrocosm, we find an exact correlation:

HIGHER SELF
(TRUTH)

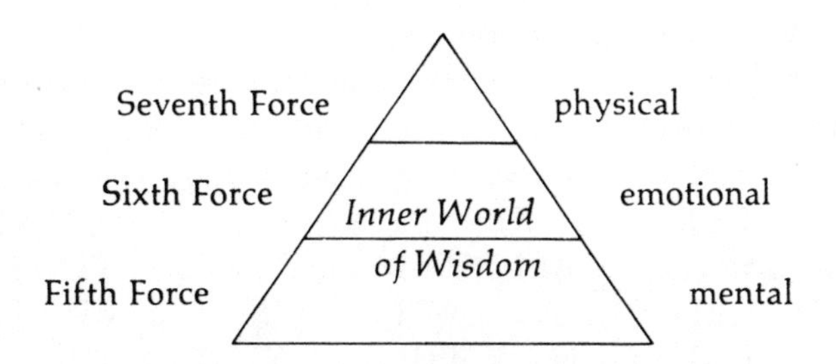

But before we explain the Upper Triangle, let's take a deeper look at our Lower Self as it travels through the stages of development that serve as the foundation for the work of Self-creation.

While in the stages of personality (ego) development, from birth to maturity, we operate in the Lower Self. We are dependent on the world outside to define us and give us what we need to survive. Consequently, the Outer World of Experience is, at first, *our only perceived reality.*

MOTIVATING FORCES OF THE LOWER SELF

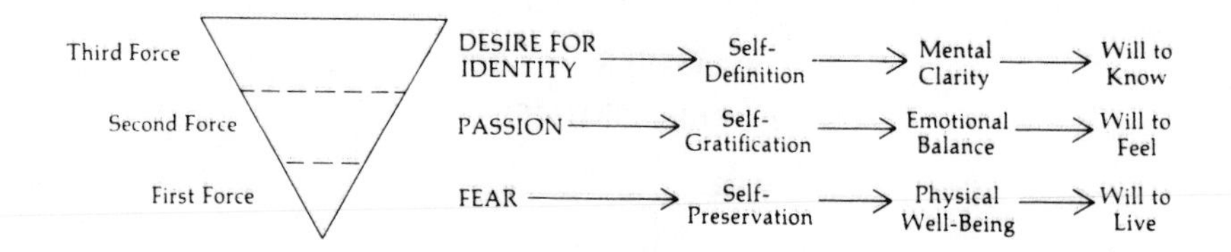

Within these three levels of reality are enacted the three basic urges of the human being toward wholeness in the Outer World of Experience. This is how the personality develops naturally as it proceeds from isolation to integration.

As we evolve toward integration, we move through three distinct levels of consciousness, each functioning as a *total universe* for the Spiritual developmental task we are to complete at each level.

The first level is the Physical/Instinctual, where we learn ORDER. When we order our lives, we learn Right Action, which produces confidence and self-mastery.

The second level of consciousness is Sensual/Emotional in tone, where we learn about PLEASURE and DEVOTION. It is "the place" where we learn to connect *with feeling* in relationship with others. Here, we learn Right Feeling.

The third level is a mental environment, where we learn through COMPARISON/ANALYSIS how to study about Life and the Self in relation to Life. Here is the training ground for Right Thinking.

WHEN THE NATURAL DRIVE AT EACH LEVEL OF CONSCIOUSNESS IS ALLOWED TO EXPRESS ITSELF, WE MOVE GRACEFULLY AND WITH EASE TOWARD PERSONALITY INTEGRATION. IF THESE NATURAL URGES ARE THWARTED, DIS-EASE SETS IN.

FIRST FORCE: THE WILL TO LIVE
(The Fear Response)

Level of Consciousness: ORDER (Physical/Instinctual)
Quality: Self preservation
Pitfall: Isolation
Mastery: Right Action

This is the primal energy force with which we begin life, our most basic need. The little baby comes into the world completely dependent upon its environment for its very life. Its first task is to discover that it is safe to be here. And from this secure feeling emerges our first solid affirmation: THE WILL TO LIVE. As it reaches for its mother, the child is given what it needs. And its needs are quite simple at this point: nourishment, nurturance and comfort. It has the capacity to draw all this from only one source: mother. Such simplicity! And so basic. So basic, in fact, that if gratified long enough for trust to develop, the little person tires of this simplicity and healthily expands to another level of consciousness. Now it knows it is safe, and has therefore laid the foundation for choosing to live. The child will now move with confidence toward the larger world of sensual and emotional experiences.

All our lives we will experience First Force as a "physical" way of functioning. And what an ingenius design! Being identified with our physical nature teaches us to listen to our own body. Our body is our little animal.... like the horse we ride. And, as with a cherished pet, we must treat it well, nurture it, feed it properly and make certain its needs are met. For, without a clean and healthy body we cannot do the arduous task of Self-creation that occurs throughout personal evolution. We could not bear the strain. Consequently, we must develop the sensitivity to recognize our body's true needs, while at the same time maintaining a certain amount of discipline in life so that the True Self remains the master of the body's appetites.

FIRST FORCE: THE WILL TO LIVE

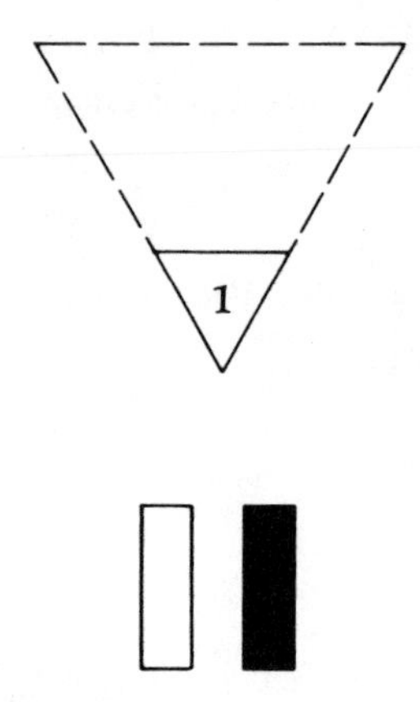

SECOND FORCE: THE WILL TO FEEL
(The Passion Response)

Level of Consciousness: PLEASURE/DEVOTION
Quality: Self Gratification
Pitfall: Duality
Mastery: Right Feeling

The child is now ready to learn about pleasure and pain, excitement and boredom, passion and contentment. Now there is a whole spectrum of emotional life to explore and assimilate. As the youngster begins to separate itself from "others," it enters the world of opposites, moving toward what is pleasurable and seeking in a healthy fashion to avoid pain. Now the child can function in the outer world, Life, and if this urge toward gratification of the senses is allowed expression in a realistic and positive manner, it becomes THE WILL TO FEEL, preparing it for a normal and lively adolescence. The person will have learned to trust the messages of its sensual nature. If uninterrupted by ignorant and neurotic others, the person absorbs each experience on its own merit, correctly interpreting what Life is telling him to be Truth. He then moves toward more healthy development — liking pleasure, disliking pain — and confident in knowing how to get his needs met appropriately. He knows how to live in the

Now, unencumbered by weighty fears from the past or anxiety about the future.

But we must remember that Second Force is our emotional "body" and thrives on passion or any kind of feeling state. Suffering interests it as much as joy for it is a *force,* and *intensity* of feeling is what it seeks. It is the same force in suffering as in pleasure! Its *nature* is to feel. It likes for you to be angry, to get your feelings hurt, to lust and be greedy, as much as it likes ecstasy and excitement. It is truly as interested in hatred as it is in love. It likes violence. It is the "self" that is curiously fascinated by spilled blood and guts at the scene of a horrendous accident or in a horror film. And it seeks constant change, for it is naturally restless. Consequently, we must learn very early in life to become the master, not the servant, of our emotional nature.

SECOND FORCE: THE WILL TO FEEL

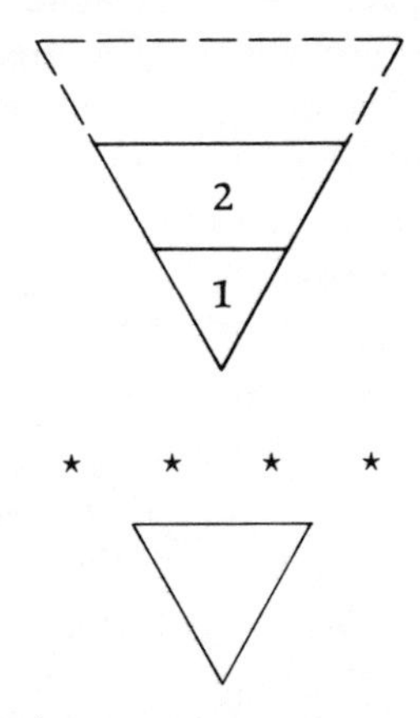

THIRD FORCE: THE WILL TO KNOW

(The Identity-Seeking Response)

Level of Consciousness: ANALYSIS/COMPARISON
(Concrete Mind)
Quality: Self definition
Pitfall: Fragmentation
Mastery: Right Thought

At this stage of development we are fully in our adolescence, figuratively speaking, and preparing for the responsibilities of adulthood. We are now becoming identified with our mental life having completed much of our emotional development. At the forefront of our emerging consciousness, ideas about who we are come into focus. We are seeking a realistic, satisfactory concept of ourselves. Here is where we begin adopting roles and attitudes we feel good about or drawn to. Conversely, we seek to avoid roles or self images that would make us feel bad. This is the level where our values are formulated, based on what we've learned experientially through pleasure, pain and comparison and analysis as we've lived our personal lives.

We have learned to live in certain ways that feel *right* to us. When something does not feel right, we experience guilt, shame, or some other discomfort. We are preoccupied at this level of consciousness with how others see us. By now we are quite formed from the learning *we have acquired from outside ourselves.*

If my natural growth is uninterrupted, I will confidently operate from attitudes and roles based on values that I trust and believe in. I think of myself as a good girl, a pleasant person, a peacemaker, sexy, a good student, a leader, a good Christian, a hard worker, loyal, practical, or whatever other images I hold that fit my ideal. If, for some reason, I try on a role that violates my self image, I immediately feel discomfort and seek to remedy the situation, either inwardly (by changing my values to fit the role) or outwardly (by changing my role).

This level of consciousness provides us the training ground for Self-definition. It is where our personality learns to express our True Self in the world — how to discriminate between roles that really fit us and those that do not. If I make it through this level naturally, I develop THE WILL TO KNOW: A curiosity is spawned concerning the deeper levels of truth about Life and the Self. Because this is a *mental* level of functioning, unbounded by concrete reality, it becomes the point of entry to an expanded way of being in the world that enables the creative imagination to work and transcendence to become a possibility. If we continue to evolve beyond this point, from learning to discriminate well between fragments of truth and comprehensive Truth, we will take a leap in consciousness which we will explain later as Fourth Force.

But here again is a warning: If we become addicted to our intellect, fully convinced that *our ideas* are Reality, we will be stuck at the mental level of functioning and fall prey to a mind that loves to keep us set apart.... to think much of itself and little of others. We will be stuck in the desire for status.

At the Third Level our intellect calculates purely for the ego, even on spiritual quests and in meditation! We need to remember that we *have* our little mind to use as an instrument, but we are *not* this mind: We are larger and grander than this wee intellect can ever fathom. It is up to us to learn to discriminate between the countless things our little ego mind wants versus the one big thing our Higher Self wants for us, which is the expression and fulfillment of our *own true and unique purpose.*

THIRD FORCE: THE WILL TO KNOW

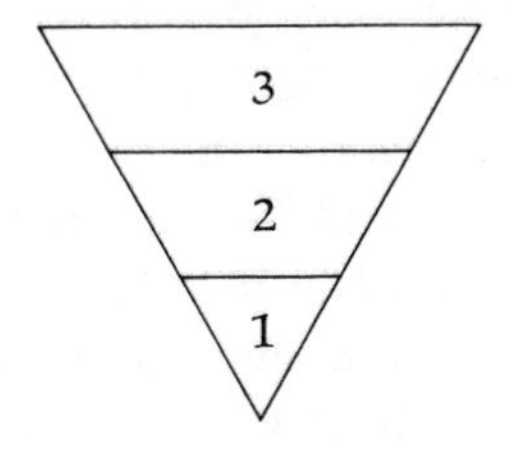

THE DEVELOPMENT OF PERSONALITY

A Summary Statement

So now we have built our "vehicle," the self designed to function in the daily world of outward involvement with people and things. I have described how this process unfolds and the forces that move us when there is a minimum of distortion or interruption. And I have also touched on how we can become so caught up in the outside world that we can lose our sense of Selfhood, in which case the Lower Self takes over and masquerades as the True Self.

I suppose the most important message I would like to express about this development of the personality is this: Each stage we have described so far is *necessary* and intrinsically *good.* We cannot move to the higher levels of human functioning if we do not develop first an integrated personality, composed of three essential characteristics: Physical well-being, balanced emotions, mental clarity. Essence is dependent upon personality for its expression in the world! Paradoxically, the Higher must attach itself to the Lower for its very existence.

> I heard a story one time about a farmer who was busily tilling a rich plot of soil when a stranger appeared and expressed amazement

at the beauty of the farmer's land. "This is truly God's country!" exclaimed the stranger in his praise. To which the farmer curtly replied, "Well! You should have seen what a mess it was when God had it all by himself!"

But, the "Lower," the earthy, must do its work properly. We all know what happens to people with sick bodies or emotional and mental illnesses; they are preoccupied with their disturbances, their lives a wreck. Physical illness keeps one stuck in a physical level of consciousness, preoccupied with one's symptoms. Emotional imbalance leads to chaos or a mental institution. And lack of mental clarity causes one to be confused and ineffective in life. THE EGO WILL CONTINUALLY DRAW US BACKWARDS, TOWARD THE LEVEL WHERE THE UNMET NEED EXISTS, *UNTIL THE NEED IS MET.* In other words, the energy the person requires for Self-creation is constricted and focused in the Lower Self — which always looks to the *outer world* for its solutions.

But we all know from our own experience that it is impossible to make it through these three stages perfectly. So the act of Self-creation need not be dependent upon *perfection* of the personality. If this were the case, none of us could ever do it. Each of us, in our own life story, has received from our personal environment a particular set of neurotic situations and painful relationships we've been required to deal with. Most of our parents, God bless their souls, have pockets of complete mental delusion they draw from in forming standards that do not fit with human nature, or crippling experiences of their own that have had enormous negative effects on them and consequently, on us. Not to mention aunts, uncles, grandmas, school teachers, preachers, bosses, friends and heroes who have influenced us according to values that had little or nothing to do with our well-being.

When we were kids, most of the grown-ups in our lives operated from the maxim "Children are to be molded and corrected" rather than "Kids are beautiful creatures designed to realize their own uniqueness." Consequently, we *had* to develop a false personality in order to survive! And this is the genesis of the multiple little "partial selves" that make up the Lower Self. As little children we had no alternative in seeking ways to avoid neurotic people who felt in charge of us. But it is *in this very battle* between Truth and false personality that each particular child learns the lesson it needs from Life that will give it spiritual staying power for later living the inner life. In other words, nothing happens by accident.

Ultimately, however, we are not intended to be victims of *anything* — even parents. We will discover later that victimhood is a myth.... a teacher in disguise to guide us to our true place in life. It is *as I recognize* my defenses and coping styles that I learn later on what I fear, who I am and where I'm stuck. These are the negatives that define the positive side of the pole for us on our journey into Self-creation.

VICTIMHOOD IS A MYTH THAT ONLY LEADS TO POWERLESSNESS. *This is the Cardinal Truth of the Transformer.* If you are a counselor and perceive your client as a victim of *anything,* refer her to another counselor immediately! You can do no one any good unless you can guide them to their strengths and to the meaning behind their negative experiences.

The world is ruled by laws that operate naturally and perfectly for our good. By my experiences, a neutral universe offers me a way to strengthen my character or my love in some manner that may not be as yet evident to me. Perhaps you've heard the saying that our greatest strengths are born out of the substance of our greatest weaknesses. If we've had a certain difficulty in life (a chronic physical ailment, poverty, a drunken parent, teachers who were hard on us, etc.), especially if the difficulties fall into a pattern, we can know these are our own personalized obstacle courses designed expressly to prod us along in our growth and to teach us the Laws of the Universe.

Later, as we are further along toward realizing our life's purpose, we will see how each negative experience contained a great learning principle. For later on, we will have the availability of the Higher Self's wisdom to show us Truth. It is only the Lower Self that operates in the dark, based on energy from the subconscious mind (the past). The light of consciousness transmutes false personality to a healthy, realistic, *authentic* person, the True Self. And this True Self is the vehicle for our Soul's undistorted expression of the world.

The most important tasks in our process of becoming are to make sense of our past — by reliving the negative parts *without judgment* and forgiving ourselves and others for any harm that we perceived. Portions of the past that still bother us represent the content of the subconscious mind, remnants of experience we have not assimilated properly, still holding ourselves away from the knowledge these experiences were designed to give us.

Portions of our past that are no longer alive to us, we have *become.* They are now part of our True Self, having been instrumental building blocks necessary to our unique creation. The experiences we assimilate are understood and let go of; they are the underpinnings for intuitive knowledge, which is a higher form of gathering information than memorizing facts about the outer world.

The past has come before, to show us where we are going; the future is there to draw us toward our eventual completion. In the act of Self-creation, we are to respect our past, draw from it what lessons we need.... cleaning up any unfinished business, and discovering the patterns and the meaning in our suffering and joys. If there is physical, emotional or mental work left to do, we evoke our will to complete the tasks, whatever they may be.... and then.... move on.

BEING STUCK IN THE PAST IS JUST ANOTHER FORM ILLUSION CAN TAKE. (EVIL IS "LIVE" SPELLED BACKWARDS!) COMPLETE, WITH HONESTY, WHATEVER IS BOTHERING YOU, AND THEN.... STOP LOOKING BACK.

3

How Addiction Unfolds in the Personality

What is addiction? We all certainly know what it feels like. The "clutched" feeling in the gut when an addiction cannot be gratified .... the feelings of sheer terror experienced when a perceived threat looms into our consciousness saying, "Maybe you can't have this anymore." Addiction is defined as "the compulsive need for something habit-forming" — (Merriam-Webster). And, again, I don't know a better prototype of this phenomenon than alcoholism. In studying the alcoholic, we can see the entire process of addiction unfold in the personality.

Experts cannot agree on a single definition of alcoholism: Some call it a disease; some say it's a symptom of a psychological problem; many say it's a "problem in living;" some call it an allergy. It's been labelled a moral weakness, a statement of immature personality, a character disorder, a neurosis. Some say it doesn't even exist, that alcoholism is merely a description of someone who drinks too much, and if she will simply drink less, the problem will go away.

In my opinion, all definitions contain some truth. Like the investigators studying the elephant blindfolded.... it depends on which part of the animal you are examining. But a common denominator in all the definitions is: The investigators are studying the Lower Self who is addicted — the *form* of the creature; i.e., the result. Alcoholism is being defined as the effect on the physical body or the outer life of the person.

Many have come up with comprehensive definitions of this kind, which are highly workable and lead many alcoholics into treatment. Alcoholism, according to most modern-day experts, is family, social, legal, financial, physical, mental, and occupational breakdown. In educational and treatment settings these terrible truths are spelled out. Often, these experts allude to the word "spiritual" but do not elaborate: the Spiritual is the *unseen* dimension, the *causative level.*

Even though the Spiritual resides in an invisible world, it is, in fact, the very ground of our Being — our true Reality, the Higher Self. And it can also be formulated. To round out our awareness of the problem, let's take a journey into this hidden dimension, this Self living in a vehicle contaminated by addiction.

Alcoholism is a spiritual predicament. It is the inner side of the beast which contains the *causative factors* of addiction! By some set of circumstances, like the sand in the oyster, it has found its way into its host, now having become a part of the personality structure — an alien substance intruding cruelly, imposing a terrible stress on the person — not a part of the True Self!

So what is the host to do with this alien creature? Like the oyster, it has several choices. It can rebel against it — "Why me, Lord?" It can lose faith in life — "Well, if this is how it is, I'm not going to try anymore." It can deny its existence, hoping the pain will just go away. Or it can suffer nobly — "This is just how I am; I'll just have to live with it."

But nothing can change the fact that the addiction is there.

The oyster who creates the pearl chooses to acknowledge the "grim intruder" and decides to transform it:

> "Slowly and patiently, with infinite care, the oyster builds upon the grain of sand — layer upon layer of a plastic milky substance that covers each sharp corner and coats every cutting edge.... and gradually.... slowly.... by and by a pearl is made.... a thing of wondrous beauty wrapped around trouble."[23]

The spiritual predicament is the felt gap between the personality distortion and the perfection our Soul is seeking to give form in the world. The presence of the addiction presents us with an opportunity for growth. It has arrived to force us to look at ourselves, specifically at those strengths and natural qualities of our Essence the addiction is masking. Addiction is more than a concept; it cannot be contained within a definition. It is a mis-creation of the Soul's intention.

* * * *

THE ORIGIN OF ADDICTION

> "In the beginning, darkness was hidden by darkness, all this was one ocean of unconscience. Universal being was concealed by fragmentation."
>
> — *THE RIG VEDA*

We've wound up in a world of duality because the Light plunged into its own shadow. The negative side of a Supreme Positive became our experience.

If we can understand this Truth, we will be able to see how all of our addictions originate from this first duality, this fragmentation mentioned by the sages of the Veda — this confusion of separating spirit and matter, the inside from the outside, Truth from untruth. But is the negative "bad?" Addiction is not evil; it is merely a narrowness of vision, perceiving a false vision of ourselves and our world.... thinking we are someone we're not, doing things we don't even have to do! Addiction is darkness.... a way of not being.

> "Our sense by its incapacity has invented darkness. In truth there is nothing but Light, only it is a power of light either above or below our poor human vision's limited range."
>
> — *SRI AUROBINDO*

The sage is saying that spirit does not abolish matter, nor does the positive abolish the negative, any more than the top of something annuls the bottom!

If we trace the use of mind-altering substances back through time, we find that all cultures have had a way of utilizing natural substances such as herbs, cacti and flowers to bring one to a level of consciousness beyond what we consider to be ordinary reality. These mind-altering experiences were spiritual experiences connected with rites of passage and initiations into the greater mysteries of the universe. They were administered by priests and priestesses, medicine men, shamans and others who were considered to be "the wise ones." These psychedelic experiences occurred perhaps once, perhaps annually, in the lives of their users. They were not designed to be used often, or without the presence of a spiritual guide!

Again, we have here the problem of separating off from the Source — taking the spiritual part out of the material. Once we decided to use these substances on our own, even simulating them in scientific laboratories, we dove into trouble. Man without God is only a half-truth; psychedelic experiences separated from their spiritual significance are half-baked experiences that can take one off his path rather than enlighten him.

Our negative man-made addictions exist in relation to their positive spiritual companions. They complete and explain each other. Each by itself cannot *really* be understood. Until I know the positive quality (a portion of my Essence) I'm withholding by hanging on to my addiction, I cannot possibly understand my addiction. I must go for the One Truth behind this apparent duality if I am to know freedom. *Who* am I? *What* am I seeking? What part of me am I withholding/expressing?

The Lower Self (our addicted selves) can only operate when Forces One, Two or Three are experienced *without* energy from any of the higher levels. Since this is only one-half of reality, the material side, and we are operating as though it is the *only* reality, we are caught in a web of illusion, incapable of realizing the larger picture. *We need this thing or person for our survival,* we feel. *There is no other reality!*

When the Lower Self and the Higher Self operate together, transformation can occur. We have a chance to break out of our limited world view. The two working together create a synergistic effect.... another whole reality. We accomplish a feat we had deemed impossible. We discover we just *are* that very person we had longed to be but had almost given up on.

But remember, *the top does not annul the bottom.* It is from having climbed from the bottom, *through* the addiction, that we transform it. The addiction is the very stuff our transformation is made of! It is because we've been hooked on relationships that we now know relationship. It is because we gave our power away to a substance that we understand our own unique potency. It is because we died that we now can live without fear! We did not choose to live like sheep who never strayed; we risked. We got our feet wet. We entered into life — got stuck, got into trouble. Now we've learned. Our new-found goodness is not built upon naivite. Our obedience does not come from the weakness of never having had the courage to try. Our knowledge comes from an overflowing of strength that has become *floodlike* in its forcefulness. There is now *life* in our understanding of addiction because we've been there. THE HIGHEST PART OF US CAN ONLY EXIST WHEN THERE IS ENERGY TO MOVE IT, AND

THIS ENERGY IS THE OVERFLOWING FROM THE LOWER LEVELS OF OUR EXPERIENCING.

We are hierarchical creatures: only when all the bodily needs are met can the energy move to the next highest level of functioning. Our higher knowledge is *rooted* in our knowledge of the lower. One may think he is a saint because he has never committed a sin. But this is not how it works. If one has never been tempted and never committed any error, there is no energy for turning inward to seek a higher way. Most saints and sages will tell you they have travelled the road you have travelled and have experienced the failures and mistakes just as you have. The only difference in them and you is they are further along on their journey, having completed, or nearly completed, the Life. They *know* and are living from their being. We are *learning,* for we are still becoming.

When we make the transition from ego-dominance to Essence-dominance, the force of the Higher Self descends and takes up the whole nature, part by part, and does what needs to be done with it, rejecting what must be rejected and transforming what needs to be transformed. It integrates, harmonizes and completes the Self. *This is the act of Self-creation.*

At this point in our growth, there is an illusion we must ward against — another pitfall: When the Higher Self begins to overshadow our meager personality, our tendency is to *throw out the Lower Self.* But the two *must* work together. This is the human condition.... our unique destiny! We, for the first time in the entire process of evolution, are to spiritualize the material right down to the very bones.... to enter fully into the stuff of Life and *make it holy (whole),* to raise it to its highest good.

There is an absolute goodness in the very heart of the things of the earth. We have been too deluded to see this, having bought into so many myths about "the evils of the flesh." The Spirit in us has not yet finished discovering itself. We are in transition. The Higher Self is still looking for all its expressions of consciousness.

Does this help you to see how your weaknesses are woven into the very stuff that makes you *you*? You've *needed* those experiences in your past that you've labelled "wrong" or "bad." They have provided the tension in your life that now makes it possible for you to Self-create. Your weaknesses and your strengths are one. Now can you forgive yourself? *We just are who we are at the moment.* And this is not a license for irresponsible behavior; it is simply a statement of fact.

Our task is to continue to be seekers of Truth in order to become *seers* of Truth.... tossed between our search for heaven on the one hand, and a rich earthly experience on the other. What I'm saying is YES. That's exactly where we are and where we need to be. We can acknowledge this without guilt, without blame. We are doing the work of being human! We are not German Shepherds, and we are not poppies in the field. We are human. Our only failure has been to set our two natures against each other.... heaven there, earth here, one good, the other evil. *This* is the original sin, the separation, the error *demanding* correction. We are to unite the two and realize one *IS* the other, to discover the infinite within the finite, the holy amidst the profane. Each weakness in us is a call to strength — our addiction, the dark side of our Truth.

And perhaps this is our final destination: to experience the joy of having been *all that is,* has been, or will be, right here where we are.... in a world of experiencing! We are not trying to *leave* life, but to expand it. To KNOW it all.

And the serpent finally comes full circle and swallows its own tail.

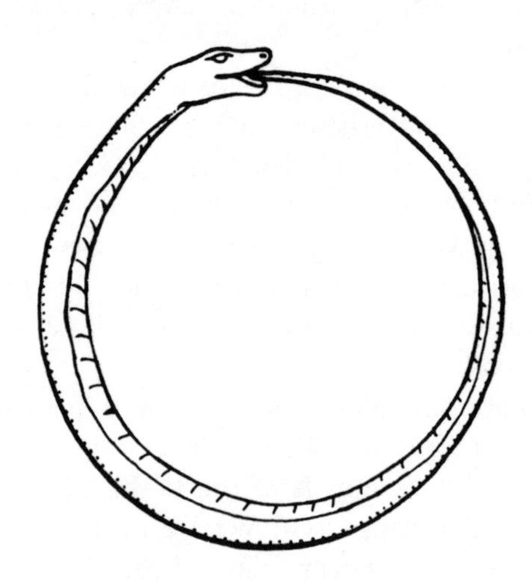

THE TRANSFORMER'S VIEW OF ADDICTION

Following are the working "definitions" a Transformer uses for addiction:

Addiction = non-growth. It is a way of staying stuck in the past, repeating like a robot the same outworn modes of operation that do not work. Habits are desires objectified, repeated by unconscious action. One cannot maintain an addiction consciously. We have to put ourselves to sleep in order to act out an addiction. Conscious awareness, moment by moment, fully in the here and now, transforms addiction.

Addiction = attachment. When we are attached to something (or someone), we have forgotten who we are. We feel we cannot be whole without this something. We experience pain and suffering whenever our attachment threatens to leave us.... like losing an arm or a leg. Attachment is the cause of suffering. *Addiction* is the cause of suffering. Non-attachment does not mean non-caring; it is non-*needing*.... non-obsessing. It is removing emotional investment so that one can truly see clearly and therefore care appropriately for the *other's sake.* Paradoxically, *attachment* is non-loving.

Addiction = postponement. Repetition is hypnosis. You did it yesterday, you are doing it today. Tomorrow will be the same. Repeating, repeating. And this is how addictions grow. The more you repeat, the deeper you carve the groove of that particular tape loop.... the more the affliction is worked into the fiber of your being. You know you want to do something else with your life, but always you feel.... tomorrow! Then I'll be ready. Tomorrow I will be stronger. Tomorrow I will have gained more knowledge; I will have more energy. I will be out of the current crisis. *But tomorrow never comes!* And transformation happens NOW! It is *this* moment. Because, you see, nothing has to be *done* for transformation to occur — no looking to the future, desiring an outcome — no goal.

Transformation is simply AN AWAKENING — coming out of a dream state — a realization that happens in the mind. It is an instant realization that you lack nothing at all! You just open your eyes and see. And the seeing transforms!

Addictions must be entered into fully before they can be transformed, because they must be recognized.... understood. Mindfulness is required. (See Exercise #3, page 236.) They must be experienced fully, recognized for what they are, understood, accepted.... then the energy goes out of them. Going into the Silence (Exercise #10, page 247) is a way of becoming mindful.

Education about the Self is the initial process in addiction counseling. Your clients must be re-educated about who they really are in order to transform their debilitating addictions. Tuning into the Self is the second phase. Then, quite naturally, your client will be ready to work through fears and resistances that block this True Self from its rightful domain as master of the personality. As these fears and resistances are understood and accepted, and the True Self takes hold, the addiction loses its power. When one operates from his True Self, a natural high occurs, because the True Self lives in the NOW, alive in everlasting renewal.

Transforming addictions means *tuning in.* We are receiving stations, designed to respond to orders from our Higher Self. There are only three positions we can wind up in: tuned in, off the channel, or receiving with static interference. Static comes from fear or illusion (resistance).

Understanding the nature of addiction is understanding the nature of desire. A desire can never be fulfilled. The more you try to fulfill it, the more you want it. This is its nature, to be constantly wanting. And the more we seek to fulfill it, the more we feed the desire, creating more and more of it. When you understand this, you can drop the future.... the wanting more and more. You can be content. You can live in the NOW.

ADDICTION AS BLOCKED CREATIVE ENERGY

ADDICTION IS NON-GROWTH.... A WAY OF BEING STUCK IN THE PAST. IF A NATURAL URGE HAS BEEN THWARTED, ADDICTION SETS IN. THEREFORE, ADDICTION CAN BE VIEWED AS BLOCKED CREATIVE ENERGY.

To free up constricted energy is the Transformer's task. He will need to know how to identify and work with each level of blockage within the personality of the client — the physical, the emotional and the mental levels. But we must remember, the personality is never really that simply dissected: all levels will be involved, but one primary block will stand out with its own particular set of characteristics.

A client stuck at a certain level of consciousness will still exhibit signs of that quality of *force* operating in his action; however, this quality — such as self-preservation, self-gratification or self-definition will seek expression through perceptual distortion. In other words, the person will attempt to gratify these natural urges in unnatural or self-defeating ways.

Blocked First Force: The Urge Toward Self-Preservation Distorted. A client stuck at this level of functioning will behave in a fearful, childish manner, for this is a very unidimensional level of consciousness — motivated by the simplistic urge for self-preservation. The basic sense of security that grounds us for living in this world is either haphazardly formed and randomly reinforced, or missing. Fear is the quality of the force that feeds this mode of existing in life, driving the individual incessantly toward meeting this unmet basic need for safety and well-being. These basic needs are *physical* in nature. This is a *concrete world, physical reality* level of consciousness.

When this initial stage of development is blocked, the world is perceived as an unsafe place, the person feeling he is alone and unprotected. Since his natural ways of meeting these needs are not predictably available for him, he will find unnatural ways to cope, become incessantly attached to any surrogate person or object that answers to the now distorted need. The child might feel panicked if out of his safe room with his familiar blanket and pillow. Or, he might appear horrified when a stranger tries to relate to him.

When older, he might eat compulsively in order to feel "full" (completed). Or he will pop a pill or load up with booze when anticipating an event perceived as "threatening." He might take on a neurotic, needy love partner to make him feel needed. Or he can become ritualistic and compulsive in his behavior, compelled to repeat over and over the same limited safe patterns, day to day. Some of these patterns are even useless, but they fill up the time and preoccupy him so that he does not have to think or feel (for most of his thoughts will be "fear thoughts" and many of his emotions will be anxiety-based).

The WILL TO LIVE, which is the spiritual developmental task at this level, is sporadic and shaky.... perhaps even non-existent. Instead, the person has become deathly afraid of life, unable to experience newness or expansion without untold anxiety. There are worlds out there to explore, but not by this one! He can't *imagine* getting off familiar ground. And please do not introduce him to new philosophies or religions. His whole understanding of the universe is predicated on his limited point of view, usually unexamined (but safe) belief systems constructed in a stereotypic manner.... "All black people are dangerous." "Only baptized Christians go to heaven." "Only people who work hard are valuable," etc.

Mistrust and fear operate in all his relationships. No matter how loving and consistant someone is in his life, he does not experience this love because he cannot believe in it. His entire world is seen through the lens of hopelessness and mistrust. Paranoia. Fight or flight are his chief defenses, depending upon his temperament. Some clients are hostile and aggressive at this level of dysfunction, while some are passive and withdrawn. All feel isolated, perceiving themselves as separate and apart from everything and everyone.... truly alien and alone.

If the client has met enough of these basic security needs, or *when* he does (hopefully with your guidance), he will begin to expand his life to new patterns of living, new relationships, or new energy in old relationships. He will exhibit a sense of self-mastery in life and will be able to give it direction. He will have discovered his own sense of potency. Cheerfulness and a bit of a sense of humor will appear, replacing the old "paranoid" view. He will show an interest in living that is exciting for the counselor to observe. Counselors, you don't have to worry about informing your client of this advancement beyond the first level; the client will tell *you*.... by his very desire for newness.

IF this level cannot be transcended, for whatever reason.... maybe the damage has been too severe.... the client is stuck in a fundamental, almost totally instinctive view of life that functions on a subhuman plane of consciousness, incapable of moving to a more integrated level. His potential is stagnated and death is his secret wish. He might choose to die slowly, through alcoholism or some other self-defeating pattern. Or, he might simply withdraw continuing to merely exist, passively or bitterly, without a real zest for life.

Some will choose death through suicide or a violent accident. If the WILL TO LIVE is thoroughly thwarted, neither the therapist.... nor anyone.... can prevent the ending of this life.

Blocked Second Force: The Urge Toward Self-Gratification Distorted. If this natural stage of development is denied or contaminated too greatly by unaware parent figures or unnatural situations, the child learns to mistrust its interpretation of sensual and experiential data. The natural yearning for self-gratification becomes repressed, or runs rampant.... either extreme causing untold emotional misery for the budding individual. Passion is the quality of the force that feeds this level of functioning in human personality. The basic needs are now *physical plus emotional* in nature. It is the emotions which take the focus now.

When this feeling stage of development is thwarted, the person does not know how to deal with his emotions. Feelings are perceived as scary, bad or unnecessary. And since our emotional life is a vital part of our humanness, we will have to do something unnatural to replace the core need for emotional expression which is going unmet. Expression of love and compassion, rightful anger, grief, joy, excitement, and the other ways of feeling naturally human are replaced by pleasure-seeking, living dangerously, creating melodrama and hysteria (to make one feel alive and important); or the opposite: denied feelings, constricted natural reactions to life situations, and repressed, stale stereotypic and rigid responses to life.

This client is confused about what his senses are telling him.... out of touch with his feelings. As a child, when he felt sad, mommy told him he didn't. When something felt good, daddy said, "shame on you, you are just imagining it." When pleasure was derived from something against the parents' moral code (which usually included anything sexual or aggressive), the child was punished. Now, the person cannot judge for himself what he is feeling or *if* he should feel it.

Clients stuck at this level of consciousness have not developed THE WILL TO FEEL. Their feelings become alienated, remain undifferentiated or forgotten, repressed or projected. The affective life will not be based on reality and will build a fraudulent self-concept and a false picture of the world. Herein lies the seed-bed for hysteria, manic-depression, depression, anxiety reactions and other forms of misdirected or unbalanced emotions. Violent rages often occur in people whose emotions are stymied. The pressure builds until something touches them deeply enough, then out it comes in inappropriate ways.

When a little child is *naturally* passing through this stage, we can see innate curiosity and a healthy desire for pleasure modeled for us. For instance, if you will observe a little child carefully you will see that she goes after a new object with all five physical senses, exploring each fully. She will taste it, smell it, look at it, feel it and listen to the sound it makes. Once the object is thoroughly examined (known), the child spontaneously tosses it aside and loses complete interest in it. This is the natural unfolding of human curiosity that leads later to Self-knowledge and knowledge of the world! The child is teaching us that we are designed to be learners.... seekers of Truth who literally gobble up our universe. Once we've assimilated a portion of it, and know it fully, we move on to something new. Onward and upward. This is the paradigm for expanded awareness in all its simplicity.

We begin by exploring our outside world, the "home" in which we find ourselves after being born into the larger reality outside the womb. Then, as we become grounded in our experience, we turn inward to explore the *inner* world, the psycho-spiritual realm that leads to total Self-realization. Gratification of our sensual/emotional needs and feeling passionately involved with life become the groundwork for relationship to others and feeling at one with our world. Feeling is good! Passion is strong feeling, it is connecting.... the cornerstone of a higher order of feeling called compassion. Sensual gratification grounds us in our feeling nature and later becomes transmuted into aspiring to serve mankind as a whole. The energy vector shifts from taking pleasure to giving pleasure.... from selfishness to selflessness.

When the client begins evidencing balanced emotions, control over useless or excessive appetites, and a desire to do something other than seek his own gratification, you will know he is moving beyond this feeling way of being connected to the world and expanding to the next level of integration, the mental level.... or, feeling wisely.

If this natural feeling stage is not allowed free and appropriate expression, the client is stuck in a level of being that is either fraught with too much emotional chaos or too little emotional response. Or he lives on a pendulum, swinging between depression and emptiness and excitation beyond the limits of balanced living. For those of you wanting more information on this failure of proper emotional development, a study of Freud, Sullivan, Horney or Jung will augment your knowledge in this area.[24]

In working in the field of addiction, I find that most alcoholics suffer greatly from a misunderstanding of their emotions. Many say alcoholism is an emotional/affective disease. (In ancient philosophy, the element of water symbolically stands for the emotions. In astrology, Neptune rules water; consequently, esoteric astrologers refer to alcoholism as a "Neptune conflict.")

When one cannot trust his feelings to guide him appropriately in life, or believes feelings are so dangerous they must be denied, so much confusion and pain result that it becomes necessary to block feelings. Severe mood swings and all-or-none thinking result. The emotional either/ors place us in a world of conflictual dualism; it's either terrible or it's perfect. I am either all good or all bad. Either God or the Devil is master-minding me (schizophrenia). You can see why many will choose a chemical addiction at this level of dysfunction: booze or pills can either put one *into* denied feelings or take one *out* of feeling anything, whichever is needed. Many addicts are seeking the "highs" or the "lows" of chemically-induced states of consciousness for excitement, because they are totally identified with their feelings. Feelings-running-rampant just want to feel! They do not discriminate *what* they feel; if pleasure is not possible, then pain will do. *Intensity* is the goal of unbalanced emotions. Being stuck at this level of consciousness, without the aid of the mental function, is such a significant part of the addiction process, we will study this level in detail in the next section.

Blocked Third Force: The Urge Toward Self-Definition Distorted. If we get off track at this stage of our development, we lose our sense of identity, becoming encased in the Lower Self. And as we probably realize by now, the Lower Self is nothing but an intricate mass of physical, emotional and mental habits, held together by a few ruling passions and desires.... associations it has made from knowledge of the outer world — a hodge-podge of self-repeating energy patterns with a few major themes. Turning to the outside world to find our identity is how we lose ourselves, not *find* ourselves: we are again caught in illusion, for the True Self is within.

Third Force is a *mental* stage of development, but it is still driven by the emotions. The motivating force in our lives becomes one of desiring status and a drive to please others — getting awards from society, or emotionally dependent on people who approve of us or make us look good. The mind's image of ourselves is in operation here. If we do not receive this needed endorsement from our societal reference group (the people whose opinions matter to us), we suffer a sense of low self-esteem or loss of identity. If we cannot succeed at gaining society's approval due to poor choices, constant failures or missed opportunities, we become neurotically addicted to something that will substitute for this good self feeling. We might seek status in a sub-culture we can fit into. Or we can compulsively collect status symbols, even when we cannot afford them — new cars, houses, fancy clothes, boats, bragging about important people we know, exaggerating titles we've held, building stories about ourselves that give us a certain image in the eyes of others. And when any of these is taken from us, we feel humiliated, even shattered, for our "story" has become who we are.

If we are finding our identity completely from things outside of ourself, we are living quite precariously, vulnerable to all kinds of conditions, for we have no control over these things or these people. The WILL TO KNOW, which is our essential developmental task at this mental level of consciousness becomes warped. Instead of going inward to know ourselves, we become an expert or fanatic in some tiny little reality we can master — the best bridge player in the club (with absolutely no sense of humor about the game), the perfect housekeeper, the expert at the races on Saturdays, Mr. Alcoholics Anonymous, etc. Authoritarianism, dogmatism, fanaticism, myopic thinking, constricted ideals.... these are several ways the mind can become stuck at this level in order to meet the self-definition demands of the ego.

And, of course, if all else fails, we can become chemically dependent. Our concrete mind, designed to bring us Self-knowledge, which is the entree into higher consciousness, has run amuck, gravitating compulsively toward more and more knowledge about the *outer* world, still susceptible to emotional imbalance. We are living in the ignorance of incomplete experiences and half-truths. Therefore, we are powerless to master life, because to see falsely is to live falsely....

"As if by enchantment, they see the False as the True."

— *MAITRI UPANISHAD*

STRIFE CONSCIOUSNESS: THE ENVIRONMENT OF ADDICTION

If my personality has formed according to principles based on the Truth of human nature, I will now have a unifying center for my identity that can function in the world with little conflict between my inner feelings and my outer life. I will have developed a healthy attitude toward myself and will consequently desire knowledge about the depths of the Self. This will attract the energy of my Higher Self, and I will be on my way toward more integrated levels of functioning .... beyond seeking merely the gratification of my deficiency needs.

If, however, I have *mis*created my reality, based on a fraudulent view of my Self and my world, I will now be ruled by my Lower Self, a false personality who functions as though it is my True Self.

The former leads to enlightenment; the latter to stagnation or disintegration. Now we can see that the biggest enemy of Self-creation is the Lower Self attempting to operate without the light of its counterpart, the Higher Self.... the ego running rampant with no master.

Perhaps it would be helpful at this point to look more deeply into the nature of this Lower Self.... the principles that govern ego-dominance.... so we can better recognize this tricky little transitory "being" that loves to take us over.

1. The Lower Self draws its data from the Outer World of Experience, believing it is the *only* reality; consequently, it thrives on half-truths.

2. Its director is the ego.

3. The ego *will* get our needs met.... one way or another.

4. The Lower Self draws its conclusions from the subconscious mind — programs based on the past, when we were *sub* (less than) conscious.

5. It only sees fragments of truth.

6. It is emotionally attached to life, based on fear, passion or desire for status or ownership. It only functions on the first three levels of consciousness.... in the world of addiction.

7. It cannot rise above itself. Like standing on a plank and trying to lift it, the Lower Self is totally *into* its experiences; consequently, there is no "self" who can rise out of it and see what is happening.

8. The Lower Self says, "My experiences *are* who I am." It feels *determined completely* by the experiences it involves in. This is the genesis of victimhood.

9. The Lower Self's three keynotes are limitation, sensation and egoism.

10. It cannot love; it can only "use."

11. Its energy feels forced instead of flowing. "I've *got* to be it; I've *got* to do it; I've *got* to make it."

12. The Lower Self keeps us locked into a sense of separateness .... isolated.

13. The Lower Self is a robot self, *re*acting to life rather than acting creatively through choice. It has many faces, for it is copying varieties of personalities.

14. Its behaviors are *acquired,* not intrinsic to the True Self.

15. By keeping our attention focused outward, the Lower Self blocks our inner development.

16. The Lower Self is ruled by feelings of scarcity: "There isn't enough for everyone. I must struggle to have my share."

17. THE LOWER SELF OPERATES IN THE WORLD OF STRIFE CONSCIOUSNESS.

Whenever you feel you are dominated by your Lower Self in a particular situation, raise your vibration to a level where strife does not exist! Seek the Truth beyond the apparent duality.... and you will find yourself living in a world of harmony rather than strife.

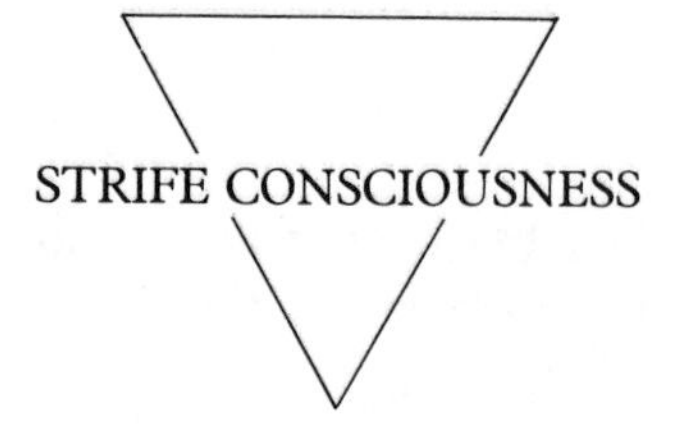

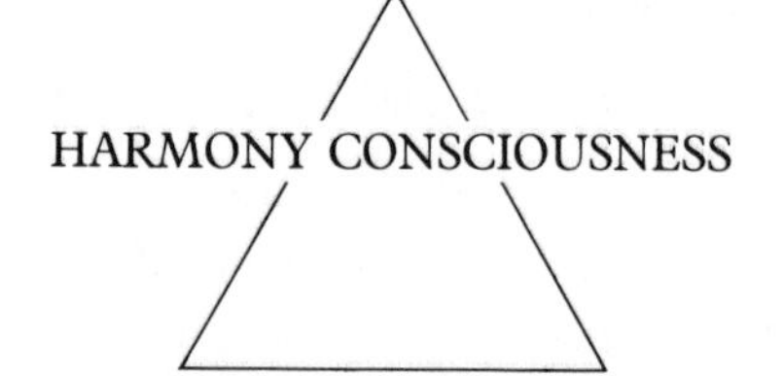

Strife Consciousness

1. Governed by scarcity consciousness.
2. Motivated by the need for self control.
3. Perceives falsely.

Harmony Consciousness

1. Governed by abundance consciousness.
2. Motivated by the need for Self expression.
3. Perceives Truth.

4. Sees fragments and *separates.*	4. Sees through all states and conditions to the overall pattern and *unifies.*
5. Utilizes the senses as receptors for taking in desires.	5. Utilizes the senses as outlets for illumination.
6. Views the body as "the truth" about who we are.	6. Views the body as a symbol, the vehicle (or instrument) of the soul.
7. Recognizes limitation and gives it power. (Focuses on the *condition.*)	7. Recognizes limitation and ignores it. (Focuses on the *perfection* behind the condition.)
8. Gets caught up in "melodramas," sees them as "truth."	8. Rises above "melodramas" and asks "What would I do if I were in perfect spiritual harmony just now?" and *acts* accordingly.
9. Feeling state: anxiety, striving.	9. Feeling state: contentment, joy.
10. Believes one must correct mistakes.	10. Knows to abide by universal Truth, which *automatically* corrects mistakes.
11. Believes things are inherited and inevitable. (Does not realize that Thought is creative).	11. Knows we will attract to ourselves everything we believe in (Thought is creative.)
12. Exalts the material world. (Man comes from experience through which he travels.)	12. Exalts the Soul. (Man comes from the One Source.)
13. Believes Man's nature must be reformed.	13. Knows Man's nature is already perfect; he only needs to realize who he is (transformation.)
14. Believes the important thing in life is material success.	14. Knows the important thing is to learn Truth.
15. Lives governed by fears of the past and future.	15. Lives governed by the present.
16. Is attached to rewards of work.	16. Surrenders reward of work to a higher purpose.

Preparing for the Life of the Spirit

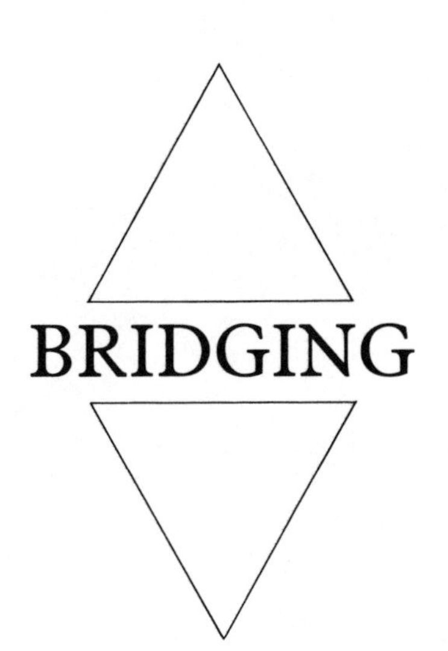

BRIDGING

4

Harmony Consciousness: Turning the Inside Out

In order to see how we redirect our energies away from Strife Consciousness (from having identified with the Outer World of Experience) toward Harmony Consciousness (becoming identified with the Higher Self), we need to study Appendix 1 on page 229 to see how the human being journeys through the levels of consciousness seeking its wholeness. This is known as "the process of becoming."

IF I DIE TO THE DICTATES OF MY EGO AND SURRENDER TO THE HIGHER SELF, THE SELF I REALLY AM, I WILL BE REBORN INTO TRUTH.

This Seed Thought represents a type of "conscious shock" that can hit us in our intellect at the Third Level of consciousness, which leads to rebirth into a transcendent state. Please note: *This thought is describing a re-birth, not a better and better way to live the old life.* If you will notice, the two triangles are discontinuous. Instead of being like this:

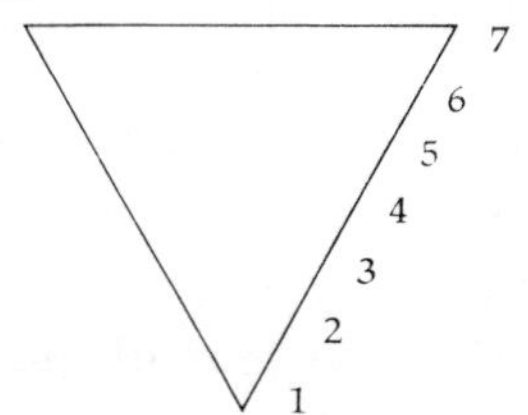

we have this:

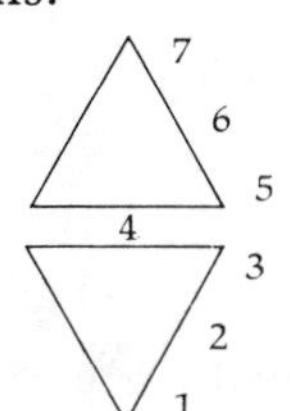

One must *die* to the old way before the new life is possible. Life flips upside down! Everything we thought we were, we aren't, and everything we thought we weren't, we are! This is such a drastic death/rebirth awareness, it cannot happen unless a spark from Level Four occurs in our consciousness. Because, as we shall see, Fourth Force is acceptance and use of the creative imagination, without which qualities we cannot bear, first of all, to even look at ourselves; and second, we will not have a way to conceive of anything other than what we already know from our past. And, of course, to judge by our present selves our future possibilities would be ridiculous. We don't even know who we are yet, much less what we are capable of being! Yet many people never make this realization. To see future possibilities as they exist in the inner world, not yet materialized, or, for that matter, to conceptualize *anything* new, requires a leap of imagination .... a certain working of the mind in its ability to create images and ideas based on what one senses might be possible — reaching up to a place that hasn't yet happened in time and space. This is the true translation of the word "faith" (from the Greek word "pistis," which means literally "another kind of thinking").

Really, what's happening is a kind of re-membering, a recalling something from a distant past, from a collective awareness residing "way back" in the recesses of our minds. Since something can never come from nothing, we must realize that on some level we already know our future.... or to put it another way, the future is already contained within the present moment. We are on the way to becoming the Being we were always intended to be.... like coloring a picture already outlined in a coloring book, or following a blueprint to its finished product. It is as though we've already dreamed the dream; and now, we are privileged to be able to experience it.

THE OBSERVER SELF: OUR AGENT OF CONSCIOUSNESS

As we learn to move into the Fourth Level of consciousness, we learn to separate the part of our mind that is constantly active from our quiet mind which is both a silent witness and a dynamic director of our energy. We realize we have been the victims of our active mind, like a laborer in a thought factory, or of our emotions, which continually mistake the force of the sentiments for the force of the Truth.

When we can experience this quieter mind, we discover we are in a state of observing ourselves *as we involve,* affording us a chance to decide creatively what to do in a given situation. The Observer Self can see what is going on without the distortion of the analytical mind or the static interference of emotional reaction.

> "To see, we must stop being in the middle of the picture!"
>
> — *SATPREM*

The Observer Self is the *key* to transformation, for it enables consciousness to work. It has been explored in many philosophical systems, known as The Fair Witness, The Watcher Self, or The Observer, defined by one transpersonal researcher as

> "That which is capable of observing the flow of what is — without interfering with it, commenting on it, or in any way manipulating it.... it simply observes the stream of events both inside and outside the mind/body in a detached fashion, since it is not exclusively identified with either. .... *Once he realizes each can be perceived, he simultaneously realizes that they cannot be his real self.*" (Italics mine)[25]
>
> — *KEN WILBER*

When we are operating from The Observer Self, we experience the various levels of naked reality without the mental and emotional veneer we've covered them with by the limitations of our Lower Self. Also, we see without judgment! Things can no longer be perceived as good or bad, black or white, but in terms of exactitude or inexactitude.... hitting or missing the mark.

The Observer Self, the voice of the Soul, is the passive aspect of the active, non-judgmental energy of acceptance. It prepares us to love ourselves by placing us in the right frame of mind. This is where mind and heart converge. It is more expansive than the intellect. The Observer does more than change our ideas about things: *it changes our level of consciousness:* If we only change ideas, we are still spinning around on the same wave length.... one more pirouette in the same mental space. To change our consciousness is to change *where we live inside....* to expand our state of Being. "As a man thinketh in his heart, so is he."

And this is no small feat for those of us who are used to feeling and mentalizing our way through life. As this beautiful type of Fourth Force first begins to work in us, we will enter a state of Self-remembering. At first we will remember ourselves (who we truly are) only now and then, as though we interrupt our daily routine to recall this amazing truth. ("This is not me! This is merely something I am doing.") Then we will go through a stage of making it a discipline to remember who we are, forcing ourselves to work harder at not forgetting. This stage will still feel frustrating, and we will fall into judging ourselves for being "forgetful." Then one day we will realize the dynamism of this effort has been nudging us right in the midst of other activities.... we will remember more and more often. And then the remembrance gradually becomes part of our conscious nature, living in the background, like a little muffled voice. All we have to do is withdraw from the outside world just slightly and there it is.... an inviolable, peaceful retreat.... a place of pure seeing.

From the Observer Self point of view we discover Life is a teaching; *all* of our experiences are leading us somewhere in our inner development. We see that if we are continually caught up in the current of Life there can be no peace or self-mastery; we will be carried off like a piece of straw. We discover we can love ourselves, in spite of our bunglings and misconceptions. And we *can* love! This is seeing from the Soul level. Reality.

The Observer Self consciousness cannot be taught; it must be experienced. In the section of Exercises, you will find two basic examples of how to lead clients into the experience of this vital agent of consciousness. They will become re-acquainted with an old friend. Once they've discovered this energy, ask them to practice one day a week being in their Observer Self as often during the day as they can remember. And do not support discouragement! Keep a sense of humor about it. At first we are lousy at being an observer; and we will find we are as caught up as ever in our emotional tumults! Yet somewhere, deep down, we will begin to experience a difference.... living more from that part of us who is never touched by Life's predicaments and who does not suffer.... just quietly watching and being. We will rise and we will fall, but each time we will rise up stronger. *The only error is to become discouraged!* We are going to be *more in the midst of Life* than those who are not seeking growth, for we are attempting to embrace *everything in our consciousness.* Not cutting off anything.... because this is the work of Transformation that we are all involved in. It is not a work for the weak-hearted!

When I can really separate my Self from the conditions that surround me, I see that apart from the faculty of *ownership* of my ideas, my perceptions, my senses, *I* am not really a part of these things — not even my body! My *Self* is in a position of observing both outer and inner events — a separate entity — that can choose its level of concern and involvement in these conditions.

And this is our primal quest: To understand the intricate interdependence between the conscious Observer and the content of our experiences.

As we stated earlier: We are not trying to leave Life, but to expand it. The Truth is right here, in the lowest material form, the body.... awaiting its ascension into the light of consciousness.... its supreme transformation. We learn to dis-identify from the content of our experiences, and with the aid of our Observer Self, remember who we are. In this state of dis-identification, we can relax and flow in and out of Life's events, seeing with clarity the meaning of them all.... realizing that each and every one, the positive *and* the negative, is part of the plan for our life. When the going gets rough, we learn to say to ourselves, "This, too, is just another experience."

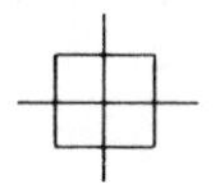

FOURTH FORCE: AWAKENING
(The Accepting Response)

Level of Consciousness: HARMONY THROUGH CONFLICT
Quality: Harmonizing Higher with Lower Nature
Pitfall: Attachment to Conflict
Mastery: Self-creation

In the space between the two triangles lies the bridge to higher knowledge, the Fourth Level of consciousness, where the Transformer does his work. Here in this "space" lives "I," the True Self.

At this level of awareness, for the first time I am able to rise above myself and see what I am doing *as I am doing it.* I am awakening! And I am beginning to love myself! I have the vantage point of the Observer Self, the one who can look *up* at my potential and harness this magnificent energy, as it looks *down* at what I am doing in the world and decides what choices to make and on whose terms. I am learning to accept myself *as I am*.... and life *as it is!*

Free, at last, of the constant constraints of my limited ego, I can *do my Being*.... acting creatively in the world rather than *re*acting mechanistically to cues from my environment. My ego is more solid now, intensifying its efforts to keep the Lower Self in the driver's seat. It will work on me to make sure I don't leave any unmet need floating loose, unattended. But my Higher Self is also a reality at this level of functioning. *I* can decide whether or not my ego is to lead, or whether it will be subservient to the me who can see what's really going on from a more integrated viewpoint. So my ego can now become my instrument. I no longer see the ego as my enemy; I am entering a world of self-acceptance.

Fourth Force is where we practice non-attachment, the art of "letting go and letting God." Letting go is an *active* force that *wills* our ego to release its perpetual judging and accept things exactly as they are. Both "the good" and "the bad" have become part of *the plan* for me. Fourth Force can love me unconditionally because it sees my real nature down underneath all its defenses, ego needs and half-truths that until now have been ruling me. I am amazed at some of the feelings I now have about myself! It feels like forgiveness.... like being calm and centered. I can feel okay about myself, even in the midst of a melodrama! I am operating from my heart, but with intelligence, the beginnings of love. Jesus' saying "As a man thinketh, *in his heart,* so is he," becomes a thundering reality to me now! This Force really does feel like thinking with the heart! It is not a naive, mushy love that allows others to walk all over it. It has dignity and discrimination. It has understanding. It seeks, above all else, to harmonize the two natures I possess. It will even sometimes seek out conflict in order to resolve a situation on a higher level.

This level of consciousness is the battleground where all of Life is fought *consciously.* The Lower Self is still able to take charge, because it is a creature of habit. We are still in the process of unlearning a set of imperatives we inherited from earlier periods of our development. And sometimes a need at Level One, Two or Three will dominate our personhood, and until we become aware of it, it has us under its spell. But the Observer Self at Level Four is always available, for it is its nature to awaken us. In fact, with practice, we discover we can tap into this resource anytime we choose.

Now that Fourth Force is awakened in us, we are always willing to see the Truth *unless* a lower need overwhelms us. In this case, we find that we must go ahead and just be where we are, in our Lower Self, running on ego power again. But it won't work for long because now we have discovered a more honest way to live. And Truth always feels better in the long run. You can count on it. Now I can forgive myself for the mistakes I've made, the wrong paths I've taken and the time I've wasted. I can see more clearly how it was all needed.

Fourth Force is the energy the Transformer uses to work from a caring position, from the heart. Here we can accept our client as she is without the distortion of our own ego's arrogance and defenses. Fourth Force can just sit there, being aware, and allowing the client to be in her space.... seeing, loving, and hoping to share Truth in a way the client can receive the benefit. This kind of relating is not goal-oriented, nor does it have to prove anything. It is comfortable just being there, understanding and accepting.

Since Fourth Force is the mere beginning of love, it can sometimes draw to itself its opposite. Remember, we often learn by contrasts. At this level I am working on being loving and learning to use my creative imagination to open myself up to new ways of being. It is natural that I will sometimes not love, and sometimes find myself in an unimaginative, robot-like state of consciousness where, again, nothing new seems possible. The difference, however, is that I now have the capacity to pull myself up by my own bootstraps and come out of this unenlightened position. I am not yet fully enlightened, but I am working with transforming energy for the first time in my life.

From here I can see with a cleared-out perspective what I *need* instead of only what I *want*. And I can also see *you* for the first time, as subject of your own life, rather than just an object in mine. I can love you even if you do not return the love. I can allow you the freedom to be yourself, even if it violates my own needs. At this level, I am in the process of transcending subject/object love. Though I still have passion and emotional energy that comes from Second Force, I also draw to myself compassion and the ability to focus on another. This selflessness comes from the Sixth Level of consciousness (which we will discuss later); Level Four is an eros/agape mixture of love, sometimes called "caritas" (meaning "charity") — a combination of the very human, passionate love, that is pleasure-directed and the Christ-consciousness love associated with Self-giving, spontaneously offered without calculating the cost or gain to the giver.

But even this level can create an addiction. When experiencing the conflict-side of seeking harmony, we can get hooked on the excitement of the ups and downs of conflict, and bring ourselves down. I've known some people who "come from the heart" so excessively that they lack the balancing energy of *will* in their lives, sometimes indiscriminately choosing a "feeling" way of living over appropriateness or logic. Then Level Four devolves into Level Two and an addiction to melodrama can ensue.... turning one's life upside down with too much change, attempting too many intimate relationships, and, in general, making one's life a mess. Since here we are attracting situations that are teaching us to open our heart, we will have lessons to learn in forgiveness and discrimination in the various kinds of loving. Having fallen into the pit of indiscriminate love, we can become polarized in love/hate, good/bad judgmentalness, expansion/constriction and problems with intimacy/isolation. Any use of drugs that accentuate the senses can be very detrimental at this level of consciousness, for it will exaggerate the conflict.

As this level becomes more cultivated and refined, we will learn to literally "discriminate with our heart." An ability to love wisely will be noticeable in our relationships — knowing when to love, how to love, and when to let go. We are now manifesting a healthy *will* to balance the softer *love* energy.

Also noticeable at this level will be the ability to forgive others who do not share our particular value system, another form acceptance takes. The quality of open-mindedness manifests in our personality. Imbalances in the physical, emotional or mental levels are no longer causing such blurred vision.... we are getting clear. We are becoming responsible adults.... letting go of childish attitudes, beginning to take our lives seriously but with non-attachment and a healthy sense of humor, with caring and concern. Self-sacrifice is no longer a negative word.

The confidence from knowing that we know how to meet our needs makes a need less demanding. This confidence stems from a new-found use of the creative imagination which operates at Level Four. Up until now, our imagination ran wild with us, exaggerating errors of the past, bemoaning perceived mistakes and abuses. Or it would carry us off into the future, catastrophizing about what might happen *if* this or that. Now, through Fourth Force, we use our imagination creatively and constructively in the *now,* discovering ways to transcend or resolve situations with a unique response. The imagination becomes brilliant and distinctive, because it no longer merely copies "the crowd." Now it can do its own thing, drawing from the higher centers where the unique response to the Soul's urge can usher forth. This is the level where Beauty emerges. The artist "sees" the higher as he utilizes the lower.

The superconscious energy is now available to image one beyond where he has already been. This kind of energy *transcends dichotomies.* A new realization occurs: Two heretofore perceived opposites can reside in the same space! It does not have to be one or the other. I can be childlike *and* mature; sexual *and* spiritual; playful *and* a serious worker; committed *and* free, and on and on! The two become One, transcended to a higher level where the dichotomy becomes irrelevant. This knowledge aids clients who feel torn apart by either/or thinking, believing they must make a drastic choice between two unwanted extremes.

DICHOTOMY TRANSCENDING

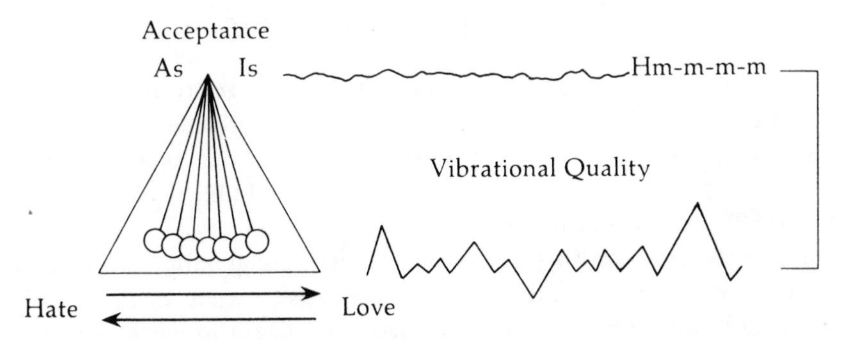

Creative imagination works in the *now,* drawing energy from the superconscious mind, offering us brand new creative solutions to Life's dilemmas. Destructive imagination works in the past and the future, motivated by programs from the subconscious mind, and its message is usually one of hopelessness. At Level Four we begin to harmonize the energies of the imagination and activate its tremendous power to transform our lives. (As one way to activate the creative imagination, see the exercise section of this book for the uses of guided imagery.)

As mentioned earlier, this is the level where Transformers work. They draw from the very highest principles about Life and human nature and then, in the therapy room, in a practical manner, they create their own unique response.

FOURTH FORCE: AWAKENING

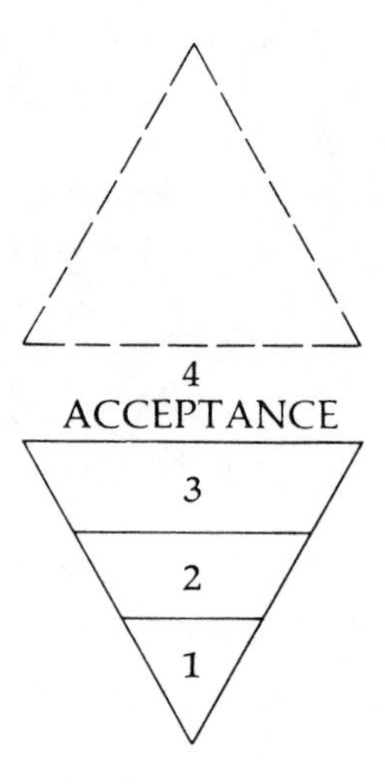

ACCEPTANCE: THE BRIDGE

Let me reiterate that Levels One, Two and Three are *discontinuous* with Levels Five, Six and Seven. Fourth Force provides the bridge. Acceptance — surrendering the need to control, judge, or manipulate Life — is the key to transformation. After Level Three is reached and Third Force is operating in our lives, the personality is getting into harmony *with itself;* the three lower "bodies" are aligning to function like a well-oiled machine. So, simply because we are beginning to love and understand ourselves, we naturally begin to work at Level Four, the Acceptance Response.... unless we get stuck in addiction.

But love and acceptance are not enough if we want transcendence! We can become trapped in a well-integrated personality! We can be the best professional in our field, the best citizen on the block, the most successful businesswoman in town, etc. But we will not live a transcended life, unless we begin to *think anew!* If you've ever talked to an intelligent, high functioning person with absolutely no knowledge or interest in the life of the Spirit, you will know exactly what I mean. Higher knowledge is not a "reality" to these people. Talk of God, destiny, a Higher Power, and the like, are considered "cop outs" or irrelevant. Living the practical life is enough. It is all they are seeking. Things must have a utilitarian purpose. God and poetry are meaningless. These materialistic people are not concerned with Being, only doing. The concrete world is their only reality. Everything must be literal. But unfortunately, *literal* understanding cannot make contact with higher understanding. "Oh ye of little faith...."

In Maslow's studies of self-actualizing people,[26] he found two types of self-actualizers: the type who transcend and the type who did not. Both types are excellent human beings. The non-transcenders were good people, fully functioning in the world of linear time. The transcenders were also good people, fully functioning in the world, but also in touch with another dimension where meaning and purpose of a larger reality, the inner reality, has been revealed to them. The time dimension might be called one's personal reality, while the other is the transpersonal, beyond the limits of the "ordinary." They are distinctly different realities, but both are a natural part of the human experience.

This is also the difference between the Western and the Eastern view of the world, the Western being concerned with the outer life, accomplishing tasks for a practical, rewarding and productive existence. The Western viewpoint rarely concerns itself with matters pertaining to the inner reality. While on the other hand, the Eastern approach views the inner life as Reality and the external world as "maya" or illusion. There is no Western word for "maya." The closest analogy is the idea of a mirage. Maya is the kind of reality where one sees something at a distance and reaches for it, but when one arrives there, "it" is gone, only to be seen again at a distance. This is the Eastern view of outer reality. The ancient Tibetans called it "glamour."

Love, compassion, clarity of vision, harmony, creativity, oneness with nature, spiritual quests.... these are the "facts" of the life of the transpersonal. Mastering inner truths, expanding consciousness, seeking ways to serve humankind are the goals the transcender seeks.

This is the world view Transformers prefer. But though they tend to transcend daily life and the material world, living it creatively, with very few external consistencies or rules, they also live in the world lawfully, honestly and with a sense of responsibility. They do not view transcendence as a license to escape responsibility; they are, in fact, Maslow's definition of the self-actualizer who transcends: they are more altruistic, more responsible, and *more* concerned about humanity than the ordinary person who is not actualizing.

Many chemically-addicted people are transcenders.... seeking to live ordinary life extraordinarily. Much of their problem is that they are trying to live in a world made up largely of non-transcenders, and seeking help from non-transcending people-helpers — left-brain-dominated psychologists, social workers, etc., who have been trained exclusively in the scientific mode so prevalent in Western thought. Transformers can live in both worlds, the right brain and the left, transcending the dichotomy between "east and west." They know how to be *in* the world, and not *of* it simultaneously. They make excellent therapists for the chemically-addicted client.

So now that we have thoroughly explored how we are intended to develop, how addictions can occur, and how Fourth Force comes into play, let's see how the Higher Triangle, when activated, creates transformation!

SYNTHESIS: HARMONIZING THE HIGHER AND THE LOWER

As the Lower Self completes its task of experiencing and meeting various needs, learning to function in the world, a very subtle event occurs.... sometimes all at once, sometimes gradually. *Personality becomes passive, and Essence becomes active.* This reversal has been observed by many and has numerous names, such as the metanoia experience, conversion, enlightenment, or being "overshadowed by the Soul." Jesus said "Lose your life and you will find it."

The physical body, the emotions and the mental life are aligned and in good health. Fourth Force is functioning, and now, as if by magic, the higher centers descend into the personality sphere. The Higher Triangle becomes activated and creates transformation! What began as two discontinuous triangles now becomes merged into a symbol we all recognize:

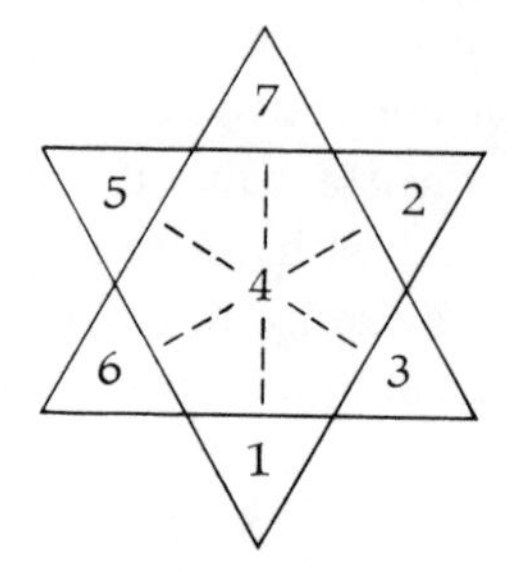

Level Seven, has overshadowed One with its dynamic qualities – Unity, Discrimination, Courage, Divine Will and Self-Mastery. Insecurity, at Level One, is synonymous with feeling alone, cut off from the world, frightened of annihilation by others outside oneself. Self-Mastery is insecurity transcended (which is what Love and Will merged together bring). One cannot fear annihilation if one is aware of being *at one* with everything, guided by the Divine Self. Insecurity, in fact, becomes an irrelevant concept. Fear is transformed into the courage to act as one's True Self. Love of God, which is synonymous with Love of Self, is the unifying force that now dominates the person.

Level Two is the organism's sensual playground.... the place where we rightfully learn to connect with our world through knowledge of the five physical senses and the personality's emotional life. At Level Two, we are completely identified with our physical senses, believing our feelings are all that we are. These needs and fears become transcended through awareness of our Soul nature. Knowledge from the intuition, which is "inner seeing," tells us we are Souls travelling through a lifetime of experiencing, which takes the sting out of ungratified physical pleasures. How can I fear lack of physical gratification when *I* am not even physical in my true nature? I *have* a physical body that prefers to be gratified, but *I am not my body;* I am a beautiful Soul evolving through a lifetime, eternal and forever perfect in all ways. When I realize I can *choose* sensual pleasure, but do not have to have it, a sense of freedom and peace washes over me, and I am content. As Level Six descends upon Level Two with its force of love and wisdom united, passion is tranformed into compassion, and self-gratification transmuted into a desire to serve others. One is now totally in love with Life. Through Fourth Force we have become fulfilled and now spill over with a love we yearn to share.

As Fifth Force pours into Level Three, the mind is transformed. Bits and pieces of Self-knowledge (acquired through the roles we've played and the self concepts we've adopted from the Outer World of Experience) becomes knowledge of the whole. Comprehension replaces discrete units of fragmented knowledge. We realize who we really are, rather than mechanically functioning like others thought we should be. We begin to express our true nature in the world, rather than someone else's idea of it. Dispassion enables us to see objective reality rather than our distorted sense of it. Action replaces reaction, and we become creators of the God-self, transcribing accurately our little part in the Divine plan. We are acting authentically. The Will to Know has become an intensely focused Love of Truth.

And all must pass through Level Four, as we cannot transcend to a higher level until we fully accept where we are now. This seems to be an inviolable principle of Life: Total acceptance of what *is* is necessary for the work of Self-creation. This is the Law of Transcendence made operational within human personality.

So now the personality is a willing and faithful servant of the Higher Self, serving as an instrument for its earthly mission. The "Master" has taken charge of his house. As you can see from the above model, One and Seven, Two and Six, Three and Five are the three polar opposites we work through, and each pole adds up to the number eight (∞), the mathematical symbol for infinity — a marriage of spirit and matter. This stands for the Divine balance achieved as a result of working through Life's teachings to gain substance.... spiritual staying power. And each set of "opposites" passes through Level Four in order to blend the two energies on each pole, making each number eight a twelve. (1–4–7; 2–4–6; 3–4–5). Twelve is the completion number in the Bible (12 disciples, 12 tribes of Israel, etc.), and other ancient teachings have also referred to this number as symbolizing completion.

It is important to note that one is never on *just* Levels One, Two or Three. For example, when one is stuck in a Level Two addiction and seeking to transform it, he is automatically working on the Two/Six polarity. The Law of Polarity is in operation here, which says we learn things by experiencing their opposite. This is why we must never ask for something unless we are sure we are ready for it! When I ask my Higher Self to give me patience, for instance, since its opposite quality will come immediately into play, I will activate all "patience tests" I need to teach me this quality. I will become invaded by rude people and given seemingly intolerable situations to master. I will be more aware than ever of how very *impatient* I am! If I ask to become loving, I will be shown in glaring technicolor the unloving side of my nature. This is how it works.

Events that happen in the outer world are totally irrelevant and insignificant unless the Higher Self (your Soul) is participating in some fashion. *There are only two types of events the evolving Soul seeks:* (1) *Tests.* Situations and difficulties that we learn from.... events that create the "sand for our oyster," designed to give us spiritual staying power or to work through a *karmic balancing;*[27] and (2) *Expressions of the True Self.* Ways to become authentic — doing things in the world that are a true expression of our natural gifts and are part of our purpose in life, and by so being, we aid humankind. Anything else we do in Life is ultimately insignificant.

The Soul delights in its work of Self-creation! You will find enthusiastic cooperation from your Higher Self when you commit yourself to the work of significant advancement of the Self. Transformers can aid clients in keeping to the task of Self-creation by guiding them away from time wasted in irrelevant pursuits that would not interest the Soul.

The following model provides another illustration of how the lower energies are transformed by the higher, based on a merging of Eastern and Western thought. You will note that the pattern of the energy flows from the bottom three levels of the top three, forms a Menorah, the seven-pronged candelabra of Judaism — which graphically illustrates the fact that the seeming polarities are *one energy,* two ends of the same arm.

When the drives of the Lower Self are brought under the jurisdiction of the Higher Self, the transformed energy brings about its evolutionary reward: Our inherent, divine ability to *know* and to *be* is realized. Effortlessly, we *are* love.

As long as our energies are constricted in the Lower Self, driven by the ego, we cannot purely manifest our true nature. Our lives are contaminated by misperceptions and unnecessary fears. Below I have outlined the Eastern concept of the "chakras," energy centers that exist along the body's main axis, to help us see where these energies become trapped in the physical body, blocking our pure expression. These centers correlate with the seven levels of consciousness we are studying, and can serve as a diagnostic tool for ascertaining where your client's energy is being dissipated. *All energy is one;* it merely expresses itself through the various centers depending upon the organism's perceived needs of the moment.

The word "Chakra" means "wheel" in Sanskrit, and is conceptualized as a spinning wheel. When a wheel spins, its outer sheath moves the fastest — more space, more diversity. This rim corresponds to our outer material self, moving about frantically in time and space. As we go inward toward the center of the wheel, we experience a slowing movement to a quiet stillness, which is the very center of our Being, the Higher Self, the center of consciousness.[28]

Symbolically, within each of these dynamic wheels can be seen a correlation of our personal physical world, our emotional energies, and how our mind and spirit function. For example, the solar plexus

ENERGY MODEL OF SELF CREATION

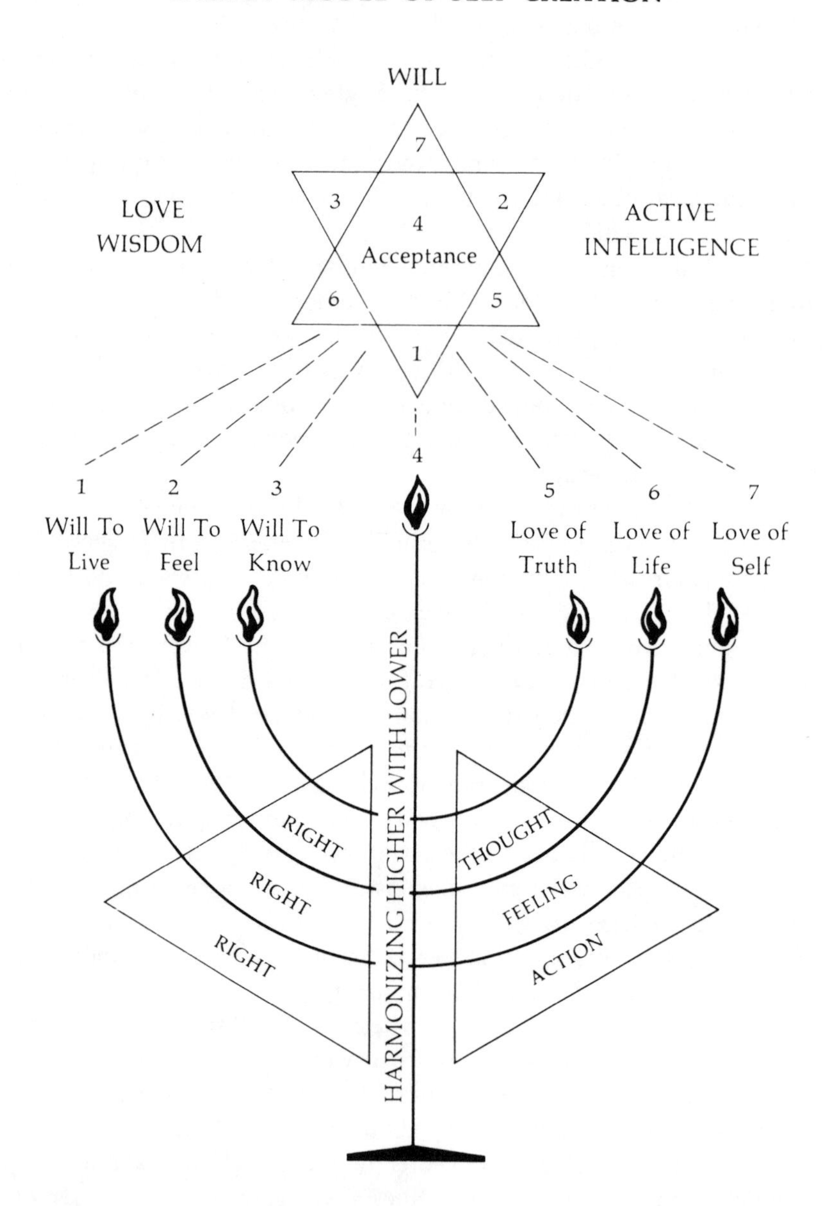

When the Will to Live is activated through Right Action, the Will to Feel through Right Feeling, and the Will to Know through Right Thought, then by the process or Acceptance (Fourth Force), we master the attributes of Authenticity, Non-Attachment (the merging of love/wisdom), and receptivity to Divine Will. The result is the advancement of the individual to a level of mastery of the physical world. He is now One with his higher nature.

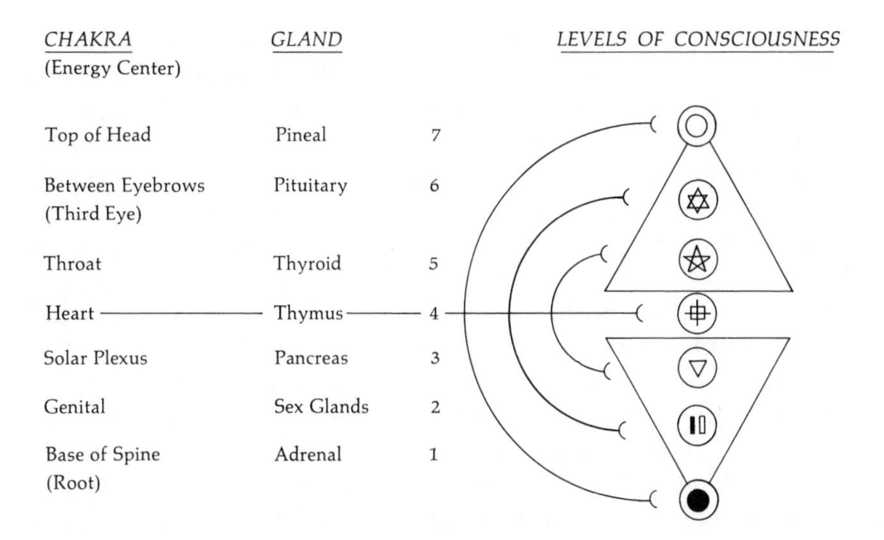

is the place where we "feel" aggression, hurt feelings and assertiveness, or physically experience digestive problems or the proper assimilation of food. The moving focus of each center reflects very concisely our basic needs and our basic nature, cutting across the dimensions of physical, psychological, mental and spiritual.

Each of these centers represents the point where a nucleus of nerves come together to form their most important functions. Likewise, each gland is represented as the major control for each center:

> "Modern medical research has established that the endocrine glands serve as strategic points of interaction between physiological, emotional and psychological functioning."[29]
>
> —*SWAMI RAMA, RUDOLPH BALLENTINE, SWAMI AJAYA*

Based on the Law of Correspondence, as expressed by the ancient Hermetic maxim, "As above, so below," the physical body is a microcosm of the gigantic macrocosm of which we are all a part:

> "These centers (called "chakras") have been rediscovered and described in many different cultures. Identical locations are noted in such cultures as far away and unrelated to India as that of the Hopi Indians in America...."[30]

As the Menorah shows us, we are required to go through life in the physical body to learn how to be whole. When we get stuck in a negative place, we are simply being tested. Now perhaps we can see why we must never put ourselves down when we see ourselves operating on the negative side of a quality, such as tolerance/intolerance. We must acknowledge our deficiency *without judgment* and remove our attention from the error, placing it instead in the direction of the positive quality that is its desired opposite, through Right Action, Right Feeling and Right Thought. If we become unloving and unforgiving toward ourselves, we get stuck in hateful and disapproving responses, which then draws hatefulness and judgmentalness into our world by the bushels. It's better to forgive ourselves. In this way, we keep our inner world clear for the positive energies of Truth, Love and Divine Will to manifest in the congenial soil we have prepared for them. A strong and active will and a desire for a pure heart are our best protection against unwanted negative qualities.

★ ★ ★ ★

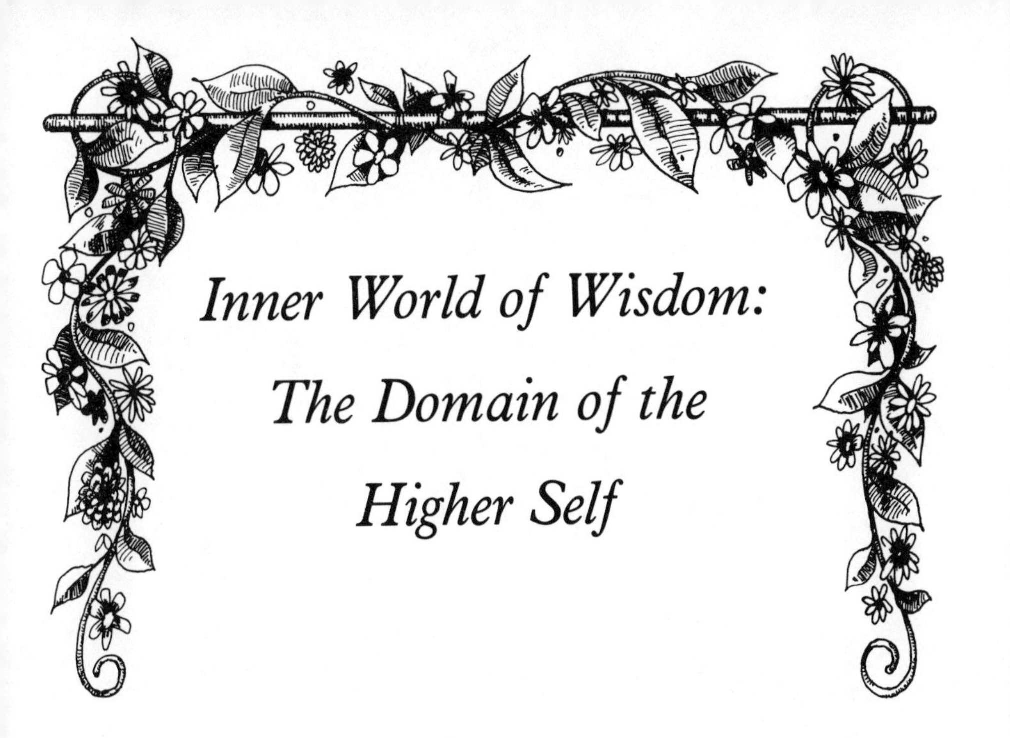

Inner World of Wisdom: The Domain of the Higher Self

BEING

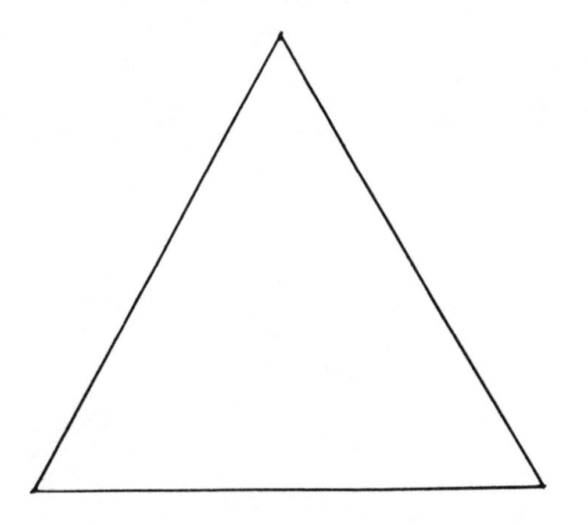

5

Being: A Description of the Higher Self

BEING AS MEANING

In our model, we now move into the formless world of Being, the archetypal energy that is our human Essence — the perfection *beyond becoming*. Traditionally we think of this dimension as the "spiritual" world, as opposed to the "material," and have considered it to defy analysis. Scientists say this area cannot be empirically defined, as it is part of a subjective, amorphous universe that may or may not exist. But the Law of Correspondence aids us here: "As below, so above." By realizing the material self is a perfect reflection of the greater macrocosm, we find we can indeed define the Higher regions of humanness. The spiritual world does not have to remain an uninterpreted mystery. This universe is identical to the one below it — only reversed. Our materialized world devoid of man-made distortions, turns out to be its mirrored image:

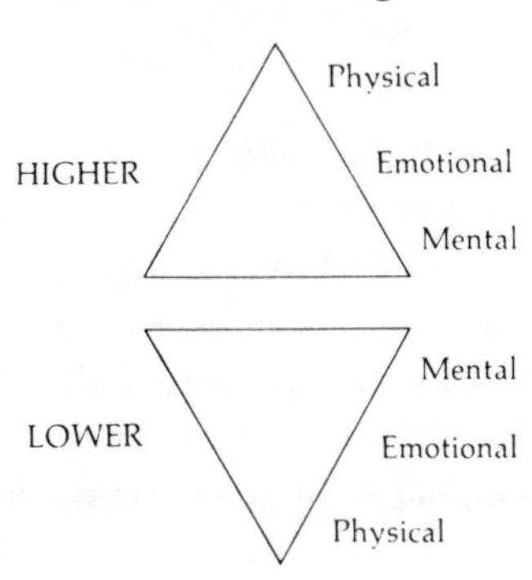

The Higher Mental, Emotional and Physical represent three distinct functions of Being, each having its unique part to play in the transmutation of the energies constricted within the Lower Self, in the process of Self-creation.

This formless world is where Meaning resides — beyond Time — already in existence before the creation of anything. This level is *not* becoming, *not* passing away; it is Being — the primal Cause of our existence. But we must "see" in a new way to experience it.

> "There can suddenly be opened within the heart or in the mind a realm of experience that is not the external world.... and we are then bathed *in the light of Meaning.*"[31] —*MAURICE NICOLL*

Discovering the Meaning of our experiences is the reawakening, the Transformation, we all seek. Meaning is another word for God. It is *curative* in nature, for it gives our Self its wholeness. It can be experienced mentally, emotionally, or "physically," depending upon which of the next three levels of consciousness one taps into.

FIFTH FORCE: THE LOVE OF TRUTH
(The Understanding Response)

Level of Consciousness: ACTIVE INTELLIGENCE (Higher Mind)
Quality: Comprehensive/Authentic Expression
Pitfall: Abstraction
Mastery: Illumination

This is the level of Higher Mind, concerned with Substantial Reality (rather than the personal self's projection of what is real). Energy originating at the Fifth Level separates the "wheat from the chaff," bringing along clarity of vision as it is learned by the organism, and weeding out false viewing, by use of the higher mental functions of abstract knowledge and comprehension.

This energy contemplates, then expresses itself in two modes, an active one of authentic Self-expression, and a passive one of comprehension. It is the level where we begin to *do our Being,* rather than taking on roles and identities that are unnatural for us. An *intrinsic* value system has now emerged, drawing its "approval" from the Higher Self, no longer needing so much endorsement from the outside world. Values and fact are now becoming one which is the mark of a self-actualizer. What we value is now being manifested in the world as observable *fact.* We have tapped into a gift of the higher mind — Authenticity.

A different "ought" system is operable. No longer are we controlled by an external "should system;" our "shoulds" now represent a natural urge coming from deep inside us, expressing our *essential* nature. We begin to express our unique purpose in life, utilizing our bodies, our emotions and our mental life in service to the Higher Self. It takes no energy to do our Being. *Stress occurs from trying to be someone we are not.* At this level we just begin flowing effortlessly toward the activities in life that are intrinsically right for us. We are following our grain. Someone once told me that when we are doing the work of the God-self, we will find it to be the place where we are the most comfortable and the most at home. I have found this to be true for me. The struggle has been in letting go of the images and expressions that did not fit, or the ones we've outgrown.

In esoteric circles, Level Five is seen as the home of the White Magician, because this type of energy can wield the power of the mind to actualize thought in the material world. This is the power to create: molding thought-forms that direct matter toward manifestation. This level of consciousness is where true understanding occurs. Its maxim: "The Truth shall make us free." It has the power to see beyond the fragmented knowledge of Level Three to the larger "whole" back in behind it all. It can see where and how each part fits together. It understands the purpose behind each "part," and how and why these particular events are manifesting right now in time and space. The Holistic Health Movement in this country is an expression of Level Five — though as with any new movement, there is ego contamination as the struggle for expression vies with opposing forces.

Level Five consciousness can see the significant in insignificant things, and the wonder in the commonplace. It comprehends the lesson Life is teaching us when we experience something unpleasant, recognizing the profit to be gained from any difficulty when taken in the right spirit. It affirms the unity in nature, seeing that "all is miracle." This person is the sage spoken of in the East, the one who sees all things with impartiality. This kind of energy can gain as much wondrous enlightenment from ironing a shirt as it can contemplating a holy ceremony or a sacred symbol. Emerson was using Fifth Force when he said "....all things are friendly and sacred, all events profitable, all days holy, all men divine; for the eye is fastened on the *life* and slights the circumstance."

At this level of consciousness, our work is to learn to image and to develop acuity of mind. Here, we listen to the world — both the inner and the outer realities — for Truth. In so doing, we manifest this Truth in our daily routine, becoming models of authentic human beings.... the one we can count on to understand and to act with integrity. (There is a danger to be pointed out here, however: to become so global and broad-minded in our approach to life that we lose the sense of concentration or discrimination necessary for the act of creating).

Physiologically, this level of consciousness is tied to the throat center, the place where we are learning to give and receive from life.... taking in Truth, and expressing it symbolically through "sounding our note."

FIFTH FORCE: THE LOVE OF TRUTH

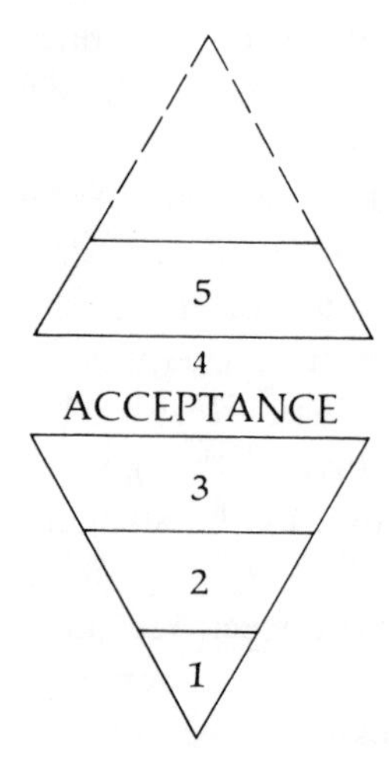

SIXTH FORCE: THE LOVE OF LIFE
(The Compassion Response)

Level of Consciousness: LOVE/WISDOM (Higher Emotions)
Quality: Intuition/Altruism
Pitfall: Over-identification with humanity's suffering
Mastery: Revelation

This drive manifests itself as a high love for all human beings and aspiration to serve, for as it looks within, it sees the nature of the human condition and the work we are to do for the Divine Plan of evolution. It comprehends with compassion. This is a "feeling" level of consciousness that takes its form in such areas of human endeavor as philosophy, teaching and healing. It is a marriage of *love* and *wisdom,* which, when really understood, must *always* be merged. Love executed unwisely becomes indiscretion, and wisdom administered devoid of love becomes cruelty or blindness.

This is the "opening of the third eye" of which the mystics speak. We cannot always explain how we know what we know at this level of consciousness, because it is *beyond logic.* But neither is intuition devoid of logic: it is a combination of all the truths we have incorporated into our being through experience as we have progressed along in Life. Intuition is a "higher kind of logic" that takes in the seen with the unseen, a *direct* comprehension of the nature of Reality that comes from the superconscious mind.

There are four ways of receiving knowledge from the intuition: the highest way is called *illumination,* which is revelation of the divinity in all things. Or, we can experience an "inner hearing" .... a voice that says, "Go, do thus and so...." and we "know" we must do it. A third way is to sense a "contact" with someone or something that indicates a relationship or a liaison with the Higher Self, an emissary from the transpersonal realms. And fourth, we can find ourselves *taking an action* that we had not intended with our logical mind, but suddenly feel must be done. All of these are ways of being in touch with higher knowledge. It is important to realize that *the intuition is never wrong.* It is the voice of your Soul! It can be transcribed inaccurately, however, because we are not totally purged of all the ego's misperceptions about Life. So there are important guidelines to follow when being led by the intuition to avoid mistakes that can occur if the concrete mind takes over the message and interprets it through distortion:

1. Uncontaminated intuition brings a feeling of inner calm and certainty, a sense of resolution that holds no doubt. There might be pain, because sometimes the revelation will mean letting go of something.... but underneath the pain will be a sense of rightness.

2. The truth of the intuitive flash will synthesize other important things in your life. In other words, it will not violate or confuse any Truth that already exists for you.

3. Intuition will feel like *flowing* rather than *forcing.* It will not require effort to follow through on what was received; every door will easily open, rather than close, as you carry out the message.

4. There is a sense of quietness and humility with true intuition. It does not boast or brag. It has nothing to defend against and nothing to prove.

5. It often comes in the form of symbolic knowledge and requires us to go beyond a literal interpretation. For instance, it may show you an impending physical death, when really what is happening is a kind of ego death.

6. Never act upon intuition without giving it the test of logic. Intuition does not live in time, so sometimes its messages come when timing is off. It is better to wait and see if the message holds for awhile, rather than acting impulsively, then test it out. See if doors open as you begin to proceed. If each step toward the goal seems effortless and natural, *go for it!* If you begin to feel you are "pushing the river," it could mean the voice of a partial self was masquerading as your intuition, and the message is off the mark.

Sixth Force receives through empathy: hearing others on their level of consciousness. It operates from the Law of Attraction, meaning it draws others to it and is drawn by others. It is the magnetic energy of the Soul, the Christ-consciousness love known as "agape."

This level represents universal love that suffers with humankind, but does not involve egotistically for its own sake. It can sacrifice for a cause and can hold forth the vision of evolution, in spite of any kind of difficulty. The motivational force is drawn from a desire to serve and the wisdom that comes from inner seeing.... devotion to God, and devotion to humanity. Good-will, friendship and affection are to this person the foundations of the human race.

Sixth Force balances the passionate, self-centered desire love that resides at Level Two. It meditates.... and sees the world clearly. It understands where mankind is stuck.... and sometimes weeps, or sighs.

SIXTH FORCE: THE LOVE OF LIFE

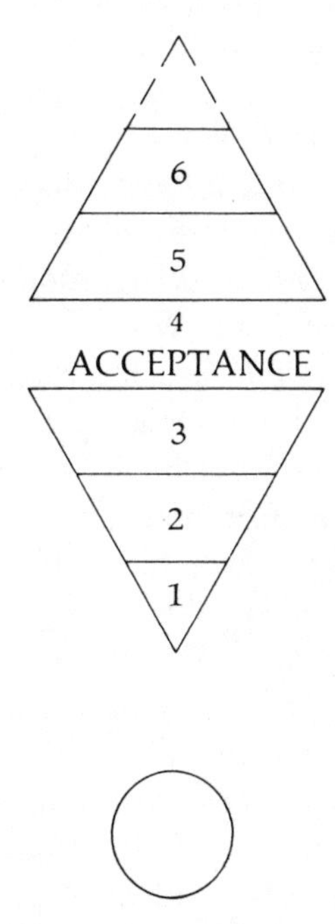

SEVENTH FORCE: THE LOVE OF GOD (SELF)
(The Unity Response)

Level of Consciousness: SPIRITUAL LOVE/WILL
Quality: Self-mastery
Pitfall: Indiscriminate use of Will
Mastery: Transformation

> "The Self is Life and the Only Reality, and whoever is initiated into the Self — and in this way has come to know himself completely —loves everything and everyone equally, for he is one with them."[32]
>
> —*ELISABETH HAICH*

This is the God energy — Original Cause. It is the force that wills us toward unity of consciousness, completion and oneness with everything. It is operating from the Law of Oneness, directing us to manifest our true nature, urging us with great power and force. This energy is so dynamic and directive, it can also destroy.... which is one of its purposes: to rip away old forms, dead matter that is getting in the way of our evolutionary progress. But if it tears down, it does so *consciously,* with a high purpose in mind.... for this is the merging of Love and Will.

This is the level of True Being — the new "body" — its urge, to manifest the Soul perfectly on Earth. Because of its unitive quality, it is referred to as a "place" — Heaven, Nirvana, Paradise. Here there is no conflict: all is One, in perfect harmony, with perfect knowing. Self-mastery is completed here. We have glimpses of this level of consciousness sometimes, but usually very fleeting. They are the moments when a soul quality such as *pure* truth, *pure* beauty or *pure* love emerge and are expressed through us. These are the "peak experiences" Maslow describes. Certain drugs have taken people here, but only to visit, never to remain. An integrated personality is a prerequisite for the proper use of this energy. Drug abusers who seek this kind of "high" do not possess an intact personality.

Disintegration can occur if one finds himself at this level before the organism is cleared out enough to handle the energy. Seventh Force enables us to know for a fact *that man is the full and final arbiter of his own destiny.* Many people are not ready to face this Truth, still caught up in the need to blame themselves or others for the "mistakes" they have made. Until blame and guilt are transcended, sometimes it is unsafe for one to rise to the level of full understanding, where total and complete responsibility for our lives resides. Seventh Force is characterized by the courage to persist and by the absolute, unswerving knowledge of one's Destiny. This is the energy that purifies and perfects the WILL TO BE that is missing at Level One. Seventh Force puts us directly in touch with the very goal which was our beginning, the purpose of our life. Like a luminous pressure, it "pushes the world and each thing in the world toward its own perfection through all the masks of imperfection." (Satprem)

SEVENTH FORCE: THE LOVE OF GOD (SELF)

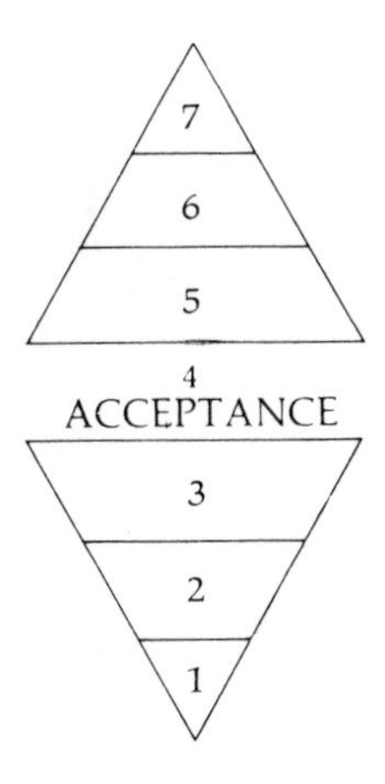

SUMMARY

I hope this gives a clear sense of the levels of consciousness residing within the domain of the Higher Self, three distinctly usable, transpersonal forces. As we can see, we truly *are* these three amazing types of energy that emanate from our Soul-consciousness, perfectly designed to serve as *specific* transformers for energy constricted in the three lower levels. The three below serve as a mirrored reflection of the three above, three in the world, and three "out of the world." The ego's will to live, to feel and to have an identity become the love of Truth, Life and ultimately, God. When the two are merged, we are able to be "in the world, but not of the world," meaning we have transcended our need to be attached to outcomes, and can just relax and be! All our willful effort to grow and expand is finally rewarded in effortlessness.

TRANSFERRING ENERGY FROM OUTER-DOMINANCE TO INNER-DOMINANCE, FROM EGO TO ESSENCE, IS THE WORK OF TRANSFORMATION. It is exciting to realize that the total key to this entire operation is learning to use the powers already contained within us. Transformers merely invite us to be who we are; nothing has to be added, only released.

★ ★ ★ ★

6

A Model of Transcendence

Transformers know that "Personality" and "Essence" are two distinctly different energies and that understanding this difference is the *key* to understanding human nature. They break through the veil of partial truths that most of the helping professions are caught up in.

To summarize what we've learned so far, the main point is to realize that man is a *four-fold being* and the causative level of his behavior in the world is the spiritual dimension — his unique impulse to live a life of significance — a life that enacts his primordial purpose.

And disease can occur at any level along the way when one gets off the mark. The Transformer checks to see where one has gotten off track — on which level the pain is manifesting — and intervenes at that level. He knows the level of intervention will be the *symptom* level, and understands the cause will be in a higher (deeper) place.

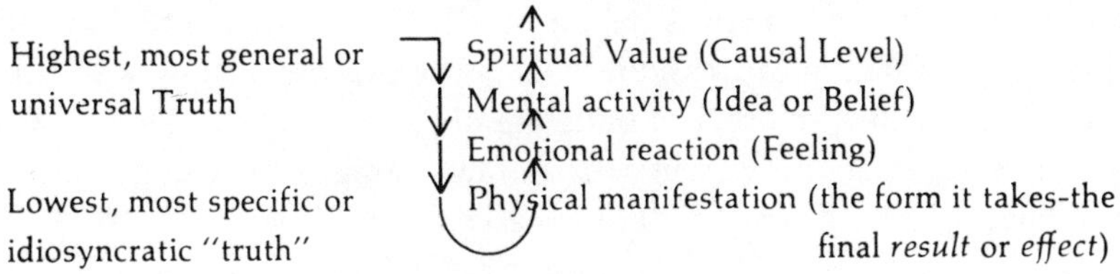

Highest, most general or universal Truth	Spiritual Value (Causal Level)
	Mental activity (Idea or Belief)
	Emotional reaction (Feeling)
Lowest, most specific or idiosyncratic "truth"	Physical manifestation (the form it takes-the final *result* or *effect*)

For example, a physical treatment, such as a massage, will not cure an emotional illness, such as imbalance caused by a temper fit; it will only temporarily relieve the stress. Emotional help *can* cure a physical problem, however, since the emotional level is closer to the "cause" than the physical; but only if the physical problem is an absolute *effect* of the emotional imbalance. We have to remember that *we are hierarchical beings,* with the physical being the lowest and the spiritual, the highest. Emotions are closer to the body, and ideas and beliefs are closer to the spiritual.

To continue our example, just as a physical treatment will not cure an emotional problem, neither will an emotional treatment cure a mental insanity. For example, emotional calmness that comes from the technique of meditation will help to formulate clear, sane thoughts, but if an insane thought still exists, even though the person meditates perfectly, the emotional stability will disintegrate every time the insane idea gets activated. Working to clear up the insane idea *will* heal the emotions, which in turn will heal the physical.

Transformers emphasize clearing up irrational thinking, releasing pent-up emotions that were built up from these thoughts, and guiding the client to new action in the world based on Truth and *harmlessness.* Because the Transformer operates within the Law of Cause and Effect *with awareness,* he knows that any action, speech or thought that brings harm to another individual will rebound upon its sender. Therefore, he trains the clients to *act rightly* in life — to live according to a realistic value system and to treat others with love and compassion discriminately.

Working on the physical level of an addiction, using such techniques as detox and Antabuse, will not help your client in the long run unless the emotional, mental, and spiritual aspects of his nature are reached. Energy constricted in the physical body will manifest as physical problems, just as energy constricted in the emotional "body" will manifest as imbalanced emotions *and* possibly, a physical imbalance as well. At the mental level, constricted energy manifests as rigid, stereotyped, unclear thoughts, which will in turn, set off an emotional reaction. And behind it all, the spiritual Self has been denied its authentic expression. This is the process of how we get off the mark. So now, in order to understand the work of the Transformer we must elaborate on viewing the human being as an energy system, and how constricted energies are released and redirected.

ENERGY: THE UNEXPLORED FACTOR IN ADDICTION

The Transformer, working from the Fourth Level of Consciousness, is fully accepting of his client's current predicament, regardless of its nature. He is working within the Law of Transcendence, which says we cannot rise to a higher level until we accept fully where we are now. He knows the client is manifesting a natural urge negatively. The first task will be to redirect these misused energies. In order to do this work, the Transformer must have a precise understanding of how the three lower energies are specifically transmuted through the activation of the three higher energies.

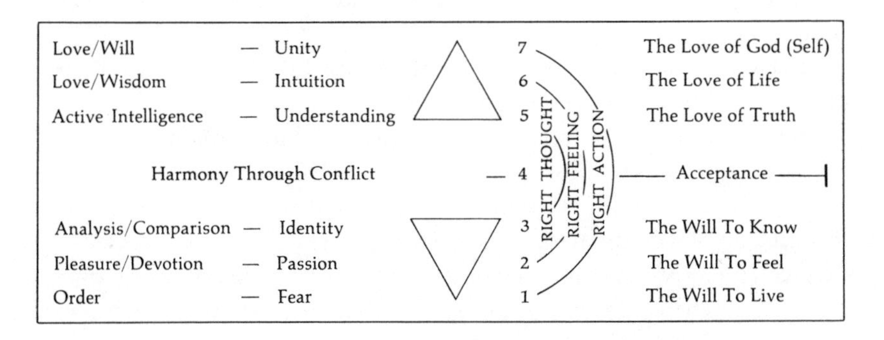

Level One deficiency transcends through Seventh Force. Both levels are considered "physical:" the *form* or *structure* of the organism — "ordinary being" and "Transcendent Being." Level Two transcends through Sixth Force, a feeling/emotional state of being; and Level Three transcends through Fifth Force, a conceptual (mental) state of being. Level Four is the transformer.... "the work of the heart." Fourth Force is activated when Third Force is operating within the personality. In other words, until a person learns to use his mind in a new way, extricating himself from mass-thoughts not based in experience there is no vantage point from whence he can perceive the "conscious shock" that awakens him to the need to get beyond ego. If he cannot think anew, he will be content to become just a "man of goodwill," a better and better person, but not a *new* person.

Fourth Force is actually *four* energies: the personality energies of the physical, emotional and mental levels combined with heart energy, the energy of acceptance. Fourth Force is the bridge — the battleground where Experience and Being meet for the first time. Its symbol is the cross, which is equated with suffering. For this reason it is called the plane of "harmony through conflict" because it is being in the world and learning not to be *of* it. This is the work that transforms our lives. It is the Path of the Heart.

We live in a universe whose nature is duality. It is through experience (duality) that we learn. When we became *created* from *uncreated* energy, we experienced our first duality, inventing a state of consciousness based on experiencing opposites. Consequently, it is not possible to be on a *single* level at any time. We will work on a pole of dualistic energy like a pendulum swinging from the lower to the higher and back again. Both the higher *and* the lower are *okay* as long as the ego stays in its rightful place and does the job it is designed to do.

Let's look again at the model used by Transformers in their work with addiction. (Refer to page 229.)

For example, as we learn to transcend a need for passion to a state of compassion, Level Two energy is over-laid by the energy of Level Six. Emotional imbalance fades away, no longer the dominant force. Guilting ourselves for natural sensual pleasures dissolves so that we are free to enjoy sensual awareness with our total being rather than just a fragment of ourselves. At Level Two, a client might have to put herself in a "seductress" sub-personality to relate to her love-mate; then, once she accepts herself as a sexual being, she will find she can relax and enjoy her sensual self naturally and easily. As you can see, the therapeutic task here will be resolving the struggle between the sensual/spiritual split within the client. People sometimes fear spiritualizing their sexual nature, believing it will mean having to give up pleasure. What really happens is the pleasures experienced at Level Two become intensified because they are now spiritualized with total meaning. WHEN WE REALIZE A TOTAL CONCEPT OF SOMETHING AS WE ARE EXPERIENCING IT, WE ARE FOR THAT MOMENT PERFECT. A moment such as this creates a state of bliss. The heart and mind have merged. A split no longer exists between the higher and lower.

Level One and Seven work together. At Level One we feel isolated, filled with dread and fear of the outside world. At Level Seven, the organism knows it is a part of a whole within which it "lives and moves and has its being," and it simply cannot conceive a thought of isolation. Isolation and fear are irrelevant concepts.

The One/Seven Pole is practical work. The therapist is working with the struggle between powerlessness and personal potency. The highest and the lowest must merge to make a new structure — a structure based on the Truth about our natural identity. The client learns that he is the *creator* of his experiences, not a victim of anything "out there." He feels a sense of Self-direction he's never before experienced. At the Personality level, this is called "taking responsibility for one's life."

At the Essence level this is the consciousness that knows one is master of his own created Universe and chooses to use his energy toward the manifestation of goodness, truth and beauty. Taking responsibility for our lives, Right Living, is using our spiritual Will, where the organism is directed by its Soul's purpose. This is not to be confused with the ego's will, which only seeks personal satisfaction.

Likewise, Levels Two and Six are a polarity, both containing the energy of our "feeling" nature. The lower emotional can swing from pleasure to pain and back again. It can get manic or depressive, or it can become hysterical. It searches for the "highs" in life by identifying with objects and people that give it a "kick." Many chemically addicted people are stuck at this level. "If I don't feel high, I don't feel alive." Going from drug to drug is really no different *in principle* than going from person to person or object to object looking for that exhilarated feeling of being alive.

So we all know what this stage feels like, even though some of us may not be chemically addicted. For instance, we might think we always have to have the most perfect and gorgeous mate by our side to make us feel excitement! And when we no longer see that person as perfect and gorgeous, we can always trade for a new model! Houses and cars can do this for us, too.... or vacations to new and exciting places, growth groups, or even spiritual paths. The way we can tell if these are becoming an addiction is if the energy goes out of them once they've been "experienced." Satiation leads to searching for a new group/object/person. Frustration of the need leads to trying to get more and more from the same outside source, until we wind up angry or depressed.

Level Two experiences — the pain we encounter while seeking pleasure — are the ways we develop a balance between love and wisdom. Learning to love discriminately, and to develop knowledge based on experience is wisdom. This kind of love is effortless — never based on neurotic need patterns. It will always be balanced and realistic, producing good for all parties involved.

On Levels Three and Five we do the mental work of conceiving the images, concepts and beliefs that truly work for us. The therapist helps the client resolve the polarity between status-seeking and expression of the True Self. We become who we are, rather than what we thought we should be. If we are thwarted at this stage, we can be extremely rigid in our thinking, or we can become an obsessive/compulsive person seeking more and more ego gratification by grasping for status from the Outer World of Experience. We take on jobs just because the title appeals to us, or marry a person just to have his or her identity. "I am doctor so-and-so's wife." It is the ego's way of trying to play the drama of life, choosing the roles and characters it wants to model from living persons or from literary heroes and heroines it has idolized.

Here, the ego is learning to express the purpose of the individuated Soul. The purpose of Life, according to the ancients, is to make our spirit Self-conscious on all levels of reality, to gather Life's experiences, one by one, and carry them back to the Source. But many of our experiences become predicaments, sometimes quite painful. If we become *identified* with our experiences and forget who we really are, we are lost. We are already perfect, but we do not *realize* it yet, so our Soul is still in transition. We are *involving* in Life so we can *evolve.* And it is through the roles and identities we choose to experience that we discover what fits for us and what does not. Oftentimes, it is through having tried and been disappointed with a certain role that we've learned to let go of seeking that particular identity. Then, other times, it is through having *fulfilled* a role that we grow beyond the need for it. Levels Three and Five are the active expression of our mental concepts about our "Self." The need for self-esteem transcends to a desire for Self-expression when we work with this energy correctly. Before, our energy was drawn in from an outside source; now the energy reverses and is directed outward from our center.

And the outward search turns inward to the contemplative life. (See Exercise #10, page 247, to aid clients in achieving this energy shift.)

Persons stuck at this level often talk a lot about the important people they have known, the titles they've had or the social or professional victories they've won. They *need* for you to notice these things, because these honors *are* their definition. Transformers can acknowledge this need in someone else and give it gladly, for they work at Level Four consciousness. A counselor still totally ego-dominated will become aggravated with a braggart, not being able to stand seeing him get the attention he is eliciting, for he, too, is stuck at this level and cannot bear to see it reflected. Level Four consciousness can see Level Three operating because it can "step aside" and disidentify from it. Then it can point out the mistaken search for the identity from the outside and gently direct the client toward an inner search. Transformers can make this point non-judgmentally.... just clear, straightforward *truthful* energy passing from heart to heart.

Acceptance, the Bridge. Transcendence through the polarities always requires Level Four energy. Acceptance of *what is* — our Selves as we are, and Life as it is — serves as the bridge to the higher centers. Without this quality we could not love ourselves enough to look at our true needs, nor would we be able to imagine ourselves as ever being any different from what we've already been. So we never just work with One/Seven, Two/Six and Three/Five. Instead our work will be with One/Four/Seven, Two/Four/Six, and Three/Four/Five.

As Transformers, we realize no Truth model of human nature will ever be absolute or linear in nature, as Life is not lived in a straight line. It is experienced more as a dynamic spiral.

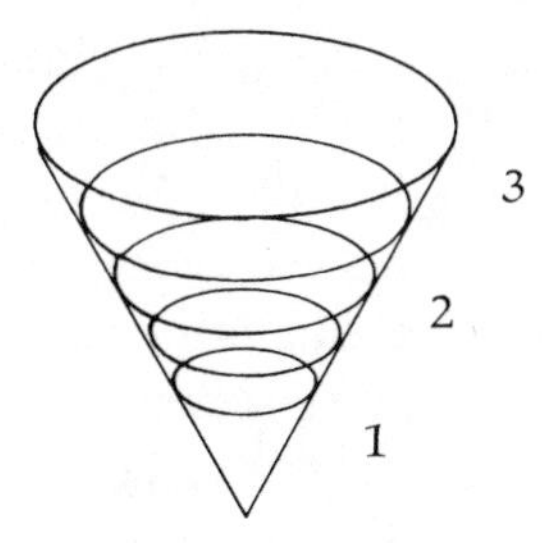

We move in and out of our experiences in a cyclic fashion until we have completed them. A particular event will keep recurring in our life "until we get it right." We are dealing with a model, *not* absolute Reality. A model can serve as a road map, but will not replace travelling through the territory. As you study these models, please remember this.

When we are still ego-dominated, we will be evidencing blocks at all three of the lower levels at once, for they all converge upon each other. But the focus will usually be noticeable on one level. People will appear to be a "1/7 type," a "2/6 type" or a 3/5 type." This knowledge can guide the therapist to the proper point of entry into his client's reality. With some clients we will want to take a very practical (physical/instinctual) approach — 1/7; with some, the emotions will be the key to the person; and with others, a concrete mental approach is the way to reach the client at the beginning of the process. Consciousness acts as a searchlight. It focuses the energy in that particular place, putting all our attention there. In other words, whatever level of consciousness I am operating on at a given time *becomes my reality.* I will tend to see the whole world from that perspective at that particular time. *It is my universe* — the context within which I view all my experience.

This is a very important concept for us to realize in our work as counselors. It is certainly okay to help someone transcend their limited viewpoint by offering them a new point of view — *but we must get their attention first.* And the only way we can do that is to join them at their level.... accepting them where they are! You can work from one level higher, and gently pull upward, but if the level you are working from is too divergent from the person's reality, they will not be able to relate to your frame of reference. It will feel like "casting your pearls before swine." Someone whose higher centers have opened can see the lower ones at work, but someone who is stuck at a lower level cannot see the levels above; they simply do not "exist." Consequently, the person at the higher level has more responsibility in the relationship than the other one. This is not an ego trip! This is a fact. The one who can see more of the whole is the one who sees more clearly; consequently, they cannot "get away with" denying the truth without experiencing some sort of consequence (karma). And no one can pretend to be at a higher level than he is. *Level means state of Being.* One just IS at a certain level on the path toward wholeness. This is not a game; this is Reality. Level Four is where we begin to know this Truth.

THE SPECIAL SIGNIFICANCE OF THIRD FORCE

Self-transformation happens *in the mind,* becoming an option for the first time when Third Force begins to activate within the individual consciousness. Before this time, the person is literally a victim of his physical appetites and his emotions. Third force is mental. And the mind (intellect) contains the ability to think *beyond itself.* When emotions "think" for us (and believe me, they do) they will only cognate within the limitations of the feelings and desires of the moment. This is why we cannot trust our emotions to make decisions for us. Haven't you ever heard yourself saying in a fit of anger, "Well, I just never want to see him again!" Or, "I don't even care what they think about it!" And other such statements that are really *the exact opposite* of how you really feel.

When we act impulsively on emotion we nearly always feel later that we have made a mistake. Third Force can get beyond emotion, even if only for a little while. And it is during these "cleared-out" mental times that we get a glimmer of the higher Truth. And we learn these Truths from comparison. "I've been worrying so much about trying to live up to everyone else's ideas about this, I am just now seeing how much I really dislike this job." Or, "I *say,* I want to be a bookkeeper, but when I'm actually doing the work, I hate it." Third Force compares actual experiencing with one's ideas about the experience. It reality tests and practices thinking new thoughts just a little bit beyond the Lower Self's desires. This is the correct use of the concrete mind who draws its data, by comparison and analysis, from the Outer World of Experience.

It can also do something even more amazing: Third Force can *shock* you into a new awareness by imbedding a Seed Thought in the mind. Seed Thoughts are concepts that contain transformation energy. They shock our consciousness into a new way of seeing. George Gurdjieff called this process the "conscious shock" that must precede man's awakening from a chronic state of sleepwalking (In bibliography, refer to authors Nicoll and Speeth for books on Gurdjieff's teachings).

The Truth Principle contained within a Seed Thought is a principle residing at a higher (more integrated) level than the person is currently operating on. But since we can *recognize* this higher Truth when we hear it — even though we've never heard it before — this proves that we are really in a process of *re*awakening rather than awakening. We are just being re-minded. In other words, we've always known the Truth, even though we've forgotten it. And Truth will descend upon us *if we are enough beyond ego needs to hear it.*

A Seed Thought is planted in the mind, nurtured, and then begins to grow, manifesting the "fruits" of its nature as we synthesize other ideas that fall into place around this new Organizing Principle. What might serve as a Seed Thought for you might not for me; they are uniquely individualized according to the level of being achieved and the contents of our personal life history. A Seed Thought *always* contains energy — "AHA!"

One of your tasks as a Transformer is to supply plenty of Seed Thoughts for your clients. Toss them out and see if they catch hold. Remember, Truth can be *caught,* but it cannot be *taught;* the other person has to be open and prepared to receive it, like fertile, malleable soil.

SUMMARY

If the ego cannot get its needs met naturally for security, pleasure and self-definition, it does something "funny".... something unnatural. It will substitute a gratifier, even if it is basically self-destructive in the long run. And chemical addiction is one of these unnatural substitutes for an unmet organismic need. Since it is a substitute, it will never really satisfy: the *real need* down under the addiction is still going unmet.... Its force still being felt.

Alcoholism, then, is a special case of addiction, where alcohol has become the chemical of choice. It is important to remember that persons recovering from alcoholism will not be able to maintain a stable sobriety unless the original need can be met and the constricted energy tied to that particular need can be redirected.

For example, a person stuck at Level One will be focused unconsciously upon his need for safety/security. And from the standpoint of his Soul's development he cannot progress until this Level One work is made conscious, faced, accepted and dealt with. If the person already has Soul-memory of the higher levels, he can transcend with meditation work, or other types of inner practices that teach him to let go of needing security from the outside world.... that illuminate this need as illusory.

But if the higher centers are not operating within the personality structure, there is no way you can reach him with higher work. He must go the "slow" way of meeting the need from outside himself: Since he is unable to use the mind in a transcending way (like using Seed Thoughts that stimulate the higher centers), he will have to work through the Outer World of Experience, plodding through the lessons of daily living. "Well, this is the fourth time I've married a woman like this. Maybe life is trying to tell me something." In this way, he learns, but it may take a long, long time!

Perhaps we can see now that there are two ways to evolve our human nature: We can evolve unconsciously, learning slowly through

Life's experiences, or consciously, the faster way. When we are consciously evolving we are taking responsibility for our own growth, not allowing our experiences to define us. We are using the mind as a magician to transform our ordinary reality into the World of Inner Wisdom. Human nature is the first level in the evolutionary chain *that can choose to evolve consciously.* When we take on this responsibility for ourselves, we become Seekers on the Path of Truth, and no longer are victims of the Lower Self. But it is through the painful experiences of the Lower Self that we gain the force necessary to die and become reborn into a life of awareness. When we opt for this individual responsibility to consciously evolve, we enter into the magnificent work of transforming humanity.

"By thy stumblings, the world is perfected."

— *SRI AUROBINDO*

★ ★ ★ ★

7

The Proper Use of Creative Force

Creative force is designed for one reason: to Self-create. Self-creation is the act of manifesting our Essence in the world.... the God-Self. Paradoxically, though we are already perfect, having to build *toward* that perfection is the very predicament of being human. There is a blueprint for me. I do have an Essence.... a pattern already designed. But since I am asleep to this fact, I must utilize this lifetime of experiencing as a way to uncover this Self that is awaiting its realization.

As I discover little bits and pieces of this True Self, I real-ize it.... give it consciousness. This process of making conscious these aspects of my true nature is exactly what evolution is all about. This *IS* the journey of Self-creation.

A Picture of Self-creation at Work: When the True Self decides to use Third Force, it becomes the Transformer and activates Fourth Force. Third Force is mental; Fourth Force is acceptance — a transformed mental energy.... The ability to accept one's past lovingly and non-judgmentally, plus imagining future possibilities.

Third Force, in the act of transformation, happens this way:

Instead of its usual position,

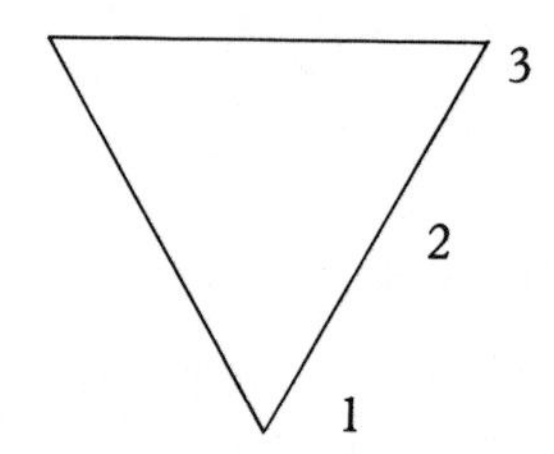

the triangle turns right-side-up and mimics the Higher Self.

THIRD FORCE IN THE ACT OF SELF-CREATION

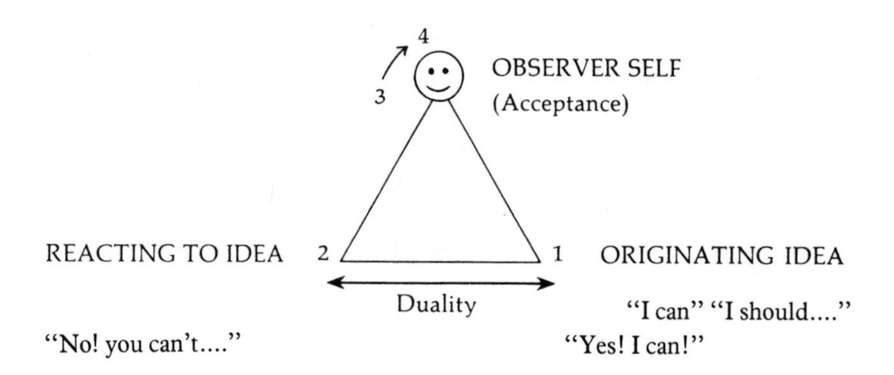

Since it is now acting "as if" it is the Spiritual Self, it Self-creates, meaning whatever it creates will be based on Truth. From this vantage point, the Observer Self shines the light of objective awareness onto the whole picture — both the originating idea and the person's reaction to this idea — and decides. It can get beyond duality, beyond judgment, and "see" both the positive and the negative in the situation *without criticism.* It can draw its conclusions from a level higher than just "how it feels." Since it is re-channeling thought at Level Three (concrete mind) to mimic thought at Level Five (abstract mind), the possibility for transformation exists.

The proper use of creative force Self-creates, enabling the energies of the Lower Self to manifest in the world authentically. Improper use of creative force also creates, *because mind is creative by nature* (we are *in* and *of* God, the creator). When we mis-create, the Lower Self — without the aid of the Higher Self — creates more and more false personality, manifesting more ego-dominated behavior as "Reality." Now there is *more* lower energy in need of transcendence, so we are moving backward instead of forward. But we *are* creating.

Creative energy follows the universal laws of energy, which say:

(1) Energy (emotion) follows Thought.

(2) When Thought and Energy come together, something manifests. Whatever the mind conceives — if it is given emotional energy — will then take form. It will "happen."

(3) For the laws of manifestation to occur, undivided attention (non-dualistic) is necessary. Thought and feeling must become one. "As a man thinketh, *in his heart* (with feeling), so is he."

As long as the Lower Self operates as an upside-down triangle, it will misrepresent Reality. The energy flowing downward will keep us DOWN, because at this level energy always moves in the direction of the densest point — like water going through a sieve, or sand in an hourglass. (Contemplate this thought for a moment, and you will see that the principle applies to your life in a very meaningful way). Tip: Water (ancient symbol for the emotions) always seeks its own level.

MODEL OF MIS-CREATION

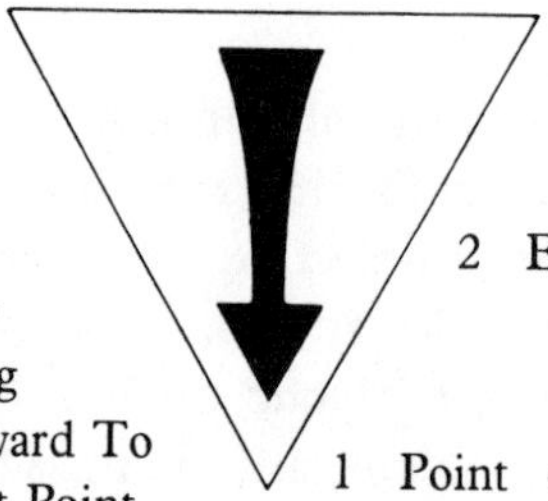

3 Concept misformed at Level 3 based on "facts" from Life

2 Emotional Energy

Energy Flowing Downward To Densest Point

1 Point of manifestation-decision now lives in physical body & will be mechanically reenacted by Lower Self as a pattern of behavior. Will keep us DOWN.

Third Force just *thinks* and draws conclusions from wherever its consciousness is focused. If it is looking "down" toward sensual/emotional gratification, it draws its conclusions from the World of Outer Experience and gets an answer based on partial truth, or illusion. "This flower smells good" (sensual truth) "....I will pick 100 of them and put them in a vase, so I can capture their essence." (Conclusion drawn from the senses which says "if a little bit is good, then more will be better.") This conclusion is false. Why? Because 100 picked flowers do not keep their essence *as blooming flowers;* they wilt and die and become a mess to clean up.

Now we can see that this is exactly how all addictions work! We mistake the substance for the essence of what we are seeking, saying, if a little bit's good then more and more and more will be better!

So now the intellect contains another half-truth, from basing a choice on the evidence of the sensual experience *alone.*

> "But the body and the man are two, and the man's will is not always what the body wishes. When your body wishes something, stop and think whether *you* really wish it. For *you* are God, and *you* will only want what God wills; but you must dig deep down within yourself to find the God within you, and listen to His voice, which is *your* voice. Do not mistake your bodies for yourself —neither the physical body, nor the astral (emotional), nor the mental. Each of them will pretend to be the Self, in order to gain what it wants, but you must know them all, and know yourself as their master."
>
> — *KRISHNAMURTI*

In this manner, the Lower Self mis-creates. Desires become habits which are nothing in the world but desires objectified and kept in perpetual motion. But let's not forget: In Truth, all energy is ONE. At the base of all our habits, positive or negative, lies the *universal desire to express Life.* This urge, which begins at the spiritual level, is the impulse to Self-create.

MODEL OF SELF-CREATION

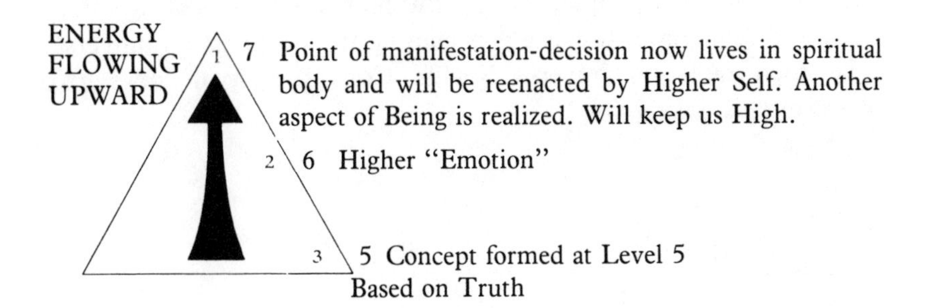

To summarize what we've learned — we are two selves — a spiritual (unified) Self and a material (fragmented) self:

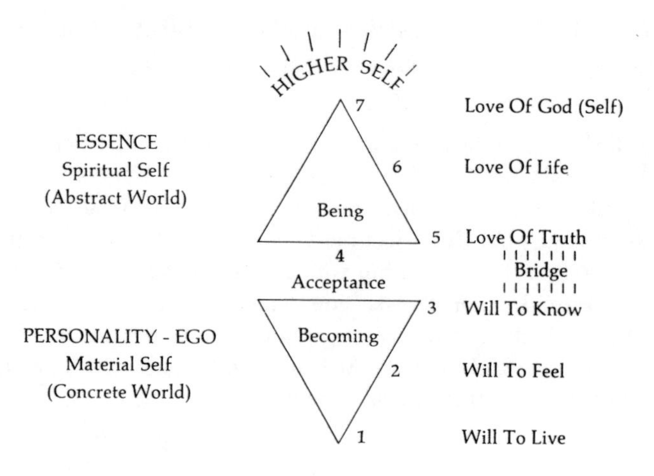

The spiritual Self is Truth because it is our original blueprint, complete though unmanifested. Our basic nature is LOVE, for God is Love and we are built in His image. The material self is illusion because, by itself, it is incomplete, misinterpreting our original design, using the will of the ego to propel it. The material self (Lower Self) tries to conclude its facts from the fragmented knowledge it experiences from sensual/emotional perceptions, *mistaking each fragment for the whole truth.* Remember, the ego only looks outward! Its knowledge is partially true, or true on a simplistic level: it is a fact that flowers smell good (to most people, that is). But its knowledge is always limited and idiosyncratic, because it is coming from a personal universe, rather than the larger universe, Reality. Consequently, it draws erroneous conclusions:

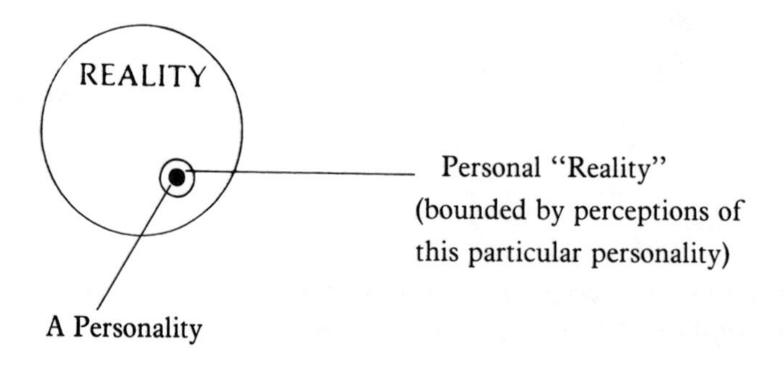

OUR SELF-MADE REALITY

In observing the origins of our addictions, we realize that we are receiving stations: *Whatever we are in tune with will determine what we receive.* So long as we are ego-dominated, we will translate everything that comes in with distorted perception, colored by lusts, greed and desires of the ego that stem from our personal history — none of which have anything to do with Reality! These perceptions create our motivation for thought and action. In this way, all addictions are born.

OUR LIFE IS THE OUTCOME OF THE IMAGES WE WEAVE IN OUR MIND BASED ON THE ILLUSORY STUFF OF THE EGO. AS IT SEEKS TO GRATIFY ITSELF IN ITS SELF-MADE REALITY, IT OPTS FOR DEPENDENCE ON OUTSIDE THINGS THAT IT THINKS IT NEEDS.

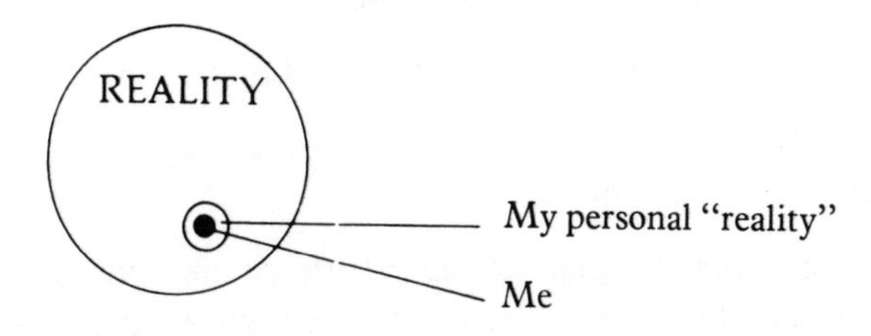

It is only when we create spaces at the boundary line of our little world — that Reality from a higher (more integrated) level can enter.

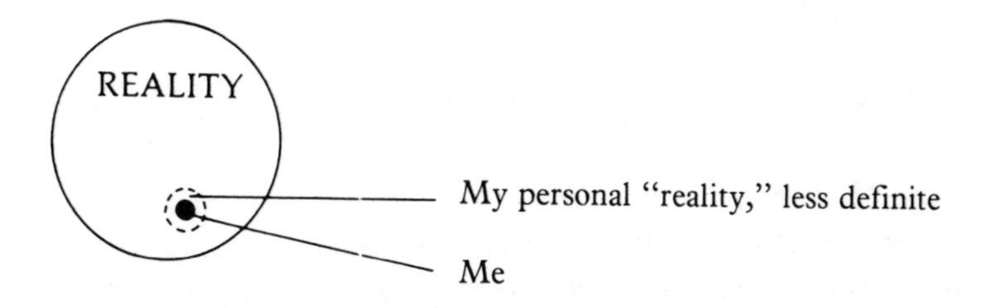

This is the process of "turning it over," the surrender associated with transformation. Surrender has nothing to do with giving one's power over to an "old man in the sky" out there somewhere. This view of surrender only encourages the concept of original sin of separating man from his True Nature — God. Surrender is not a negative statement about the Self, but a positive one: "I am turning my life over to the Real Self that I've always been, letting go of my ego-limited viewpoint. My Higher Self will now guide me, for it is my *personal link* to the Higher Power, the Source of All That Is."

> "Man has freedom; he can choose God or reject God, he can lead the world to perdition or to redemption. The creation of this being Man with such power of freedom means that GOD has made room for a co-determining power alongside of Himself. Man is the crossroad of the world."
>
> — *HENRY SLONIMSKY*

Here are the steps to the process of a true surrender:

1. Awareness of the illusion we were caught up in;

2. Desiring with all one's heart and mind to know the Truth;

3. Opening to this Truth as it begins to show itself — in *total* sincerity, not as a blind for our ego;

4. *Remaining* open as the Truth enters, purging all negativity and illusion that cannot be maintained within the Light (even when this becomes extremely painful);

5. And finally, by *being* this Truth in our every action in Life (and here is where most of us break down from lack of courage or staying power).

ESSENCE IS DEPENDENT UPON PERSONALITY

The Higher and Lower must work together to make us whole. And interestingly enough, the Higher is dependent upon the Lower for our advancement. *The expression of Essence is dependent upon the development of a strong ego, an integrated personality.*

Self-expression, comprehension of the whole, intuition, compassion, seeking wisdom, and spiritual Will are irrelevant concepts to persons starving for personal gratification.

If I am still mistrusting of Life and needy for ego satisfaction, I will be preoccupied with my needs, gathering data solely from the outside world and focusing on the lack I am constantly experiencing. I will be swinging from the good to the bad, the right to the wrong, the highs to the lows. Think for a minute about the people you've known with weak egos. They are either functioning in Life unrealistically, or they are not functioning at all. Their energies are necessarily so taken up with matters of personal survival, they have no energy left over for the higher work of transcendence.

We are like the little acorn, striving to become an oak tree. It begins as a raw little seed (Essence), unprotected by the tough hardy acorn shell. This little seed — already destined by nature to become a strong beautiful oak tree — is doomed if it cannot build around itself a strong acorn shell. The seed represents the raw material we are born with.... our Essence-potential, containing the God-energy that leads toward perfect completion. The acorn — tough and hard — is like our personality, the home of our ego, a protective covering for us to use while we are developing in the world. At some point in time — given the right conditions — the acorn breaks open, shedding its protective boundaries, allowing its Essence to pour out from the center, rising up toward the sun, pursuing its destiny. And the finished product does not even vaguely resemble the acorn! Isn't that interesting? But it now produces other seeds, complete with their protective coverings, and so propagates itself.

And this, too, is our story.

BOOK TWO

THE PRACTICAL WORK OF THE TRANSFORMER

The Therapists of the Future

Our philosophical mindset determines everything we do vis-à-vis a client. Consequently, this underpinning serves the most fundamental purpose of grounding us in using ourselves as instruments in the life of another. The more secure we are in our own philosophical base, the more we emit the quality of Potency,* one of the counselor traits that research has found in high-functioning counselors.

The Transformer has a world view that works with the highest, most synthesized universal principles, drawing them down from the abstract into manifestation in the concrete world, then creating their own unique response. The Transformer works with the future *now* .... taking a *pro*active view of man, which focuses *forward* toward his wholeness that is trying to emerge, rather than backward toward the fragments of his past errors. He uses a model of helping that contains four levels, as man is a four-fold being. This manifests as four different settings and therapeutic models that become the appropriate line of work within the context of the client's life.

The Transformer utilizes a higher viewpoint of the various stereotypic therapeutic issues all psychotherapies are familiar with — such as the problem of resistance in a therapy session, etc.

Transformers work with three natural laws of energy that determine how the human being utilizes his energy flow. It's just now being acknowledged in the field of human behavior that human beings are energy systems. This knowledge is coming in mainly through the area of transpersonal psychology, holistic health, and the new physics. Energy, color, light, sound — these will be prominent themes in the therapies of the future. The Transformer is learning to work with an energy model, including an understanding of the subtler levels of these energies affecting us. The three laws of energy that directly affect us are rooted in Hermetic principles — knowledge that was prominent in ancient Egypt and Greece but has been almost lost to us today. These laws are the Law of Motion, the Law

*See author's earlier book, *Becoming Naturally Therapeutic,*[33] especially the chapter on Potency, Eupsychian Press, 1981.

of Use, and the Law of Free Will. In this next section, these Laws will be explained.

The therapists of the future use their knowledge of the superconscious mind, along with knowledge of the subconscious mind, the level where most therapists of the past have focused. The superconscious realm contains the key to transcendence, or the ability to transmute Lower Self constricted energy into its Higher Self positive counterpart. For instance, my addiction to something "out there" was merely the mis-use of my precious creative energy searching for an outlet.

The Transformer understands the mechanism of transmutation and brings about transcendence of addictions rather than merely *overcoming* addictions (whereby we grit our teeth and still focus on the same indulgence, though we no longer indulge). The Transformer teaches us to turn the other way, feeding energy into the positive side of the pole that has been blocked in its expression by our complete and compulsive concentration on the negative.

The Transformer knows that what we've thought and fed energy to, consciously and unconsciously, is what we've become. AND BECAUSE WE CAN CHANGE OUR THINKING, WE CAN CHANGE OUR LIVES. HEAVEN AND HELL ARE NOTHING BUT STATES OF CONSCIOUSNESS.

In this section we will travel through the spirals of the hierarchical journey through the self-created "hells" we invent as we become attached to things and people outside ourselves to "find the answer." And each level of consciousness will contain its positive antidote — the *way through* the addiction. Therapeutic tasks at each level will be explained.

And finally, the journey beyond addiction, which becomes an extensive interpretation of the Twelve-Step Program of Alcoholics Anonymous will be explored. The Transformer is familiar with this twelve-step spiritual path, for it is the universal path we all follow when we move from personal egoistic living, through completed relationships and on into a world of serving others caught in the predicaments of Life.

The Transformer brings us to that inner Reality that is everybody's true nature.... that place we *really* call "home." All of these principles and issues will be dealt with in Book Two, to aid the Transformer in making explicit her mental and spiritual grounding.

8

Utilizing the Higher Knowledge

As conceived by Aurobindo, the Transformer works "From the top, down," or from an enlightenment model of human nature. He sees us in our perfection and then attends to the blocks and misconceptions that are stopping us from realizing this potential wholeness. He recognizes quite easily where we are stuck and chooses his method of intervention to match the level where the client "lives."

When translated into the everyday world of the client, this becomes four different settings, or models of helping, hierarchical in nature.[34]

PHYSICAL	EMOTIONAL	MENTAL	SPIRITUAL
Medical Model	Psycho-Social Model	Self-Actualization Model	Enlightenment Model
		client → ○ (Norm)	No Norms No Limits What Is *Is*
	(Norm) client → ○		
(Norm) ↑ client → ○			

THE FOUR MODELS OF HELPING

When a client is physically ill, we work within the medical or healing model that we know heals the physical body. The client's physical health is "below normal" and our goal is to bring her up to physical wellness.

When a client is well physically, she will naturally seek relief on the next level, which is the psycho-social; i.e., her intrapsychic (inner difficulties) conflicts and her interpersonal relationships. The goal, again, is normalcy, or balance.

Once this level is achieved, clients seek to rise above their "normal" level of functioning; they begin to seek the actualization of their potentials. Our goal here is to turn a client on to her strengths, talents, wishes and dreams, helping her live life more fully, enhancing what is already healthy and functioning. Growth groups, marriage encounter, the human potential movement, are examples of this kind of work.

When a person has advanced into the self-actualization level of functioning, if she continues to grow, she automatically begins to seek enlightenment (total conscious awareness of the human being and the universe). Spiritual paths are individualized at this level depending upon the "type" of individual Seeker. There is no *one* path appropriate for everyone at every stage. At this level, one finds that ordinary "rules" tend to vanish; there are no longer norms, comparisons, or even limits. This level of growth has a broad perspective that takes in all other perspectives. In other words, it can utilize the medical, psycho-social, or self-actualization models of intervention when appropriate, not having to pit one against the other, judging one as "bad" while another is "good." Enlightenment means total acceptance with relevance and discrimination of whatever another might need at a particular time in life — seeing clearly how everything relates to everything else. Since it is the "highest," most expanded viewpoint, it can look "down" at the narrower levels and see it all. As stated earlier, the higher can see the lower, but the lower has no awareness of the higher. The following analogy helps us understand what enlightenment is:

> Imagine yourself suddenly trapped in a cave, hundreds of feet underground, in absolute darkness — encompassed by a sense of fear and unfamiliarity. Then you discover you have a pack of matches in your pocket, so you strike one and it lights up your

> immediate surroundings. This affords you the data you need to know you are okay right where you are standing. But you still don't know what's "out there." So, cautiously you move forward a few feet and you strike another match, now lighting up another fragment of your "reality." The light goes out, and you move to another point in the cave and strike a match. Now you have three different portions of the cave that are "known," but you still don't know the "Truth" of your situation down there. Then, suddenly someone enters and turns on a light switch! Now, the entire underground cavern is ablaze with light, every nook and cranny illuminated! This is enlightenment.[35]

For this reason, Transformers tend to approach intervention into the life of another from the enlightenment point of view, even though their client may not "be there" yet. Language does not lend itself to a full description of working from the enlightenment level, for language is too limiting. One has to intuit what I am attempting to describe just now. A paradox exists here: One does not have to be enlightened to work from the Enlightenment Model! He only has to be committed to bringing as much light and openness *as possible* in any given situation.

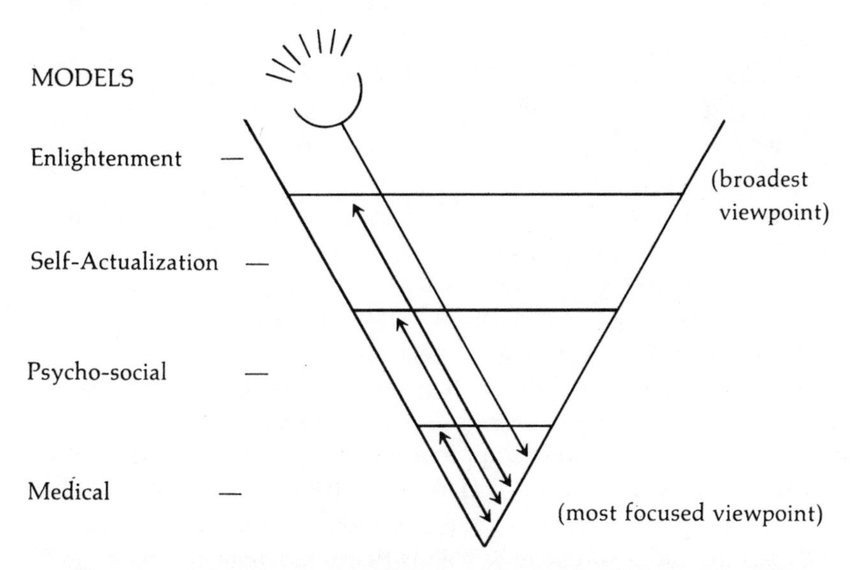

Let me elaborate, to avoid misunderstanding. I am *not* saying that people who work with the medical model are less enlightened than anyone else! Some of the wisest people on this planet are healers, medical doctors and researchers concerned with the physical body. I *am* saying that when one utilizes the Enlightenment Model, he may very well choose to work within that medical arena for an expressed purpose, and he will know what that purpose is.

The same is true for all the other levels. However, if one is *stuck* in the physical/medical model and has never seen beyond this level, he will interpret his entire world through the lens of the medical approach, seeing the physical/medical reality as the *only* reality. Whereas, if one has only advanced to the psycho/social level of work with clients, he will see the medical and psycho/social as the only reality. The self-actualization level is still limited to personality development. Enlightenment transcends personality, seeing the larger meaning in every situation, taking it all in, but might choose to focus on any one of the levels *for a specific purpose, for a specific client.*

I think all of us have experienced how this works. Have you ever tried to talk to a closed-minded medical doctor about your fear of taking drugs for a cure of something? She simply cannot "hear" you; she sees a medical answer as the *only* answer possible.

Have you ever tried to talk to a social work professor or a psychologist who does not believe in anything but his own model of intervention; seeing everything in life in terms of a psychological or social problem?

Or, have you ever been in a human potential center where the panacea seems to be personal gratification, total honesty-in-the-moment-for-the-sake-of-honesty and total expression of the ego? "I am I and you are you and if by chance we meet that's cool; if not, it can't be helped." In the name of enlightenment, this is an ego-dominated statement from people who are "stuck" in self-actualizing. I am not meaning to sound critical; but it is true that every level that looks at the body, the emotions, or even *the personality as a whole is still* too limited to explain all of our human potential!

Transformers are attempting to stamp out limitation! — by learning to let go and accept *everything* as helpful, including knowing how to discriminate about what's appropriate for whom and when. And remember: ONE DOES NOT HAVE TO BE FULLY ENLIGHTENED TO WORK FROM THE ENLIGHTENMENT MODEL CONSCIOUSNESS. The only rule is that one has to be committed to bringing as much light as possible into the here-and-now at any given time, on any given subject.... committed to seeing the whole and remaining open to newness. And if we will go within and ask our Higher Self to give us this expansive point of view, it is given to us.

THE TRANSFORMER'S VIEW OF MAN AS ENERGY

Because the Transformer views the human being as an energy system and addiction as blocked creative energy, he utilizes three laws of energy as guidelines for the release of the creative potential in humanity.

We will now explore these laws to gain the knowledge we need to aid our clients in the proper use of their spiritual potency.

The Law of Motion. Life is motion. Even in absolute calm, there is movement: Stillness is movement in repose — in perfect tune with the flowing of a motion-packed universal force.

And since life *is* movement, there is nowhere to stop! We are a process — *in* process — the process of becoming. The universal energy, of which we are a part, is directional, taking us upward (inward), heading toward the Source. It is a natural law of physics, discovered long ago, that everything returns to its source.

So we can count on the knowledge that even our trials and our errors are temporary, taking us where we need to go. Our Higher Self will lift our energy constricted in animalistic, subconscious behavior right on up and into the higher centers that manifest the essential Truth of our unique nature. You can transcend your Lower Self, for that is how you are designed. And when the Lower Self rebels and gets its way, you can know it is only a temporary victory. The Higher Self will ultimately prevail if one continues to choose growth, for this Truth is in the master plan that governs the larger Reality.

The Transformer works with this knowledge as a chemist might — transmuting "lead into gold," the lower drives into their higher qualities. He knows that all energy is One, but can manifest through any of the seven different levels of consciousness. When we understand this, we can use this knowledge as a diagnostic tool. The body will tell you where the energy is flowing, consequently, its purpose — or where it is stuck, consequently, its fear.

For example, recently I went through an emotional churning that was created by thinking I was losing a loved one. When I would catastrophize about the future without him, I would feel the energy in my solar plexus: He has been very important to my ego's sense of confidence, a necessary mentor to me. When I would reflect for a moment on his needs and become aware he might need to leave for his own sake, the energy would leave my third center and my heart (fourth center) would hurt. As I was reflecting, I was walking along a path in a beautiful park. My consciousness became captivated by a gorgeous blooming tree, and for a moment the glory of nature fell in upon me, juxtaposed against my sadness. I felt the energy go up into my throat (fifth center) as a desired expression of tearful joy and meaning. For a while I was seeing the whole context of death/rebirth and the natural Law of Cycles in operation in my life.

Your energy is like the varied colors that flow through a prism. All of it is Light; the colors are its distortions, shaded by the multidimensions of desire.

The Law of Use. The ability to co-create life force is the organizing principle of human nature. This act is what gives us our form. This is what is meant by living (vs. dying). We have the capacity to constantly create new energies, even to the point of regenerating new cells every seven years of our life. And the moment this activity ceases, our body dies.

The paradoxical human predicament is that we continually manufacture new energy, and then we don't know what to do with it! So we have to throw it off! If this energy just sits in us, unused, it ferments and makes us sick. *It must be used.* And since most of us have lost touch with what it is to be used for (Self-creation), we throw it off. We relieve ourselves of it through the seven centers we have studied — the seven levels of consciousness — through fear, passion or seeking ego status if we still are identified with the Lower Self. When enlightenment begins dawning, and we are able to utilize our higher centers, we can then harmonize our energies, making our lives creative, even blissful. The choice is ours as to how we use or misuse our energy.

The saints and sages taught that we are channels, drawing energy down from the Source that contains Truth seeds designed for one purpose only — to enlighten man as to his true and rightful nature and purpose. This energy is designed to come in through the top of our head and out through the heart into the world. And this is how we teach and learn from others. When we are sharing our Truths, we are using our energy correctly, efficiently. When we harbour it — through greediness or self-doubt — we feel dissatisfied with ourselves and we sicken. The energy must be put to its rightful purpose!

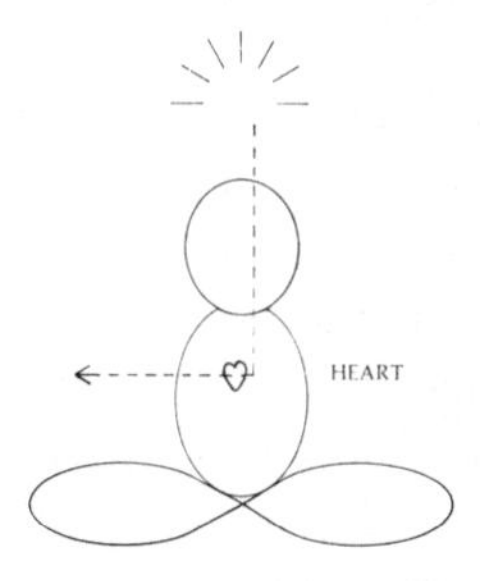

Transformers concern themselves with their clients' right uses of energy and teach them this principle of service to their fellow human beings. They must never horde a piece of Self-knowledge, no matter how small.

The Law of Free Will. We cannot move to a higher level until we accept fully where we are *now:* We do not grow by changing into someone we are *not,* but by becoming more and more of who we are.

Yet everyone does not seek growth. Certainly, plenty of us resist Self-knowledge. And *all* of us do it some of the time — even ardent Seekers of Truth. It is an observable fact that we are free to choose growth or not to. At least, so it appears. But are we really?

Human beings are evolving in a process of *conscious* evolution. The levels below us (mineral, plant and animal) are evolving with no effort — completely in tune with nature, and with no conscious *intention.* This does not mean these levels do not have their own kind of consciousness; but it is a consciousness operating *un*consciously.

At the human level we are operating with the ability for Thought. We have become "Manas, the Thinker." (Manas is a Sanskrit word meaning *man.*) This "Thinker" in us is the immortal individual, clothing itself with personality, but larger, grander than personality. It is the "I" who is evolving, the True Self, able to observe its process as it passes through the human experience it is seeking as it ascends up the ladder of Being.... a thinking entity imprisoned in a body.

> "Try to imagine a 'spirit,' a celestial being, whether we call it by one name or another, divine in its essential nature, yet not pure enough to be one with the ALL, and having, in order to achieve this, to so purify its nature as finally to gain that goal. It can do so only by passing *individually* and *personally,* i.e., spiritually and physically, through every experience and feeling that exists in the manifold or differentiated universe."[36] —*ANNIE BESANT*

We can choose to evolve, or we can choose to remain "mindless," asleep. But the tension is in the Essence of each of us to make the choice. Free will is part of our nature.... not just a happenstance occurring at random. And since we contain this tension (growth vs. non-growth) *within the very core of our being,* perhaps we do not really have a choice. I can *choose* non-growth but does this relieve the existential tension within me? No! If even a tiny part of me is awakened, it will observe the unawakened part with *concern* and seek to force it out of its sleep state. The only way I can feel absolutely *no* tension is to be *totally* asleep — totally unconscious. But then, I would be an animal, not a human. Could it be then.... a human being simply must evolve, and *will* at some point in time.... no matter how distant the event? We are free to choose when and how we will move forward, but perhaps not free at all to choose that we will indeed move.

A Transformer works within the Law of Free Will. A client can choose his own timing and method of growth, but the Transformer knows he *must* grow, as it is his nature to do so. He keeps the tension alive and focused on the growth choice.... aware that the client is merely choosing how long to postpone an existential reality. We *will* evolve — with all the joys, sorrow and trials this journey entails!

The Transformer knows instinctively that this journey, for each of us, must occur individually. And further, no one can relieve us of this personal responsibility. We must do it for ourselves. We leave the "many," the society that sleeps, and we venture into the lonely world of the Seeker. The Transformer sees this aloneness as a fact for each and every one of us, for he is aware of its Truth within himself. He knows, and he feels compassion. NO ONE CAN BECOME CONSCIOUS FOR US!

SPECIFIC THERAPEUTIC ISSUES REVISITED

Psychological textbooks are replete with information about certain therapeutic issues that become recurring themes for counselors and psychotherapists in their work with clients. Following will be some of these, redefined according to the Transformer's theoretical stance.

Resistance.

> "Force does not become creative until it meets resistance. Light does not become visible until it strikes an object."[37]
>
> —*LAMA GOVINDA*

Resistance is a gift. And we must learn to respect it. Often the Higher Self uses resistance to step down our energy. We are moving too fast, in too big a hurry to evolve. At times like this, the Higher Self will mediate to keep us from blowing a fuse.

Resistance represents the beginning of a change.... something new is trying to emerge from our unconscious. If it is coming from the subconscious, we might feel fear at seeing this "monstrous part of ourselves" that has never seen the light of day. So we resist, not knowing what will happen if it rears its ugly head. We may need time. Or we may need to be treated gently. It could be we are not ready to make the life changes that will be required once we see this fragment of ourselves clearly.

If the energy is coming from the Superconscious, it means a new quality of perfection is trying to emerge, to be expressed through us. Often, this new quality will also require some life changes we are not prepared to make. What if I do become a leader? What if I let go of my defenses against being purely female? What will happen if my spontaneity emerges in full force? You can see how many of these higher traits, the glorious aspects of the God-self, can be indeed frightening if they come upon us unprepared.

The therapist can determine the origin of the resistance by eliciting symbols and imagery from the client's imagination (See Exercise 14). Just for a moment, ask yourself, how do you experience resistance in your life? Perhaps there is a habit, an addiction, you are being asked to let go of, but you resist. How do you resist? What behaviors of resistance do you use, what ideas, what feelings? Look at each, first of all, as getting in your way.... each resistant behavior, feeling or idea. Now, look at each for the *value* that it has for you! Are you surprised! You see, there is a gift there. Resistance can point you to where you need to grow.

In order to allow this new Superconscious quality to come into my life, what strengths would I need to develop? Am I willing to begin developing them now? Why not? How can I more consciously cooperate with my consciousness so that my own evolution can advance more evenly and rapidly? This resistance is giving me the opportunity to contact this part of myself that is scared, hurt or deluded. When I choose to experience pain and watch it consciously, it begins to give me its message. I can see what is needed. If I only look at the pain, I do not learn anything. But if I hold both views at once.... seeing the pain, and seeing the *meaning* of the pain.... both the worldly experience and the higher knowledge.... I become a channel for Truth.... I am Understanding.

> "Let me not beg for the stilling of pain, but for the heart to conquer it."
>
> — *RABINDRANATH TAGORE*

Problem Solving. Transformers do not believe they have the answers to their client's problems! They know the answer resides within the client. But the answer must come to the True Self from the Higher Self. If it is coming from a partial self, it could be simply an emotionally-laden reaction to the situation that cannot be relied upon as the whole truth.

When a client asks the counselor what to do about something, a Transformer usually says, "What does the wisest part of you say to do?" or something to that effect. If the client cannot immediately begin speaking to the issue from an objective space, the counselor will put the client into a state of relaxation and have the client get a message from his Higher Self (See Exercise #1). Then the two of them will discuss the results of this work. Or the counselor may ask the client to go into the Silence (Exercise #10) and discover, without any guidance or interruption from the counselor, what Truth emerges.

If an answer does not come, or the message is too garbled, ambivalent, or vague to be helpful, the Transformer begins to work with the client's interference patterns. What is blocking this client's awareness of the answer to his problem? Fear, need or illusion is often a way of keeping the client from moving too fast, or from having to face the next step that is beyond the solution to this current problem! Perhaps the client is not emotionally ready to face this answer, or maybe physical illness is occurring that has weakened his ability to cope with the stress of the particular change in his life. Trust the resistance and work with it. It will give 'way if it is supposed to. *Trust the process.* The only "wrong" is unconsciousness. As long as the client is conscious of his resistance and is willing to take responsibility for it, things are proceeding according to the process of Self-creation.

Changing Another. Transformers don't try to change anybody for a very simple reason: They don't believe anyone needs changing. Everyone is responsible for his own evolution.... the seeds for our own advancement are already within us. Since transformation occurs from within, Transformers know that to interfere with another's way is to become a toxic agent in that person's life, leading him *away* from himself rather than toward more Truth.

A Transformer thinks in terms of "opening" rather than of "changing." To open means to become more and more of what one is — the very essence expands as it receives from Life the requirements for its unfoldment. Like a flower who knows when its time is ripe for blooming, a client moves toward fuller expansion of his nature in the presence of the Transformer, for he is being encouraged and endorsed for being himself. Fears that have blocked his awakening are dealt with — entered into and found to be empty of meaning. One's opening is blocked only by the fear of going on in and meeting one's fears face to face. When we stand at the portal of our fears, afraid to peek inside, our fears become powerful.... demonic. But they can only hold their power so long as we fear going in to see what's there. Once we do, we discover an emptiness.... the void. *There is really nothing there at all!* Our fears are illusions that exist in the mind. Transformers know that the power of the mind can overcome any fear totally — even the fear of death. Opening is the key to Being.... for we already *are* who we are intended to be; we've just been closed to this realization!

The Transformer is like a lantern; her light flows naturally from within, guiding others by its very nature, absolutely effortless. *Re*-forming is effortful, tiring, and never really accomplishes anything. TRANSFORMING IS EFFORTLESS BECAUSE THERE IS NOTHING TO BE DONE; THERE IS ONLY SOMEONE TO BE. The Transformer believes that if she continues to work on herself, seeking higher and higher levels of consciousness, that is all she ever needs to do. The result is that she becomes a light unto others, because she is a reflector of Truth.

Morality. The therapists of the future will not be so hung up on "morality." The Transformer views moral issues as man-created; God is seen as impartial. The Transformer does not see things so much in terms of opposites. He has come to know that life has to be accepted in its totality. When one is filled with moral concepts, he becomes extremely judgmental and condemning. He misses the point of life. Morality belongs to the Outer World of Experience; love, wisdom and acceptance are the Truth of the inner world. A moralist becomes a constant vigilante — a sentry of life, not a master of life. He is so busy guarding, judging and labelling, he dissipates his energy that was designed for experiencing and expressing Spirit. And because he has suppressed his very Being, he must condemn yours.

The Transformer adopts as his maxim the ancient Vedantic saying: "Don't pay much attention to the doing, pay attention to the Being. Don't think of what is to be done, just think of who you are." And another, from St. Augustine: "Love God, and do as you will."

He says *as you are* you are welcome. The problem has never been that others are rejecting you; the problem has *always* been that you are rejecting yourself. You make mistakes in the Outer World of Experience, *not* because you are "bad," but because you don't understand Life. There is no improving to do, no place you have to get to. You merely have to learn to look within and *realize who you are.*

YOU HAVE FORGOTTEN YOURSELF, AND THAT IS YOUR ONLY FAULT.

The Here and Now. Like most true Gestaltists, the Transformer believes the here and now is the eternal moment, the only place where transformation can happen. To be totally in the here and now, one must become goal-less, desire-less. If suddenly you became aware that you have forgotten time — that you just passed through a space where time vanished — you were in the here and now. And where was desire? Desire is always longing for something you do not yet have, so it is always in the future. Or it is stuck in the past, dwelling on some fantasy of what might have been, if only....

Desirelessness is the key to here and now living, getting fully into the moment with fascination. It matters not what is fascinating you; if your Spirit is involved totally, you are present, living and being.

The here and now is the central apex of the cross — being in the middle of the river:

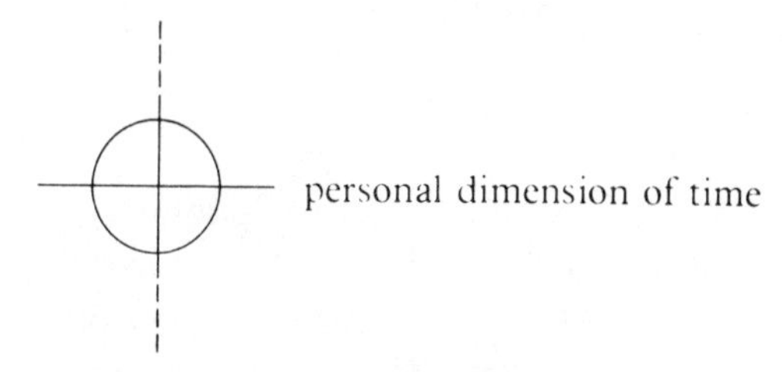

Life flows past you, experiences come and go, and you are there *receiving* them, feeling them, allowing them to flow on past. You are right at that place where the personal dimension of past, present and future *happen,* as the transpersonal dimension enters you from "above.'"

Jesus on the cross is the model of authentic existence — living and being fully himself, in the eternal *NOW.* It is the stance we are all challenged to accept.

The present moment is a chance to meet head-on the tests and trials of our past actions (causes). We can choose to dissolve the stresses and strains we've collected within ourselves by the thoughts, feelings and actions we've created over the years. To the extent that we can become conscious of these tensions, we can free our constricted consciousness so it can become identified with our true and rightful nature and purpose in life. A wise man told me once: We are here purely for one reason.... to dissolve all anger, fear and repressed resentments we've built up through living our lives.... so our light can shine clearly.

Self Knowledge. The Transformer is ultimately concerned with only one kind of knowledge: knowledge of the Self. For she knows that this is the only form of knowledge that is transforming. Other types of knowledge teach us to be practical, to live more effectively in the mechanistic world. But Self-knowledge brings leaps of consciousness, synthesizing fragments of truths we already know to a higher octave. This is how higher and higher levels of integration occur.

The Transformer lives by the maxim: "Man, know Thyself."

> "The Self — at one and the same time the Self of all living creatures, and therefore my Self — knows no bounds; so the entire universe is within me, and my Self fills all the universe. Everything that is —

> I am! In everything I love, I love my Self, for the only things we think we don't love are what we haven't yet come to recognize within ourselves!"[38]
>
> —*ELISABETH HAICH*

Our business is to turn resolutely away from earth-bound ignorance and listen to the wisdom that, whatever anyone may say, is sounding within us *at any given moment.*

The Seeker must have the sort of courage that holds her firmly in the certainty of her inner aim even when she is being censured by others in the outer world.

> "He who hesitates on the brink of the dangerous waters of this knowledge, wishing for assurance of his safety before plunging, will never achieve inner certainty. One cannot learn to swim without swallowing much water."[39]
>
> —*SRI KRISHNA PREM*

The Seeker distinguishes Self-knowledge from religion per se. Religion can be a path toward Self-knowledge, but the two concepts are not synonymous. SELF-KNOWLEDGE IS KNOWLEDGE OF THE SPIRIT AND DOES NOT BELONG TO ANY SECT OR RELIGIOUS GROUP. It is the birthright of humankind — whether we choose to claim it or not. Spirit is the very core of our Being, and knowledge of this sort provides the roadmap for the journey into Self we all must make if we are to evolve.

Historically, the priests of the various religious orders have very grudgingly divulged Universal Truth, preferring the safety of teaching only the standard dogma of their particular framework, presented in a socially-approved manner. Teaching the *real* Truth about the Self is moving into wild and dangerous territories for it gives man *the key to his power and responsibility,* rendering him unfit to be a passive follower of any limited orthodoxy. The power of the priesthood is thereby often compromised and consequently, ineffective.

It is recorded that the great Christian mystic, Meister Eckhart, was excommunicated for teaching the Truth to his people in lay language that they could understand, thereby placing the keys to knowledge directly into their hands.[40]

Transformer's View of "Family." Little babies are born into this world already advanced in certain areas of character, and deficient in others. Researchers have noted great variances in talents, likes, dislikes, genius, modes of expression, needs, that offer the suggestion that we are indeed *not* born "equal."

Our original family is the context (training ground) wherein our basic patterns of thoughts, feelings and behavior emerge. A functional family minimizes weaknesses and builds up strengths of the child, thereby aiding him/her in forming a strong, effective ego. A dysfunctional family unintentionally maximizes the weaknesses and fails to build upon strengths from a lack of awareness of the true needs and potentials of its members. This creates a "karmic predicament" for the person to be worked out. The adult family unit we choose to form in later years gives us the opportunity to correct the unenlightened attitude and the mistakes made within the original family unit.

If we've learned our "lessons," we become agents of transformation for our children; if we do not, we continue that particular family's chain of "neurosis" in a robot-like fashion, and no evolution takes place.

Some of us are "quantum leaps in consciousness" for our family chain, having gotten into the business of Self-creation and advanced so rapidly, we did the work of Self-creation in one generation that usually requires several generations to accomplish.

As we learn to be an enlightened member of our personal family, we are elevated to a level of serving the larger family of humanity, in whatever area we've prepared ourselves.

Questions Transformers use in aiding a client to learn the Truth of his/her family:

(1) What skills did you have to build in order to defend against a particular adult in your family unit? And, how is that skill now useful to you as an adult in your personal development or in your work?

(2) What kind of models (negative or positive) did you have in your family that add to your knowledge of personality development? How have these models aided you in developing strengths you needed in order to actualize your unique potential?

(3) What role did you play in your family that now has meaning for you as an adult in a new way? Were you a hero, a peacemaker, the "clown," etc.?

(4) Quietly reflect on your original family unit for a few minutes. Now, give me a symbol that, to you, represents the unit.... What does this symbol elicit in you? What *meaning* does this symbolic information hold for you today?

(5) Think of your family in these terms (and see what enlightenment you get):

(a) You *chose* your family (on a superconscious level) — before you were born.

(b) Your family gave you exactly what you needed (for your Soul's advancement) — not what you *wanted,* maybe, but what you needed.

Your reflection upon these questions will provide important clues to your unique purpose in Life.

Primary Relationships. Transformers do not view all primary relationships as "made in heaven" and designed to be for a lifetime. *Some* are, for sure, but only those that were committed to *consciously.*

Many people marry for neurotic, egoistic reasons, having nothing to do with matters of the Soul. She was pregnant and needed a father for her baby. He was scared to live alone. She was wanting prestige, so she married into a wealthy family with tradition. These kinds of ties are karmic, not cosmic! They contain lessons for the personality to experience that are sometimes learned to completion and transcended. Then the relationship may die a natural, *spiritual* death. (The Soul needs for it to die so room can be made for another relationship that is more appropriate for the tasks of the present).

The Transformer views all primary relationships as *one* continuation of the *one eternal relationship.* The form may change, but the principle remains one of seeking wholeness.

Transformers look for the purpose behind a relationship, and help their clients come to terms with the Reality of the situation. They do not encourage divorce, nor do they encourage staying together; they merely promote clarity of vision and the courage to act on the principles of Love and Truth.

The Paradox of the Intellect. Over-intellectualization is a danger all counselors and other people-helpers have noted, both in groupwork and in individual counseling. Paradoxically, we are to learn to use our minds to rise above emotional overreacting, and yet we have all noticed that understanding a problem merely from the cognitive level doesn't always help.

Here is an insight into this paradox, with, perhaps, a key to transcending it: The intellect does not operate in isolation from the two lower bodies, the emotional and the physical. I can understand something with my mind, but my emotional body and physical body can still contain the negative message I'm trying to overcome. I can *know* I shouldn't feel jealous and rationalize that jealousy is a Lower Self emotion that is based on illusion; but my emotional reaction still occurs, and my body hurts. *Sometimes we must experience the mental concepts at all levels of being before they will fade from our consciousness.*

When knowledge of the negative event is contained in all three bodies, they must all receive the light of consciousness in order to transcend the negative state. And it quite often happens in stages: I might get the intellectual insight on Monday. The following Monday I may feel the energy again, but this time, my intellect and emotion connect simultaneously, and a catharsis occurs. I believe I've conquered the problem after this, only to discover a month later that I am experiencing a nervous stomach when this same situation again presents itself. So now what? I begin to feel hopeless. Will I *ever* get over this? And the hopelessness begins taking me down into negativity about what a jerk I am — just a Low Consciousness Stupid Female! Well, the key here is that I am judging myself, being unloving, therefore *stuck,* based purely on ignorance of what's happening in my consciousness. I have indeed purged the mental, and partially the emotional. What's left is lack of awareness at the cellular level of my existence. My cells still have not gotten the message.... so a little partial self persists in holding on to a past program, based on memories stuck in my subconscious memory bank. My brain still is not enlightened about the nature and purpose of this particular problem. Since this is a problem with the *un*conscious mind, I will need to use a "right-brained" technique to bring about this enlightenment. (For example, see Exercise, #12).

Though our minds try desperately to run off and leave the emotional/physical difficulties we face in life, it simply won't work. We must enlighten the wholeness of us! Mental, emotional, physical.... it *all* must be lifted up, spiritualized. In many spiritual or religious philosophies, the body has been viewed as an obstacle, incapable of spiritualization, being viewed as a heavy weight holding the Soul back. These people have attempted to teach us to leave the body behind, to turn loose of our "animal nature" that is so gross and lustful.

This philosophy sees the earth as a field of ignorance, and the earth experience as a purging of our animal nature, a place to withdraw from forever. This philosophical attitude, however, violates the message that we are here to spiritualize the worldly, and keeps us in a dualistic consciousness.... heaven is good; earth is bad. The highest Truth has always been ALL IS ONE. Matter *is* Spirit made concrete. Man *is* God in Expression. We are charged with the human responsibility of finding the Supreme Positive even in the most negative. The high must meet the low, the limits of the past become the ingredients for a future completion. So long as we attempt to leave a part of us behind, unconscious, *something remains.* And if something remains, it means it must be reworked again and again. We will be doomed to repeat the same patterns in order to have, again, the opportunity to enlighten the remnants that are still in the dark.

ENLIGHTENING

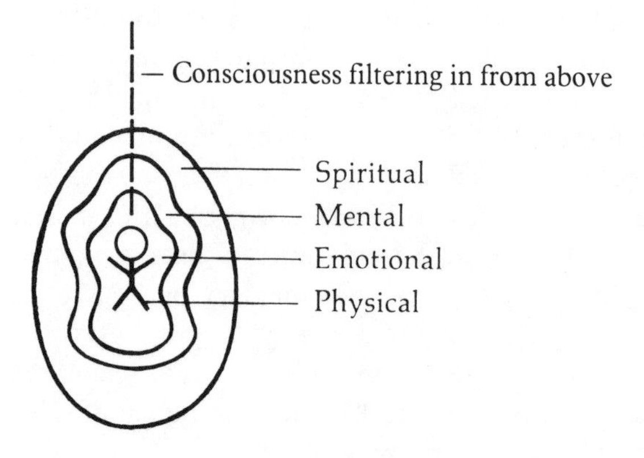

Mentally, our clients need clarity. We do this with the Third Force, the concrete mind, by a process of analytical, critical thought. This activates Fourth Force which enables us to view our past, *without*

judgment, until we understand it. Then, we draw out the feelings that are stuck with the memory. We assist in the work of catharsis, a purging of the emotional body.

Many therapies teach cathartic techniques. But all effective ones share in common a focusing on the feeling, connecting with it, and getting it on out. (See Exercise #9, "Focusing on a Feeling"). Now, the body must *express* the pent-up feeling. If it is anger, a striking out, or beating, or yelling must occur. Clients need permission and tools for this kind of work. If you feel you cannot do it, refer your client to a body therapist.... a Neo-Reichian, Bioenergeticist, Rolfer, Feldenkrais practitioner, or someone trained in the Lomi technique. There are other tried and proven body therapies. These I've mentioned are merely a sampling. If the body still contains the memory, there will be symptoms such as tightness of muscles, rigidity, pain or illness.

Even though we do not perform all the work ourselves, we must realize the importance of completing the process from the highest to the very lowest, finally making conscious every little cell in our bodies. Otherwise we fall back again and again on our journey toward wholeness.... one step forward.... and two back.... doomed to repeat. Perhaps the players will change, but the script will be the same old boring melodrama, the shadow without awareness of the light.

In my practice, I have found that some clients are extremely emotional, with no problem at all in contacting their feelings. And others have excellent use of their mental faculties, but with little success in getting in touch with feelings. With over-emotional clients, it is good to help them mentalize, so they will have concepts that synthesize and attribute meaning to their emotions. I ask these clients to face me, eye to eye, while they learn to use their minds to cognate. Sitting directly in front of someone, maintaining eye contact, facilitates thinking. We work with Seed Thoughts that lift them out of their limited viewpoint. Or with affirmations that re-program negative, vague or incomplete thought processes, such as "I already contain within me the seeds of my perfection; I need nothing else." Or we reality-test our ideas and think it through together.

With clients who tend to mentalize their feelings, I ask them to lie down and close their eyes so they can describe their painful experiences without using their intellect so much, getting them into a state of relaxed consciousness so they can live for awhile *very close to their recalled experience,* without the interference of my personhood to deal with. In this way they can reach their emotions more easily, and relive the experience without feeling drawn into communication with me, or into intellectualizing their experience. Music and guided imagery work well to avoid over-intellectualization. Also, silence. To learn constructive uses of guided imagery, you can study *Psychosynthesis* by Roberto Assagioli, and a delightful little book by Shakti Gawain entitled *Creative Visualization* (see bibliography).

Please know that these techniques are extremely powerful. It is imperative that we work these on ourselves before we attempt to guide a client through an imagery experience. If new to you, you may feel a little shy at first in utilizing these techniques that work on the unconscious. Practice with your friends, or clients with whom you feel most comfortable, and you will discover their power for yourself.

As Transformers, we must aid others in descending all the way down.... through the densest mental fog, into the emotional churnings, and deep on into the subconscious, to the very cellular core of the difficulty.

It is as though we seek to avoid the dark half of the Truth, when actually, all of it is one thing. Our perpetual torment seems to be that we believe we have this "blackness" within us, this ugliness we call sin, evil, whatever. But here is how we view it if we are to transform ourselves: The very blackest shadow in us, the very most painful to face, has its exact same degree of corresponding light. We will carry in us the very obstacles that we need in order to *make real* our perfection. Always we will find that the shadow and the light go together. It is our special work to recognize the Truth of our dark side in order to know the light. *As long as we reject the one for the other, we will continue to fail in our mission of transformation and miss entirely the aim of our existence.*

MY PROBLEM IS A TEACHER TO ME — A VITAL CONTACT WITH MY PAST THAT I AM TO ATTEND TO AND MAKE CONSCIOUS. IT HAS SURFACED SO I CAN KNOW IT.

9

The Transformer's Therapeutic Task

A Transformer is a catalyst for activating and directing the natural process of Self-creation, making Personality passive and Essence active. A channel for higher truth received from the Higher Self, she merely gives the message a concrete form.

The client has gotten off the mark and has begun mis-creating. His energy, which is designed to create and express knowledge of the Self, has become constricted and misdirected by the ego. Consequently, he is stuck, with energy spinning around going nowhere. When this energy build-up happens, we often label it anxiety or fear. Energy polarization will occur within Level 1/7, 2/6 or 3/5 depending upon many factors — the level of development of this particular person, his unique past history, and his natural gifts, strengths and weaknesses.

For instance, if one is polarized at Level One, Level Seven energy, designed to manifest Essence directed by a zealous and persistent Spiritual Will, is flowing instead through the constriction of Level One consciousness. Can you imagine what this energy must feel like? It creates a fearful, isolated, mechanical person, passing through a constricted life space, afraid to risk the movement required to expand. This person is operating from a consciousness dictated by instinctive compulsions, reptilian in nature, meaning his very *life* feels threatened. Fight or flight will be the response, coiling up or slithering away. He is either in this state temporarily due to an emergency in his life — a regression — in which case he can rise above it with the Transformer's assistance because his higher centers *are* available to him. Or he lives in this state most of the time because this is the consciousness level on which he lives due to his limited level of development: He understands the physical, concrete world but not the subtler worlds of the psyche or the mind.

It is no wonder this person feels so bad: The highest of all energies (Level Seven) is trying to flow through the smallest possible amount of consciousness creating untold tension (Level One), having to misuse a potent willpower to hold onto a distorted belief that the world is scary and the life is threatened. And since this is a purely egoistic fear, this person's energy is involved in mis-creating an illusion, holding onto a life separate from its true Source. The holding on is what hurts.

Likewise, Level Six energy, designed to express the higher emotions of a compassionate yearning to love and serve humanity, is attempting to express itself through the highly-charged sensual energy of Level Two, which is drawing its "data" from the experience of the physical senses and the emotions. Emotional disturbances will be the theme for this person. Since our outer experiences are only one-half of who we are, we are living from a half-truth falsely perceived as the whole Truth. This can lead to a type of hysterical devotion to causes, attachment to people and/or objects needed for gratification, or a frantic search for the "highs" in life.

Misuse of the senses and emotions completely dissipates the organism's ability for peace of mind. It totally exhausts the person's energy. It is love turned to lust. Satprem refers to emotional energy as "fog incarnate," for it distorts Reality in favor of the sentiment's notion of what Reality is. Passion gets caught up in diversity, thinking each single event or method of gratification is essential.... completely absolutizing the experience: "If I can't have this particular thing or person *right now*, I can't stand it!" This consciousness is animalistic in nature — like a male dog in the presence of a bitch in heat.

Compassion, its higher counterpart, draws diversity back into itself: It becomes great enough to include diversity in the realization of unity. *Passion is emotional reaction without realization of the meaning of the event. Compassion is where emotion and realization merge.*

When the higher mental energy of Level Five becomes constricted through the fragmented consciousness of Level Three, it causes the person to become preoccupied with desire for status, for he is seeking self definition. The Will to "Know Thyself" is looking in the wrong direction for its identity. The ego's view of itself (which it is getting from the outer world) is threatened. This is the archetype of the immature human — a self acting in the world as false personality, not knowing who it really is. As we are becoming conscious, we can only tolerate so much phoniness and self-deceit without complete breakdown. Trying to be something we are not causes undue stress on the organism because it takes so much energy to pretend. It feels like *me against myself....* which is exactly what's happening. There is constant fear of being found out (often unconscious).... and a nagging anxiety about not knowing who we really are, or what we really want. We usually feel okay if we are getting approval from others, but the moment the approval is withdrawn, we panic or feel depressed.

Polarization at one of the three lower levels means using the lower without its higher counterpart — Level One without Seven; Level Two without Six; or Level Three without Five. Half-truth is the result. The Lower Self is real and holy; but without the energy of the Higher Self, it deceives, sometimes viciously.... *experiencing* devoid of purpose and meaning. The Transformer works from Level Four, as a catalyst and a balancer, making sure both the energies from the higher and the lower are utilized. Channeling higher truth is a calm, dispassionate energy, but does contain a certain joy that comes from expressing one's true nature — Truth! Thought is limiting when we think from our Lower Self; thought is creative when we are channeling from the Higher Self.

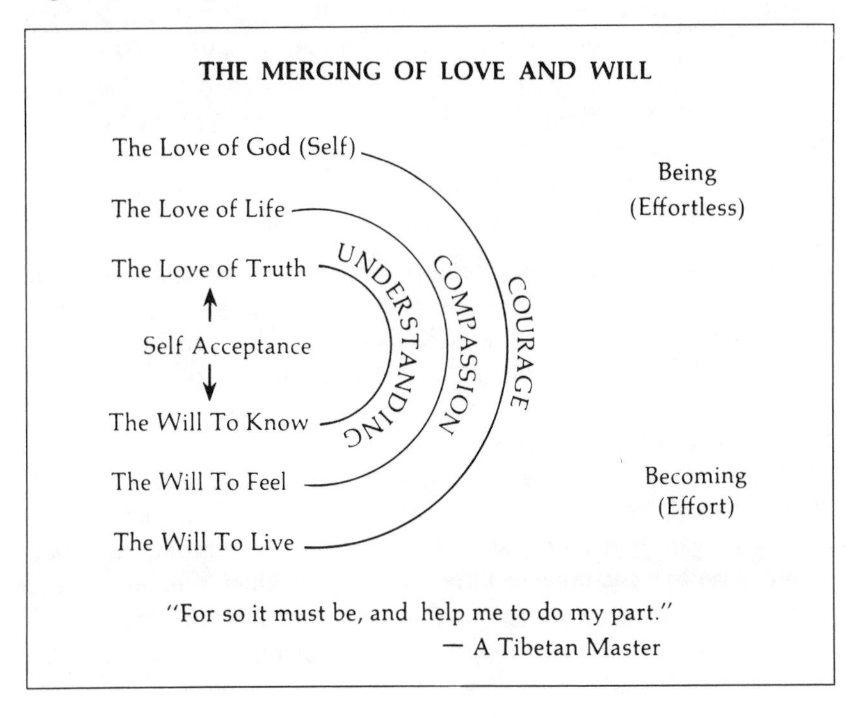

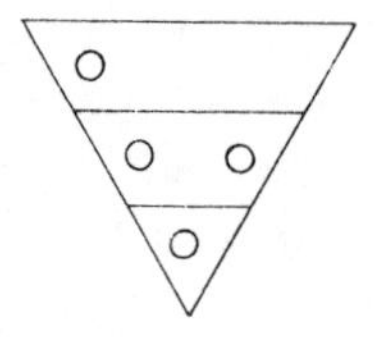

THE HOME OF THE PARTIAL SELVES

Levels One, Two and Three are where the fragments of our personality live, our partial selves. They are activated by the needs of the ego. When the higher counterpart of one of the lower centers is operating, the partial selves are under the supervision of the True Self and will not get out of control. When we become polarized, however, in Level One, Two or Three, we become "victimized" by a little subpersonality. We are its victim because we have gone unconscious and allowed it to take over. A fear, passion or identity response won out while "the master" was away. Remember, the partial selves function in order to get an ego need met, and they are indeed a part of our personality — *we created them.* And we created them because we needed them at the time! But they are *not* the True Self.

It is anti-therapeutic to try to rid oneself of a partial self, even an extremely negative one. We can never rid ourselves of a part of ourself! The more we try, the more force this little self will have and the more trouble it will give us. This phenomenon has been noted by all major psychological theories. We must, instead, integrate these little selves by a five-step process: *acknowledgement or recognition, understanding, acceptance, coordination/cooperation and synthesis.*

Acknowledgment or recognition. Before anything else can happen, we have to become aware of a particular subpersonality operating in/on us. A good clue is the feeling of a "personality change" that happens instantly, brought on by a certain cue from the outer world. And there will be a pattern to it: "I *always* act that way around male authority figures!"

Once we "see" the little character and realize it has literally taken over our eyes, nose, mouth and ears, then it helps to picture this self as a real, honest-to-goodness character. See him/her in your imagination in a costume, or uniform, with a distinct look on its face, a certain stance, a certain describable way of being. The more detail, the better we will work through this stage of recognition. Give the little character a name. Humorous ones often are very effective: "Mafia Mom," "Whooshing Witch," "The Great White Glub," ("Glub" for short), "Superstud," etc.

Understanding. Once we see this little person, we must find a way to get to know it. Have a dialogue with it in your mind. Or, watch yourself acting from this characterization *with awareness.* Whatever.... just get to know it. Ask it what it wants, what it is trying to do for you, how it feels, where it comes from. Treat this personality exactly as you would a new person coming into your life that you are indeed fascinated with.

Once you understand this little self, you will find, *without fail,* that it is trying to do something good for you. Sure, it's distorted. And maybe even off the wall, but it is trying in its own way to help you because it does not trust *you* to help yourself in this particular situation! Part of the understanding stage is to help your little partial self gain confidence in you.... that you definitely appreciate its concern, but you will show it that you can handle the situation just fine. You may even have to strike a bargain with it. That's okay, too.

Acceptance. Acceptance springs forth spontaneously from the process of complete understanding. We begin to love and appreciate these little partial selves, for we see how in their own distorted manner, they have been struggling to help us. They have been a part of our personality structure *because we have needed them.* Acceptance now allows them to be seen fully in the light of day, enabling us to utilize them realistically for the tasks they are meant for.... and, at the same time, keeping them from overstepping their bounds.

Coordination/Cooperation. Once acceptance is achieved, judgment will fade away. You will see this little self as having a purpose in your personality, though misguided in its expression. And you will know when you adopted it (probably when you were a child). Now you can begin the work of personality restructuring wherein this part of yourself can begin working with other parts *in harmony.*

This type of work immediately puts you into the fourth level of consciousness. Let's say you have a subpersonality that becomes rude and aggressive with male authority figures: "I *have* to show that son-of-a-gun he can't run over ME! I'll show HIM!" But with more Self-knowledge, you discover you also have a little part in you that sometimes becomes too submissive to a strong masculine figure, and you wind up letting him run all over you. Quite often you will find these little selves work in pairs (opposite extremes). In this stage of integration, the two little extreme selves can learn to work together to strike a comfortable balance vis-à-vis this type of situation.

Synthesis. A synthesis occurs when you no longer feel any need for a subpersonality to help you out with a theme, such as "Male Authority Figures in My Life." Once you have become completely balanced and comfortable with these types of people, there is no longer a need to put energy into the concept "Male Authority Figure." You will just *be* someone who relates to persons in those roles as easily as you would with anyone else. The "split" no longer exists; you have integrated a segment of yourself. The way you will know this stage is by the *absence* of energy (interest or reaction) in the entire subject.

Emotional over-reaction is always the clue that we are operating from a partial self. The True Self has no need to over-react to anything. It knows who it is, and it has no need to prove anything to anyone.

Subpersonalities are *Re-minders.* They are set off by particular circumstances in our lives, and they will always represent a pattern. Each time one pops up, it gives us another chance to see the Truth about this particular predicament we are caught up in. Re-minders offer us another chance to complete a little piece of illusion operant within the personality. We can appreciate them for the opportunity they give us to become whole.

What has been described here is the process of *dis-identifying* from these little subpersonalities and *re-identifying* with the True Self. This process has three steps.

(1) Observation: I HAVE YOU.

(2) Dis-Identification: AND I AM NOT YOU.

(3) Re-Identification: I AM pure consciousness and the impulse to (Self-Realization) act... my True Self.

"The words 'I am' are potent words;
be careful what you hitch them to.
The thing you're claiming has a way
of reaching back and claiming you."
— *A. L. KITSELMAN*

"The basis of all Self-realization and inner freedom is dis-identification. We are dominated by what our self becomes identified with, and we can direct and use whatever we dis-identify from."
— *ROBERTO ASSAGIOLI*

WORKING WITH POLARIZATION

So now we will examine the therapeutic tasks involved at each level of polarization, exploring in detail how to work with clients when they are stuck at a certain level. Before we begin, it is crucial to point out that a particular client is never consistently stuck at any *one* level. Depending on the external predicament he is caught up in, he can be stuck in Level One at one time, Level Two at another, and Level Three at some other time. Clients do, however, usually have a certain preferable mode of "stuckness." In this sense, you can categorize them by their usual behavior. But I caution you in trying to make this model too rigid. As Alan Watts said once: "Human nature is wiggly." Any theory of personality that tries to set generalized rules in concrete has to be illusory: Each client will demonstrate to you his or her unique way of operating in Life. You must have the eyes to perceive this uniqueness.

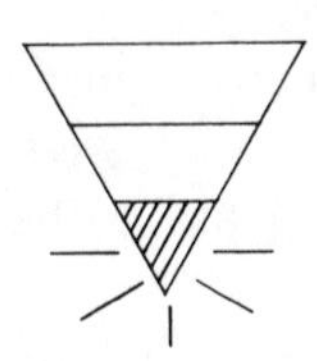

LEVEL ONE POLARIZATION
(The Fear Response)

Allow your eyes to glance over the above words, which symbolize the essence of this type of client's predicament. This is an *intuitive* process, so do not attempt to analyze or separate out any portion of this word picture.... just let it have its way with you for a few moments. Allow the *pattern* and *feeling tone* of this client to come in on you. When you begin to "feel" this, let a symbol come into your mind that represents this unique individual. In so doing, you will get a sense of how to proceed with your client who is stuck at Level One. Remember this: *Acceptance of Self and of Life as it is* will always be the primary task of all levels of polarization. But beyond this generalized acceptance of what is, the three lower levels diverge in the necessary tasks of therapy. Following is a suggested guide to working with a Level One polarity.

As already mentioned, when a Level One polarization is occurring, this client is caught in the illusion of separateness and isolation, having no sense of connectedness with humanity — no sense of purpose or meaning in life, no reference group to belong to. This client will be angry or depressed, exhibiting a great need to control life, or just to forget it and withdraw. Since she is connecting with the outer world solely through fear and impotence, she feels paranoid about life and the people in it. Her experience has taught her that this is a dangerous and unpredictable world, and she must not let herself be vulnerable. This belief resides in her subconscious mind, determining the way she experiences her reality. Because of this belief structure, you can be sure this *is* indeed her reality! Therefore, you must enter into this perceived reality with her until rapport is established. Otherwise, you will become just another one of "those people out there who cannot understand." And you will have reinforced the very thing in her you would like to help transform — her lack of faith.

A Reformer would argue with this client about her reality and try to convince her to believe the way the counselor does, leading to more polarization and increased resistance. A typical Reformer response would sound like this: "That's not really how your life is; you are just imagining it." Or "I hear you saying you are a victim of your life, and that is simply not true."

A Transformer, on the other hand, "goes with the resistance" and unhinges this person's defense mechanism, freeing her energy to explore other possibilities a little further down the line. "It's as though everything around you just doesn't seem to work out very well. I can sense your desperation." Or "I sense you are really afraid you don't have much power over your life. That must feel awful."

Entering into this client's reality with her does not mean you believe it to be the whole truth; it means you believe that *she* believes it to be the whole truth. It just means you will *believe your client....*

using *her* world view as the starting point from whence to launch the therapeutic process. Then you can lead her into a wider, more realistic and hopeful world as she gradually begins to trust that you do indeed understand how she feels.

At some point in the first session, a Transformer will elicit from the client portions of her "story" where she has been successful... even if only small successes... and draw attention to these times when appropriate as the client opens. This creates a "success platform" for her to stand upon from whence to view the "failures" in her life with more balance. This is highly effective in building hope and a new point of view.

Empathy and Self-disclosure* are two counselor traits that are very helpful with this kind of client. Especially share any times that you have felt these "paranoid" feelings about your own life, if you can be genuinely sincere about it. And your mode of communication should match the client's as much as possible. If the client talks in terms of problem-solving and goals, you do the same. If she shares a lot of feelings and emotions, or talks in metaphors or images, follow her lead as much as possible. Your communication is your tool for blending into her reality.

Description. Often you will notice that this client has a retentive stance in life.... holding on, holding in. Body movements will usually be stereotyped or restricted. The person may suffer from constipation or lower back problems, or trouble with the legs and feet.... in other words, her foundation. These Level One energies are tied to the anal/adrenal area of expression. This client will be either a withdrawer or a fighter, depending upon the particular personality style.

This type of client can be born with the physiological weakness for alcohol addiction, what is referred to in this book as "cellular alcoholism." The knowledge of the disease resides in the genetic structure of the organism, manifesting itself once alcohol is consumed on a regular basis. This type of alcoholic never drank normally. Alcohol affects her body chemistry differently than it does other people's. From the first drink, she felt something others do not feel, which set up a craving and an immediate compulsivity about drinking, as though the cells are starving and the alcohol intake relieves (deceives) this deprivation into thinking it is gratified. And often, with

*See the author's book, *Becoming Naturally Therapeutic,* especially the chapter on Empathy and Self-disclosure, Eupsychian Press, 1981.

this type of client I have observed a difficulty with sugar intake, diabetes or hypoglycemia.

THERAPEUTIC TASKS FOR LEVEL ONE POLARIZATION

Your first task with this client is to establish rapport. And it may take a while. A statement like "You couldn't possibly feel like that" is toxic because it lacks respect, discounting the client's perceived reality. It would cause her to mistrust you. You come across as a preacher or a judge. On the other hand, a statement like "I really do believe you when you say you are miserable and life seems to be just awful for you" will lead to her opening up and trusting you, consequently expanding her world a tiny bit to now include you. This is the main task at this level.... to assist your client in expanding her viewpoint and discovering that it's safe to do so. In other words, you will use Level Seven Force to counteract the constricted negative side of Level One Force. Level Seven teaches that we are a part of a larger whole, and we each have a unique purpose here.... that there have indeed been times (and will be again) when we have used ourselves creatively, following the will of our nature, and that we *can* be safe and feel united with a larger energy that gives us a sense of belonging. It teaches us to release the fear we are holding on to and to have faith in the total process of humanness, even when security, pleasure or self-esteem of the Lower Self *is* threatened.

To this client, you must impart this knowledge concretely, not abstractly. One way is by creating a way for her to talk about some of her successes in life, no matter how small. "What have you done in life that you are proud of?" or "What has happened in your life that has made you feel good?" Help her to see the conditions that led up to this success. Point out to her that she can have this kind of result again if she can understand the process. Then you can always go back to these recalled successes when she moves into spaces of hopelessness.

Concreteness is crucial. Most clients stuck at Level One will not understand a mini-lecture about cosmic consciousness, but they will understand the principle of oneness and of feeling their own power if you can help them recall successes. You can also help create some new successes for them to experience. When you understand the principles to work with, it will occur to you naturally and easily what to do and say with each individual client. And even though the work may sometimes seem slow (after all, these clients are often limited in their ability to explore), you will succeed.

To be more specific, a client stuck in the Fear Response needs to discover that she is not alone and that life is worth living.... that even her suffering can have a purpose! She must tediously begin expanding her point of view so that her experiences can broaden. Just as the baby learns to leave the crib and eventually even the safety of its house, this client must be supported and understood while she ventures out and finds her "group," or her place in the sun.

Alcoholics Anonymous is an excellent tool for this process for alcoholics, unless even this is too frightening. Sometimes a person at Level One has to begin relating to just one other person (you!) before she can overcome the group phobia that is symptomatic of the extreme paranoia. But if AA can be accepted, it will be a good beginning for developing a sense of belonging to *The Whole,* being part of it all. Her "whole universe" may become Alcoholics Anonymous for awhile: "All alcoholics understand me; others do not (outside world)." She will see the world divided into alcoholics and non-alcoholics. If she likes you and you don't happen to be an alcoholic, she will feel you *must* be an alcoholic but maybe don't know it — or maybe you just never drank!

As this client begins to venture out, help her do it gradually, with as little risk as possible. Encourage her to expand, but avoid extremely scary things at first. Slowly desensitize her to the fear of new experiences by helping her pick new situations that will be fairly safe and easy. If you want to put her in a group, for instance, make sure it will be a group on her level, with people who are somewhat like her. Putting her with others too dissimilar will make her feel even more alienated. You are dealing with the polarity struggle between powerlessness and an appropriate sense of power and unification with others.

As you talk with her, implant the realization that we have created our past and will therefore create our future. Help her to see specifically how she has created her past by the choices she's made, *given how she viewed the world at the time.* If she goes back and recalls the exact points in time when she made choices that she now views as mistakes, she will see that *given* how she was perceiving her alternatives, she made exactly the right choice each time. This awareness will often relieve her guilt feelings entirely.

In fact, take a little time right now and recall a choice you once made, seeing yourself at the decision-making point in time and space (e.g., that day I was in the parking lot about to get in my car when I realized I had to move.) Be this specific about the point in time.... and review how you were perceiving your world then, the choices you felt you had, the people in the predicament with you, etc., and you will see what I mean: It was exactly the correct choice *then.* (Certainly, now that you are several years older, and several degrees wiser, you would have done differently, but this is irrelevant because it is not Reality). Work with Fourth Force. This will model love and forgiveness, and also the use of the creative imagination.

After rapport is established and the past has been reviewed somewhat, study Exercise #7, *Transforming Resentments,* and lead your client through this process with however many persons are necessary. Begin with *self*-forgiveness.... Her energy used to hold onto resentments needs to be freed up for moving forward in life.

Once past resentments are dealt with and have been cleared out, she must learn a new skill so as not to build them up again: the use of the Observer Self that can watch without judgment what she does *as she is doing it.* In counseling sessions practice the Observer Self exercises in this book. As she discovers how she has chosen her past by her reactions to others and to situations, she will gain confidence in choosing her present (which creates her future) choices. She will realize she is free to choose safety if she wishes, or she can risk at her own pace.... but she *must* learn to do this consciously rather than seeing herself as a victim of life. You must help her transcend *any* feelings of victimhood, because this is the enemy of personal freedom.

"Victimhood" is only perceived as reality when we are operating from a mechanical consciousness without awareness. When we learn to be aware, we cannot be a victim of anything: we are *creators* of our lives, not victims. Teach this to your client.

For a homework assignment, ask her to walk around for fifteen minutes each day for a week observing her actions, feelings and thoughts, and asking, "How am I setting this one up?" or "How have I attracted this to myself?" And get honest! *Be insistent and firm about honesty.* It's exciting to really get to know yourself! You must model this enthusiasm and faith in the process of awakening.

This client has to learn how to stay in the here and now rather than spending so much time catastrophizing about the future or worrying about the past. For awareness on this, have her draw on a piece of paper three circles of varying sizes to show how much of her energy she spends in the past, present or future:[41]

Examples:

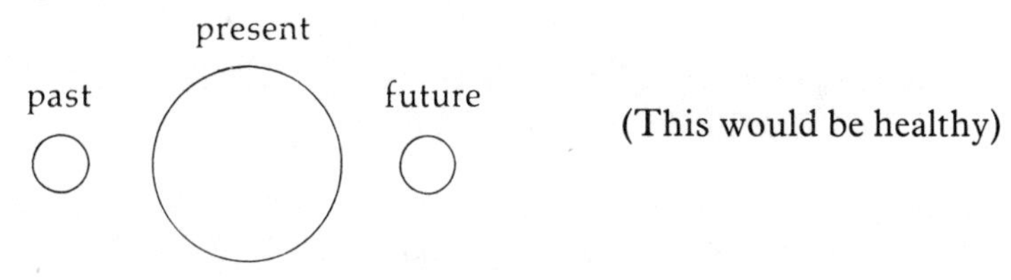

(This would be healthy)

Some self-defeating ones would look like this:

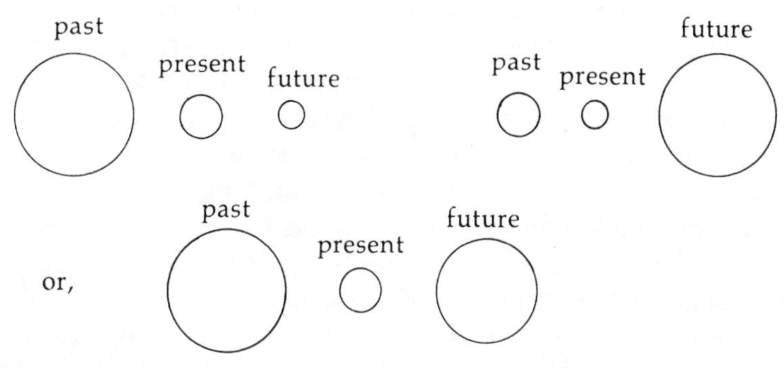

Sensual/emotional awareness (Level Two consciousness) is a wonderful way to guide this client up a notch. As we begin to live more from our actual experiences, we make better contact with the world and let go of the paranoid delusions we are creating with our minds. THE BODY KNOWS, AND THE SOUL KNOWS; ONLY OUR MINDS CAN LIE.

When our true feelings are suppressed, we create symbolic needs, having gotten completely out of touch with our *real* needs. So we will go after a symbolic need, such as food, drink, etc., and it will not fulfill us, because it is a *false* need. I don't really need that food or that drink; I need safety or love. But now our minds are telling us an untruth, so we begin to create a false reality, getting further and further away from our real needs. Helping a client get in touch with *real* feelings, *real* needs, is a healing event.

And as you move along together, hope is gradually built. Hope and trust. And you do this by using yourself as an instrument. *You are the one she can trust and who models a hopeful attitude.* Your ability to be empathic, genuine, warm and honest about yourself will provide the groundwork for this therapeutic relationship. With a client like this, no confrontation is used at first. She needs to open up and explore, *not change.* At least not yet. Once rapport is established, you can begin to confront lovingly.

STAGES OF THE THERAPEUTIC PROCESS FOR LEVEL ONE POLARIZATION

1. *Empathic Listening.* Begin by listening to your client, entering into her *reality,* slowly forming a bond. ALWAYS BELIEVE YOUR CLIENT! Never argue with her about how she sees things. Just listen, empathize, and if you want, add some things from how you see your world, if you think she can relate to them. Otherwise, don't confuse her by bringing in too much about yourself, especially at first.

Draw out your client's "story" as a way of establishing rapport. This will also give you a sense of how she perceives and responds habitually to her universe. It will also enable her to vent some pent-up energy. As you learn her patterns of thinking, feeling and acting, you will be able to assess how to enter into her life space therapeutically.

Listen to the way your client uses language and metaphor and respond in similar fashion. For example, if she speaks in terms like "I have to decide a course of action soon," respond with something like "What decision seems best to you right now?" rather than "As you are sensing your world, what image do you get?" She is showing you how she thinks, which is concretely and concerned with practical problem-solving. You must meet her on her level.[42]

2. *Releasing Constricted Energy.* Once rapport is established, help her begin to release the pent-up emotions that have built up from past unfinished and misunderstood situations. Letting go of guilt and resentments and building Self-acceptance and forgiveness will be the main tasks. See Exercises #8, 9, 11 and 13 as especially valid for this stage.

3. *Attributing Meaning and Purpose to the Past.* As your client is bringing up this old material, help her redefine her past with purpose and meaning. Everything that has happened to her was for a reason. And it all makes sense now, if together you can both look at the patterns and events through the lens of understanding and acceptance. Help her see that *given how she viewed the situation at the time,* there were *no mistakes;* that there is no such thing as blame or victimhood.

4. *Transformations.* Once this more "remedial" work is done, you can begin guiding your client to higher levels of functioning by connecting her with the more integrated True Self. She must begin by utilizing the Here and Now appropriately. Here are some of the exercises that will help:

a. The Observer Self (#5) will give her a larger perspective on her activities, helping her transcend judging herself negatively and seeing the world through the distortion of fear.

b. "Seeing Yourself Completely" (#13) will give her a larger, more loving perspective on herself.

c. "Evoking an Ideal Model" (#15) will enable her to begin practicing how to be in the world in a way that is effective and desirable. This will, in turn, build her self-esteem.

d. "Evoking a Positive Quality" (#16) will teach your client how to work with the positive side of a negative habit pattern, and will also give her a great sense of accomplishment and order in following the instructions and experiencing the results.

5. *Right Action.* And finally, emphasis should be placed upon the client's everyday life — the actions, feelings and thoughts she is consciously choosing to focus on will be examined and corrected by Right Action — doing *the next right thing.* She can begin practicing "Harmlessness" and processing with you the situations that occur in her life that are troublesome or exciting for her to share. She will have some successes to report. In this work, be sure to continue to build up her successes and play down the failures, redefining them as "tests."

6. *Transpersonal Focusing.* As therapy progresses successfully, gradually guide your client "out of herself" into serving another. Help her discover her particular strengths and talents in serving. No matter how small, each of us has something worthwhile to give another, and this is how we learn to be part of a whole, relieving isolation and feelings of meaninglessness.

7. *Disengaging.* Toward the end of the process, begin acknowledging more and more your client's own personal power, disallowing dependency on you and transferring her dependency to a larger group or activity. Help substitute interdependence for dependence, where others are dependent upon her sometimes. Help her understand that

dependency/independency are both natural and can be used appropriately and interchangeably in life as we learn to recognize the cycles of change within ourselves.

QUESTIONS AND ANSWERS

Question: Addiction at the cellular level.... where did it come from?

Answer: For me, two theories will explain cellular alcoholism. Perhaps either of these will help you understand this phenomenon: (1) *Genetic memory.* This theory says we pass on to our offspring certain traits, strengths, and weaknesses. A "Factor X" may or may not exist that causes a proclivity toward alcoholism. Allergy and diabetes also seem to fit into this category. (2) *The Doctrine of Rebirth.* This concept is fairly new to the West, but long recognized in the East. It is beyond the scope of this book to delve deeply into this philosophy, but briefly, it says we have lived before in other times, as our Soul seeks many experiences through various personalities in order to evolve its nature. Through many lives we build up a chain of cause and effect relationships whereby lessons are learned, or not learned, from our experiences. We will be drawn toward lessons we need in future lifetimes in order to balance everything out. According to this theory, the alcoholic would be born alcoholic with something very fundamental to work through in this lifetime, either through a family chain of cause and effect (group karma), or personally (individual karma).

There have been some clinical studies in past life regressions that tend to support this theory:[43] Many people report having had spontaneous recall of past life events, people, or even abilities, such as foreign languages or ability to interpret foreign symbols from other times or other cultures. According to this theory, the Law of Cause and Effect is not a punitive Law, but a benevolent one, offering us time and time again the opportunity to advance in the areas where defects or ignorance reign within the personality. Our Souls opt for the circumstances where the necessary lessons can be learned. Disease, in itself, is viewed as benevolent, for it brings the Personality face to face with the urge of the Soul. Its objective is coming from a Higher Purpose, such as getting the attention of the Personality in order to correct something within the person that is illusory. Or the disease can serve as a teacher to someone else in the life of the sick one. Coping with alcoholism would be a seedbed of knowledge about the Self and its desire nature. Transforming this addiction would lead to the development of many beautiful, Soul-enriching qualities.

The Doctrine of Rebirth is often confused with the superstitious doctrine of Transmigration of Souls, the view that people become animals, insects, or inert matter as punishment for wrongs. Personally, I consider this to be a false theory because it violates the natural process of evolution, taking us backwards instead of forward. We are evolving, not devolving! We *can* get stuck! But it is unlikely, since we are human, that there would be lessons of a *non*human nature to learn.

Cellular addiction can also occur later on in a lifetime, rather than at the beginning, simply by continuing to drink so much that the disease pervades the spiritual dimension, then the mental life, then, in progression, on down into the emotional nature, and finally, still unchecked, it enters the body's cellular structure as "Truth." (Now, the body thinks it is alcoholic.) The cellular addiction then becomes a *result* of the lifestyle, rather than the cause of it. And since the cells now believe they need alcohol to survive, the body follows their orders and craves the substance.

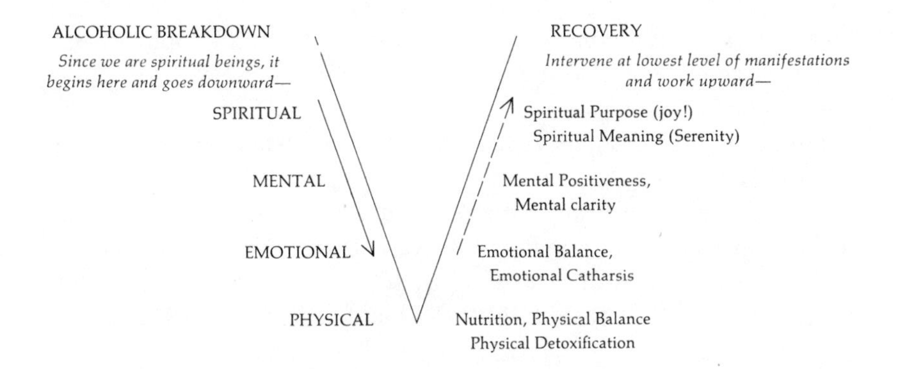

The body will control the mind if an organic deficiency is present. Some very current research tying hypoglycemia to alcoholism, as a *cause* rather than a result, validates this point even further.[44] Investigators Paulos and Stoddard found that some 100 alcoholics voluntarily kicked the alcohol habit following treatment for their hypoglycemic condition.

Also, in studying 73 alcoholism cases where lithium was administered to combat depression (a common symptom of hypoglycemia), a marked decrease was found in serious drinking bouts from the group taking lithium. Twenty-five per cent of the lithium patients returned to problem drinking compared with sixty-four per cent who did not receive the lithium treatment.

When a cellular imbalance occurs within the organism, the body will dictate to the mind its needs and will seek gratification, regardless of the irrationality of its choices: e.g., going after sugar when sugar is the problem; craving the very food one is allergic to, etc. It is as though the body is crazed from its deficient condition, seeking instant gratification, and tells the mind what to do, "thinking" it is telling the Truth.

You will recall that the physical is the densest, most basic level of human functioning. When illness has reached its "bottom," we must begin there and climb back up again.

Question: I am comfortable with genetic theories, but the idea of reincarnation scares me. I've noticed, though, that I'm fascinated with the subject. What do you suggest I do to help me believe in it?

Answer: Instead of trying to believe in a particular philosophy, I would suggest that you examine the facts you already *know* about human experience.... and then be sure you hold a philosophy of life that is large enough to contain what you know. A philosophy of life always underpins our knowledge and experiences. Sometimes we are living out of a philosophy that we have never even verbalized. Have you ever had an experience that does not fit into this particular time frame? Or does your intuition tell you there has been something before your birth that is influencing you? If the Doctrine of Rebirth fascinates you, by all means study it. If it is a Truth for you, your study will set off a spark deep in the place where *you know.* If not, you can reject it.

Question: Can a client be addicted at the cellular level and be further along than Level One emotionally or mentally?

Answer: Yes. I have had clients where this was the case. It depends on how highly advanced the Soul was when it "fell into" the alcoholism. We can progress and fall back, progress and fall back.... at least at the current level of human existence as we are experiencing it. (I don't know yet what happens to superhumans!) The way you can tell if the client has progressed above the First Level of consciousness is that he will "recognize" Truth at the higher levels. It won't be like talking to a blank wall when you speak of creativity, service to humanity or following the Soul's urge. These clients are, to me, the most beautiful and touching to involve with, because they know on a very deep level the trouble they are in, and they have a desperate desire to rise above their dependence. They usually do not feel they are "victims" but realize they must take responsibility for their own health or lack of it.

Intervention begins at whatever level the client is showing the most symptoms. Then we facilitate the progress upward. When a client realizes he is a spiritual being, his higher centers begin to open, and a new kind of energy is available. (Not really new at all; it's been there all along, unrealized.) To quote Maslow:

> The "higher circuits" already exist in the human personality, as does the subconscious, determining a lot of our pain and joy. Peak experiences, creativity, aestheticism and spirituality are functions of these higher energies. These levels are the natural flow toward the realization of our emerging perfection.

When I work with a client stuck at Levels One or Two, it helps to remember that EMOTION FOLLOWS THOUGHT. And thought, fueled by emotion (energy), manifests in the physical world. "As a man thinketh *in his heart,* so is he." Synthesizing the mind and heart (what your client thinks and how he feels become one) creates a healing event in the life of a person in conflict.

Question: So you are saying that addiction at the cellular level can come from the past, even before birth.... or it can come from falling all the way down through the dimensions during one's lifetime, all the way down to the physical level. Is that right?

Answer: Exactly. And I would speculate — and this is pure speculation — that if one falls all the way down to the cellular level during his lifetime, and then begets children, the children may inherit the weakness. Food for thought.

Question: Does it fit into your philosophy, then, to say that alcoholism is a disease.

Answer: Certainly.... disease on many levels. Look at the word "disease." It means "lack of ease." And I would define disease as a conflict between the Soul and the Personality, which can never be eradicated by merely directing curative measures toward the body alone. It requires a spiritual, mental and emotional effort as well.

Focusing purely on physical "cures" is falling into the trap of materialism, believing we are *only* a body. This is why we've not progressed very far in eradicating alcoholism. We only superficially repair damage, leaving the cause still operative in the person. In fact, apparent physical recovery can even be harmful.... arresting the disease at the physical level.... as it hides from the client the true cause of his problem and enables him to fall short of discovering the deeper aspects of renewed health if he were called upon to continue working at the higher levels for total cure. Again, food for thought.

Disease is our teacher, and if we rightly interpret its message, we are guided to an awareness of a virtue we are being asked to develop by our Higher Self. Suffering is a corrective that points out a lesson we have failed to learn, and it will continue to reappear (maybe in varied forms) until we learn what we came here to learn. Once we *get it,* we no longer need the suffering. And, in fact, we can prevent or divert suffering or disease when we realize at its onset what is actually happening. As long as we still have physical life, no matter how diseased we become, we can know our Soul is still not without hope.... that we can advance beyond our stuck point.

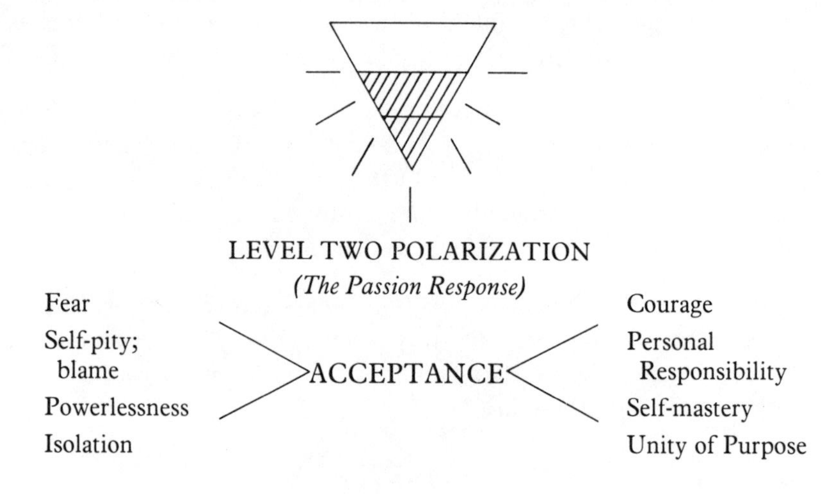

Again, do not attempt to analyze or dissect the above words — just let them wash over you as an intuitive response emerges within you toward a client stuck at this level of consciousness. Then, slowly, allow your particular client to come into focus and let a symbol representing this unique person come into your mind. This symbol will contain the energy and the meaning of the *whole truth* of your client. Use this information to guide you in your work.

This is the client who is addicted to seeking sensation (or avoiding it, if too much pain has been experienced at the emotional level.) In fact, this client *defines* himself by the degree or type of sensation he is feeling (or missing). When he is not "high" on something or someone, he feels depressed, or dead. At the extreme end of the continuum, it would be the manic/depressive syndrome (a combination of physical and emotional imbalance). Mood swings are a fact of life for this client, as though his life is lived on a pendulum, swinging from one end to the other, needing constant stimuli from the external world .... up, down, pleasant, painful. Often this client will have experimented with every kind of mood altering phenomenon he can find.... anything rumored to produce a "turn on."

Please keep in mind, I'm talking about *an addiction* to this emotional quest. It is natural for all of us to yearn for a transcendent experience, as we are spiritual beings seeking to merge with that "something" greater than we are. But healthy people are content with gradual evolution toward these "highs" and do not feel the urgent need to push the river.

This client experiments with life with the same furor that he experiments with chemicals.... often even flirting with death. He has untold amounts of pent-up energy, restlessness, nervousness.... always on the move. He avoids learning to meditate or anything else that helps him be still.... and yet, this is exactly what he needs to learn to balance out some of this supercharged energy he is attempting to handle. He will talk to you in emotional/feeling language, as though his whole world is viewed from the level of sensation: "That didn't feel good to me." "I'm bored stiff." "Boy, what a thrill." "I had a big blowout last night." "Life is flat, dull.... I may as well be dead," etc. It is as though this client really needs a way to blow off steam — he produces so much of it!

Fritz Perls teaches that there are only four ways to release emotions: anger, grief, joy and orgasm — and that a healthy person can utilize all of these "explosives," appropriately, of course.[45]

In the teachings of Gurdjieff, we learn that our emotional center is the most difficult to work with, because we become so very identified with our feeling states. We take for granted our emotional states, as though they *are* us — rather than seeing them as something we are to observe and separate from. He compares our emotional center to a mad elephant who needs a tame elephant on either side of it for balance, one intellectual and one instinctual.

The starting point in the work of balancing our emotional states is self-observation, the work of the Observer Self. Can I observe my emotional state *as I am experiencing the emotion* and ask what brought it on? In what connection did it arise? If I can learn to do this, I can begin to bring my emotions into alignment with my Higher Self.

Clients stuck in their emotions are stuck in the past. Most people continually nurture such a great reservoir of unhappiness from their past, it takes a great deal of personal work to clear out these habitual pathetic responses. They are used to feeling pathetic, which of course only gives rise to continual negative feelings. We must eventually cancel out our past, and not allow it to control us. But before he can believe it possible to let go of the past, your client must learn he has control over his present. And we begin this by learning to watch our habitual ways of responding to stimuli coming from outside us or from our own thoughts and belief. Our habitual responses, based on a lack of understanding of Life, are creating the emotional imbalances we get caught up in.

So, Level Two addictions are the *misuse* of the emotional energy. Emotion is our way of experiencing feeling/motivation. It is our love energy. But this Second Force without the balance of Sixth Force is love turned to its extravagance.... lust. The rules of lust are: "If a little bit is good, more will be better," and "I don't care what tomorrow brings; I'll just have all I can get right now." Love and attending to the now are natural. Lust and being addicted to instant gratification are natural urges turned to their opposites, and will eventually lead to pain.

When one seeks pleasure solely from the "things" of life, only one of two possibilities can result: satiation or frustration.... and enough of either leads to hopelessness. The first time I try a sensational gourmet delight I am thrilled by its taste. The second time, I still am, maybe. But what happens if I eat the same menu 10 times in a row? I become satiated. Suddenly, it has lost its allure. In fact,

I can even become repulsed by the thought of this once-cherished flavor. Satiation feels awful, because of the letdown. Something I thought would "give It to me" no longer does. And recalling the first thrilling exposure to this delight makes me feel even worse. What happened? Is something wrong with me? Can I never be satisfied? So the message my organism records (the sense-awareness) is that nothing lasts; everything fun eventually fades away. Nothing is worth going for. I can never be happy.

On the other hand, if I continually seek out a certain delight and discover I cannot find it, or if I find poor substitutes but not the real thing, I cannot satisfy my desire. Then I continually long for it, pitying myself that it cannot be. And, in my imagination, this desired object becomes the grand unreachable perfection that I now compare my ordinary experiences with and find wanting. Frustration is the result.

Both satiation and frustration are ways to experience failure and hopelessness.... an inability to be present to my real existence. Through making these processes *conscious,* I can let go of my need to re-experience over and over again the same gourmet delight. It is now possible for me to flow with my present experience, whatever it may be, trusting that the future will bring more diverse and pleasant experiences.

Clients polarized at Level Two can turn sour in another way besides seeking the highs from objects in life. They can also become emotionally attached to causes and ideals, over-aggrandizing their values. When they cannot live up to the exaggerated "cause," they create suffering for themselves and others. This is a misuse of the beautiful and good devotional energy that resides at Level Six, becoming devoted to a cause representing a *fragment* of Truth (an exaggeration). This can lead to dogmatism, fanaticism, arrogance, closed-mindedness, or even cruelty.... the very opposite of love and compassion. The "cause," especially if it is designed to serve mankind, becomes a way to feel self-righteous, and the human dignity of an individual not worshipping your same cause can be compromised or brutally ignored. Extremism will always eventually turn to its opposite.

In the area of child abuse, there are many heart-breaking examples of this kind of distortion of Truth. I once knew a preacher who tied his children to the table top for hours at a time and wouldn't let their feet touch the floor as punishment for disregarding "God's rules." The earth, to him, had become so evil, he didn't want his children's feet to get dirty. What we label child abuse, he would call righteousness.

So, how do we help this person? Shaming a client for his excesses or mandating him to stop some behavior leads to more abuse. Experience has taught us that trying to prematurely force one's Lower Self away from an addiction always fails. Apparently, the person still needs the experience in order to learn something about Life or about himself. Does this mean we encourage the continued abuse? Seems like either way becomes a trap for the therapist. This whole question of guiding clients toward transcendence of Lower Self excesses is indeed a very big issue for those of us in the chemical addictions field.... the very core of our work. I have devoted much time and thought to this question, as I'm quite sure many of you have. And I don't pretend to have a formula that is fool-proof for working in this area. The following information has helped me to understand this client, and has greatly assisted me in feeling less urgency to *fix* him, or to blame myself when I couldn't. So, even though it is not a panacea, I offer it to you as a helpful suggestion.

First of all, clients at Level Two tend to fall into two categories: One type seems to be "young" and inexperienced in the worldly life, as though his Soul just hasn't had enough of certain sensations and events. This client, to me, is still at the stage of development where he is diving down *into* the world, craving more of Life's experiences. Classical Buddhist psychology (Abhidharma) provides a good source of practical wisdom for this type of client when he suffers from his experiencing. The work of "Mindfulness" gradually removes the energy from the coveted source of pleasure. The client continues to involve in the excessive behavior, but *only with awareness.* He watches himself non-judgmentally as he is indulging himself. *He does not judge; he watches.*

> Mindfulness is bare attention, or keeping present, with accurate, non-discursive registering of the situation taking place, without any reaction to the situation through mental evaluation, comment, labelling, behaving. It is deliberate observation of the body processes, emotions, and thoughts as one is engaged in the activity.[46]
>
> – *NYAROPONIKA THERA*

Thera speaks of our everyday activities as being like events occurring in a dark room cluttered with garbage, where a large portion of our activities occur in a twilight state of semi-consciousness. In this sleep state, unwholesome, neurotic behavior can thrive without our having to take responsibility for it. Ignorance and lack of awareness settle in the mind like dust that accumulates year after year, reducing the living space in the room.

Just like a child with a new toy, if we are fascinated by an experience, we will continue to crave it — even a negative one — *until we experience it fully with total involvement.* This is why Mindfulness is a technique that can lead us out of a negative compulsion. In the past, because of our judgment about the behavior as being "bad," we've turned our attention away from the event as we were involving in it, thereby never letting ourselves complete the experiencing. We've gone through the motions without taking responsibility for our actions; i.e., without making *conscious* what we were doing. Remember, we are here to make it all conscious. Mindfulness focuses our attention totally on the action, enabling us to complete it. When something is completed, it is *perfected* — no longer requiring our energy. Now we know it. And when we know something, it fades away and our mind moves on.

As your client gains proficiency in utilizing this method of watching, he will discover for himself that healthy mental states are antagonistic to unhealthy ones: they cannot reside in the same space. And he will gradually learn to substitute the positive counterpart for the unhealthy behavior when he is not caught up in the negative side. When the negative side *is* operating, he uses Mindfulness again. For example, when he overeats, he watches himself without judgment. When he is not overeating, he practices moderation in diet, choosing behaviors that lead to healthy food selection and eating habits.... such as substituting non-eating activities, breathing adequately, trying new healthier foods, being around nutrition-conscious people, etc.

One must realize in working with the Mindfulness technique that this is a gradual, slow-moving process, carefully supervised and sometimes taking several years.

The other type of client in this category seems to be "burnt out" on already having passed through so many years of excessive living. He knows about the world and is feeling somewhat defeated, or perhaps the best description is *tired.* You will sense that he is begging you to help him quit indulging himself. The pleasure is long gone and really holds no appeal for him, yet he still seems stuck, like a broken record, in some defeating habit pattern. He isn't just saying these things, either. He really is *through*.... but hasn't the strength or the skill to stop doing his mechanistic dance.

This client is on the way *up* and *out*.... needing to transcend his behavior. A Seed Thought for him (and you, to assist him) is: THE SELF IS GREATER THAN ITS CONDITIONS. And the Way of Negation will be this client's path, rather than involving with Mindfulness. He no longer needs to watch his excesses and run them out; they no longer hold any fascination for him. Instead, he needs to practice denial of the experience, gradually learning to withdraw this behavior pattern from the world of the senses. With your help, or the help of others you refer him to, he will respond to meditation, yoga, spiritual knowledge about the senses. He will be willing to practice the rewards of aloneness, or communing with others who are choosing a life of negation. This is a difficult path, but one many of our most saintly people have travelled. And one must be ready and prepared for it. Practiced prematurely — when there is still a strong fascination with the behavior in question — it will only lead to downfall.

The Path of Negation is a true Spiritual Path, but only when experiencing is *completed;* otherwise, it becomes a false teaching which bids us to leave our physical senses before we have learned how to use them properly. For example, one does not go from unhealthy sex to no sex. If he attempts celibacy prematurely, he merely carries his misunderstanding and frustrated needs into his celibate life with him, manifesting neurosis. One must travel from unhealthy to healthy sexual encounters, then evolve gradually into a celibate state, if this is so desired by the Higher Self. These matters are *states of mind,* levels of consciousness one has reached through personal evolution —*not* physical events. Spiritually and psychologically we cannot pretend to be where we are *not.* Only the Lower Self can pretend! The True Self just IS.

Again, this is a very touchy subject, one containing many fears and controversies. We are talking of the split most of us feel between our "animal" nature and our "spiritual" nature, as though the two are poles apart. It helps resolve the duality if we remember that we do not denigrate our animal nature simply because it is like a high-spiritual young colt, wild and unbroken. Its vital energy is God-given, as it is its nature to be full of life. Instead, we attempt to give this little creature the room it needs to be itself, while all the time exposing it to the more domestic life of the trained animal. And we do this with love. Often we are so frightened by the raw force of our passions that, in our fear, we attempt to flee madly from our unpurified nature. It is a far sounder policy, however, to equilibrate the battling forces within us by learning to understand both sides of our nature, experimenting a little here, a little there, *with awareness,* until we discover the energy is transmuting to its positive counterpart, and our unruly team of passions calms down.

Our greatest teachers have taught us not to fear plunging into Life: we are here to experience and to gain knowledge, which can only be done through facing realities and seeking to our utmost the Truth of human nature and of this universe we populate.[47]

The pleasure and pain we experience as Second Force in us becomes the data for developing Level Six consciousness — a merging of love and wisdom that leads us to the trained life of the intuition, the world of inner sensing.

STAGES OF THE THERAPEUTIC PROCESS FOR LEVEL TWO POLARIZATION

1. *Non-judgmental Listening.* Listen to your client without judgment as he describes to you his excessive behavior. Once you have really heard him, ask him this: "Do you *experience* this behavior as a problem?" (Some people complain about an excess they are involved in, because they feel they ought to, but they really delight in it and are not about to give it up.) "You talk about this as though it should be a problem, but let me ask you again, do you actually *experience* it as a problem?" If the truthful answer is "No," then I would invite you to work with your client on discovering why he needs to complain about it. Whose voice is inside him serving as "the judge"? Is it Dad, Mom, the Church? Who is disapproving?

If the answer is "Yes," he is having a great deal of trouble with this, and you believe him, you would then begin helping him transform this behavior, depending upon which type of client it is, either through the Way of *Mindfulness* or the Path of *Negation.*

If the client is ambivalent about whether or not he is "through" with this experience, have him begin practicing Mindfulness as a part of his lifestyle, and evoking whichever positive qualities he desires to manifest (See Exercise #16), and you will see a gradual change in the energy attached to this behavior. This approach requires patience, monitoring, journal-keeping and non-judgmentalness on both your parts, but it is highly effective if you are willing to pursue it.

2. *Bibliotherapy.* Reading materials that contain transformation ideas will be crucial as an adjunct to this client's therapy. *Sexual Energy and Yoga* by Elisabeth Haich is excellent for understanding sexual excess. (Read it yourself first.) *Handbook to Higher Consciousness* by Ken Keyes, Jr. is also excellent for dealing practically with compulsive behaviors. The works of Bhagwan Shree Ragneesh are very loving and helpful for a better understanding of the sensual pleasures and how to transcend them by learning to live in the here and now with awareness. Avoid literature that is preachy or judgmental. This client needs to *understand* his addictions, not flee from them. He is seeking transformation, which can only come from a seedbed of self-love. Self-hatred leads to increased energy in the undesired behavior or to symptom substitution.... and an added burden of guilt that takes him down rather than up.

3. *Proactive Focusing.* Therapy sessions do not need to focus continually on the negative side of the excessive behavior. Gradually withdraw the energy from the negative and stress its positive opposite. (See Exercise #16) What virtue is attempting to emerge in your client that would *naturally* solve this problem? If it is moderation, concentrate on time and exercises developing this quality. If it is patience, utilize theory and techniques that breed serenity, a slowing down, and a steadfastness in thought and action. Always allow the client to work with you in defining the positive opposite quality. To me, the opposite of excess might be moderation. To another, it might be learning to appreciate whatever he is involved in at the moment (impartiality). These are qualities we are working with, not quantities. Qualities, if you recall, are part of the True Self, gifts of the Higher Self. Consequently, we cannot know these about another person, as they are invisible and belong to *his* particular, unique evolutionary schema, not ours. We are individualized Souls evolving toward our unique perfection.

4. *Thematic Life History.* When your client is beginning to experience results in transforming the excessive behavior, have him write a life history of this particular indulgence so he can get a clear understanding of the lesson he was learning from this particular difficulty. This will be a theme-centered life history, not a general one. Once he

discovers the purpose of his affliction, he will be able to love himself in spite of it and finally let go of it forever. During this stage, if he feels he has harmed another by his past behavior, or feels the need of forgiveness from someone, you can help him do this.... either directly with the person involved, or symbolically in imagery or Gestalt work. (See Exercise #7, "Transforming Resentments" for one way to work with unfinished business from the past.)

5. *Connecting Mind and Heart.* Utilize Gendlin's method of Focusing on a Feeling (Exercise #9) as a way of aiding this client in learning about his feelings. He will begin noticing when and how feelings occur in him — how he uses his feelings, etc. You can teach him to breathe deeply and evenly, and other centering and meditative techniques which you are familiar with to bring about a balancing of necessary emotions that habitually run rampant within him. Once he becomes familiar with his feeling nature, help him discover ways to tie meaning and understanding to the feeling reactions. He can also learn to use his mind to control his feelings when appropriate. A good use of restraint and reserve can be excellent qualities for this client to develop. You can teach him to evoke these qualities, as explained in Exercise #16.

"You are not your feelings. You have feelings, and you are not your feelings." This is the disidentification affirmation you can use effectively with this client. Because he is so identified with his emotional body he can't even tell the difference in emotional reactions and reality, he is often confused about what is really going on. Help him understand this enormous difference between *being* a feeling and *having* one!

6. *Transpersonal Focusing.* Transmuting passion to compassion requires a training ground for this switch in emphasis to occur. Have your client begin to serve others in some movement, group or "cause" he believes in. Remember, this client is naturally "devotional" by long association with his emotional nature. He will benefit greatly by having something or someone to concentrate upon besides himself. Self-preoccupation has been one of his main difficulties in life, holding back his progress. An excellent positive quality for him to develop is Non-attachment! (See Exercise #16). His use of The Observer Self will serve as his guide for balancing extremes and seeing the world more clearly. Also, learning to get messages from his Higher Self will enable him to learn the difference between acting creatively in Life

and over-reacting emotionally from outworn, exaggerated negative habit patterns.

QUESTIONS AND ANSWERS

Question: I assume we are working with a 2/4/6 continuum with this client, right?

Answer: Yes.

Question: I think of Level Six as developing the intuition. But you mention devotion as one of the higher emotions. How do these tie together?

Answer: The intuitive person is elevated to Truth about the Self and our correct relation to the universal scheme. This means he has transcended limited sense-awareness. He gets his "data" from the Inner World of Truth and he is perfectly focused on devotion to one aim only.... that of serving his Master, the Higher Self. We can think of this Higher Authority as God, the source, or any projection of a "Master." An intense devotion to The Totality of all-that-we-are is more integrative than being fanatically devoted to an earthly "cause," a fragment of Truth, such as Presbyterianism, vegetarianism, meditation, even World Peace, or eradication of hunger or disease.... all worthy, high causes, of course, but still only particles of Truth. Please understand me: I am not saying they are untruthful or unworthy projects to put oneself into. I am saying they are fragments of the Truth that are appropriate for persons at certain times, but *not* for everyone at every stage of unfoldment. They are means, not ends. Partial truths can become dogma or pet projects that limit our vision and cause us to emotionally over-react to Life, losing sight sometimes of the higher, more synthesized Truth that resides above it. Higher Truth always supersedes lower truth; it takes it into itself.

These partial truths do lead us to the higher, however, unless we become stuck and addicted to the lesser ones. This is the teaching about not laying false idols before us. Devotion is a lofty calling, if the devotion is not carrying us off on a tangent of half-truth. Intuition leads us to very high levels of discrimination about what is proper devotion. Pure devotion to the teachings of one's Higher Self leads to a balancing of the qualities of Love and Wisdom. Sixth Force does not merely know Truth; it *feels* it as well. It is the emotions of the Spirit.

Question: What if the excessive behavior is harming others? I'm thinking of someone addicted to something horrible like child molesting.

Answer: First of all, we need to discover what unmet need the client is attempting to meet through this acting-out, intolerable behavior. The *need* will be valid, though the *behavior* is harmful and cannot be condoned by society. The person is endorsed, not condemned for having the *need* underneath the action.... even though we most certainly condemn the behavior. This client is taught to see the correlation between the behavior and the unpleasant consequences it has for himself and his victims. He is taught to meet the need in appropriate ways. If criminal behavior is involved, the appropriate societal consequences are his rightful experience. He earned society's reprimand and must pay *for his own sake.* But, if you can, help him pay mindfully — understanding the lesson he is to learn. Then, if he is motivated, he will learn how to evolve beyond this stuck point and not repeat the error.

I feel humbled sometimes when I realize how quick I am to judge another who is acting out in criminal behavior which appears so very atrocious to me. But often I fail to see the subtle, pervasive harm I sometimes do with my psychological character assasinations, gossip, false teachings and acts of selfishness. Crimes against the inner self often go unnoticed by the masses; only our Soulmates and spiritual teachers can see these. We must not be too quick to judge others' errors. "Judge not, that ye be not judged" (Matt: 7:1) means we will attract to us the very lessons we are judging others for. Obviously we have not learned our lesson in this particular category or we would not feel energy in the subject in the first place!

Question: How are we to know whether a client needs more "digging into the earth" experiences, or whether to work on transcending them? Seems to me, we have to make a judgment here in order to know which way to guide.

Answer: I never feel I can make this judgment, but my client can. She has to be taught this point of view first, of course, or she will not have enough understanding to contemplate her life from the standpoint of cause and effect or her soul's growth. Clients know where they are on their path, if you know the right questions to ask them. "What do you want?" is a very good question to ask, for instance. Does she want an *experience?*" If so, help her transmute the energy from a negative one to a rewarding, total one. Is she sick of experiences? Is she seeking knowledge? If she truly is tired of bogging down in the same old mess, perhaps she genuinely is seeking to negate this particular behavior.

The Soul has to complete its human experience before it is ready to transcend into unity with its Higher Self. But there comes a point on our path where we pass the nadir of the "descent into matter" and begin the Path of Return. To attempt to escape from our experiences before we have learned our lessons is evading our training. We must *fulfill* the conditions of liberation from the trials of Life, which means we shirk nothing we are to learn. WE CAN ONLY LEAVE BEHIND US WHAT WE HAVE MASTERED, BALANCED OR OUTGROWN.

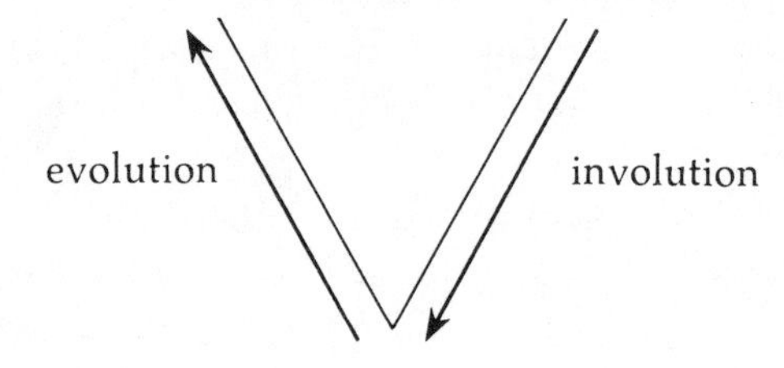

If an experience is still hanging around incomplete, a portion of our energy will constantly feel pulled backward, seeking to complete the experience. Pretending we know something we don't is another way we try to short-circuit our training. But this only leads to unripe ideals not grounded in our experience and does not make us better teachers. This is what Jesus called the unprofitable servant. We attain by the process of *natural growth,* not by repression, avoidance or denial.

Question: It seems to me that all chemical addictions are Level Two addictions. They are, just by their nature, aren't they?

Answer: No. Some people are more addicted to physical safety or mental ideas of themselves than they are to seeking "highs." Not all addicts are the sensual/emotional type. *Chemical addiction can occur at any level as a substitute for not getting that particular set of developmental needs met.* I do believe that Level Two addicts come to our attention more frequently, however. They are often fun-loving, gregarious, exciting to be with.... out there where the people and the action are.... living it up.

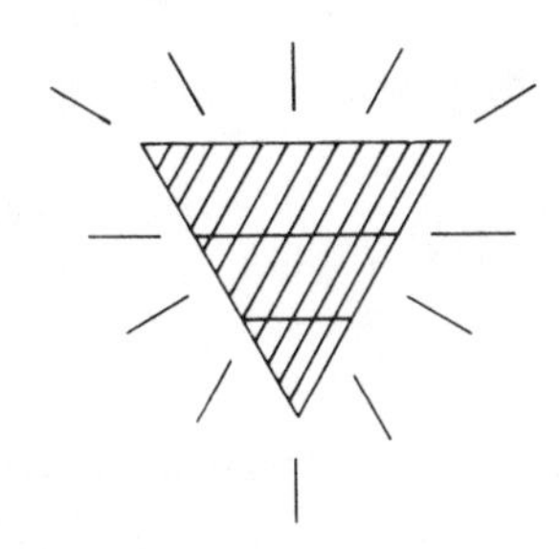

LEVEL THREE POLARIZATION
(The Identity-Seeking Response)

As you glance at the above word-picture, let your intuition tap into the essence of this client who is so starved for approval and lost in her search for Self. Absolutely caught up in how others see her, she is nervous and uncentered, feeling at the mercy of whoever chooses to define her. Close your eyes, relax, and allow a symbol to come into your mind for this client. See her with your inner eye, and let the symbol give you the key to her essence.

As you will recall, this is the level of consciousness where the mental life becomes activated. This person is becoming quite sophisticated, as she now has at her disposal the full functioning of the physical/instinctual, the sensual/emotional, and now the mental centers. This is the level just before the personality becomes integrated and highly organized.... designed to be the servant of the Higher Self.

The mental aspect of the Personality is the energy that gathers facts from Life. It is still contaminated by emotional attachments, but the intellect is coming to the forefront. It sees things in fragments, rather than as wholes, caught up in the particular part of experience that contains the ego-gratification sought at the moment. But it is beginning to cognate and attempting to make sense of its world by the use of the mind.

Concepts at this level are born from experience in Life.... from the senses. Those Self-concepts fueled by emotional energy are the addictions at this level of consciousness. For instance, if I have always idolized movie stars and beauty queens, I will have an ego lift every time someone calls me glamorous or beautiful. If I have valued great scholars, my ego will light up when I accomplish titles and tasks pertaining to the intellect. At this level, without its higher Level Five counterpart, *I will glorify the identity Life gives me.* I am enslaved by public opinion, and the public's (or someone's) approval of me is my addiction: When I have it I am at ease; when I don't have it or doubt it, I am dis-eased. I have made the Outer World of Experience my "God" because I've given it power over me.

When evolving naturally, this is the level where the organism develops its self-definition. Paradoxically, it is often through experiencing the not-self that we learn who the Self is. Since we live in a world of duality, we learn by experiencing opposites. I may try on certain roles, job titles and "characterizations" during my life only to discover after practicing them for awhile that they were someone else's idea of who I was rather than a true part of myself. Our day-to-day experiences are examples given to us as teachings that illustrate the laws governing Life's natural flow. Not one of us can learn without times of trial and error, confusions between fact and fantasy, or other tests that can take us away from ourselves. The true test for us is to rediscover, over and over again, the Truth behind the veil of illusion.

By using Fifth Force, which completes Level Three, we will uncover the larger picture.... the wholeness which is the ground that contained the fragment of Life we were fixated on at the time. This fixation, of course, is taking us away from ourselves. One can never find her true identity as long as she is totally defining herself by a fragment of the outer life. She will become less and less authentic as she focuses on being like others want her to be. These are the "shoulds" and "ought to's" we've often found so troublesome. A woman becomes the leader of her organization because "she just couldn't say no," when in reality, she is a shy person who serves better than leads. Or she might join a social group because "Everyone she admires belongs to it," when in fact, the goals and functions of the group do not interest her. In this Level Three reality, one's self-esteem suffers every time she receives a slight or an insult from another.... especially if the slight deprives her of her status or role in life.

Alcoholics stuck at the Third Level of consciousness have often been leaders in their professional careers, or have had honors, power or money. Listen to them and you will hear much talk about past accomplishments or important people they have known. They cannot see beyond the fragmented reality this honor actually represented when they did have it. They are stuck in limited thinking and stuck in the past.... and dangerously addicted to identities that reside outside themselves.

Level Five consciousness is the higher mind. It sees Reality all in one piece, comprehending the whole Truth. It can grasp the unity of things, because it is part of the *essence* of the person. It can broaden the mind and carve out a variety of paths in Life, paths that match the True Self's urges for expression. It is not stuck in compulsive conformity or limited thinking. Fifth Force can contemplate Life, then fix in the mind a perfected thought that comes from the True Self and finally mold that perfected thought into a correct action. Level Three consciousness sees the fact about a thing *devoid of its meaning.* Fifth Level consciousness relates the meaning to the fact. For instance, I bring you a bouquet of flowers as a gift. Level Three consciousness will have the facts about which flowers last the longest, which are in season, etc. Level Five conscousness will understand what the gift of flowers symbolizes for you, their meaning in your life. Level Three knows facts; Level Five understands.

In teaching your client to use his mental powers, you will need to direct him away from piecemeal thinking into wholistic thinking. He will need to study his life and comprehend its meaning. Meaning in action. And he must learn to direct thought toward the dictates of his True Self. Once he gets a glimpse of the powers of his mind and *realizes* that thought is creative, he will become more inner-directed and less concerned with the outside world's approval. On the surface this may seem to be irresponsible, but quite the opposite is true: He will be becoming responsible for himself.... *claiming* himself for all the world to see! Thoughts from the higher mind can lead him outside the boundaries of his ego to a more loving, more integrated expression. He will become a model for others.

STAGES OF THE THERAPEUTIC PROCESS FOR LEVEL THREE POLARIZATION

1. *Reality Testing.* In listening to this client describe his failures (according to society's or family's standards), you can begin wedging a space between his idea of what ought to be and how the experience actually felt. Example: "Father wanted me to study medicine, and I've failed miserably by flunking pre-med classes." You ask: "Were your pre-med classes interesting to you?" "Do you want to be a doctor?" Help him to see there may be a discrepancy between his idea of medical training and how it actually felt to him. Actual experience is our teacher, but only if we have our mental self tuned into the experience to draw a conclusion and comprehend its meaning. Experiencing without being able to attribute meaning to the experience leads nowhere but to repeating the same old patterns again and again. So we begin connecting the experience in the world with the ideas that fit the experience. We look for patterns, themes, pictures, associations, wishes, hopes, dreams. And we begin tying together the client's mis-creations of the past with the potentials for creating the future of his choice.

The Observer Self is paramount to *Reality Testing.* Please refer to the sections of this book that speak of the Observer Self, including Exercises #4 and #5. Seed Thoughts that will lead the client to more knowledge about who he is are offered (and caught, if they strike a chord in the receiver). Levels Three, Four and Five are activated while this work is being done. The pendulum will swing between Three and Five with Four used to provide the balance between self-acceptance and self criticism. As more understanding and acceptance of Life emerge, Stage Two is begun.

2. *Evoking an Ideal Model.* At this stage I like to teach my clients to become acquainted and identified with their Higher Self. One way to do this is explained and experienced in Exercise #15. Once they have a clear picture of what their Higher Self looks like, they begin practicing responding to situations as this wise Self. When confronted with an emotion-packed negative situation, your client can learn to say to himself "What would Higher Self do now?", picture it, and act accordingly.

3. *Practice "As If."* Support practicing the True Self in action in the client's daily life. If this is a bank clerk yearning to paint pic-

tures, help support his creative urge to paint. If your client is a quiet, shy person who has been pushing himself into leadership roles or aggressive jobs, help him acknowledge his truer nature. Provide him with reading materials and models that reinforce his quieter side, while at the same time encouraging some growth of his more assertive, outgoing potential. If he feels awkward practicing the new roles, remind him to act "as if" he already *is* this new Self, and to begin picturing himself being the new way. This is how Truth becomes manifest.

Please note, there is a big difference in pretending we are someone we are not, and practicing "as if" we've already achieved a desired quality we are learning to manifest. The former is phony, unconscious and repressive, leading to more false personality; the latter is done *with awareness,* constructive work-on-ourselves that leads to Self-creation.

4. *Mental Transformation.* As clients begin to express themselves more creatively in the world, they seem encouraged about Life. They are extremely ripe for mental transformation. I like to implant Seed Thoughts containing transformation energy.... thoughts that shock the consciousness into new ways of perceiving reality. (Thoughts like "You are not who you think you are." "Quit trying to control everything and you will master Life." "Yes, love even *that*!" "The person with the most authority is the least authoritarian." "The less I need approval from others, the more I receive it." "This game is a lot bigger than we ever imagined.") The capitalized sentences in this book can serve as Seed Thoughts for your clients. You will find them summarized in Appendix #5.

The True Self stands between the outer and the inner worlds, both containing a certain kind of reality for him. The outer world offers knowledge gained from the senses; the inner world contains all of the knowledge gained from the intuition. All of us are somewhere on the continuum of learning to let go of the outer world's dominance over us. And as we accomplish this, the sensual knowledge we've experienced passes into us as internal experience. All of us are existing within a certain ratio between these two realities. We learn that the outer life does not satisfy the deepest yearnings within us, and we begin to awaken to a different kind of knowledge.... *understanding,* rather than just knowing facts. Seed thoughts carry transformation energy and produce understanding. They are the "aha"s we experience during moments of enlightenment. And it is at this Level 3/5 that the client can begin making the shift from being guided solely by his senses to being guided by his inner Truth.

5. *Provocative Questions.* Provocative questions provide an excellent tool for mental transformation. These are questions that, on the surface, appear mundane, but contain deep spiritual significance. Some of the most fruitful questions I've used are: "Who are you?" "Where do you come from?" "Where are you going?" "What are you here for?" "What quality is trying to emerge in you?" "How did you manage to attract *this* experience to yourself?" "What are you doing?"

6. *Thought is Creative.* Once a client realizes that her thoughts are creating her reality, she is awakening to the inner life, which means she is becoming dominated by her Soul's purpose rather than society's wishes for her. She is now ready to begin replacing habitual programs and tapes with the thoughts she wants to rule her life. WHATEVER WE FEED TO OUR MINDS AND THEN NURTURE WILL GROW! Either positive or negative. Until we arrive at this level of consciousness, we are powerless over our minds, being literally victimized by unmonitored thoughts that rush in from everywhere. I am constantly asking my clients "Where did that thought come from?" Until we gain knowledge and control over our minds, we will not discover the real solution to our difficulties. The correct answer always lies in the direction of knowing oneself, which leads to a change in consciousness. As long as a person is turned outward and believes the problem and the solution lie "out there somewhere," he is caught in the world of appearances, cutting off the possibility of inner change.

A therapist's task at this level is to help him feel that there is more to life than what is apparent to the senses, that deeper meanings and interpretations are possible. Then an openness and a sense of wonder can occur. Also, one can bear up under tremendous difficulties if he knows there is meaning in the suffering; it gives one a sense of purpose larger than himself — transcendence. He will see that the outer world needs adapting to, and we must become proficient at doing this when it is appropriate. But he will understand now that the real Truth of self-transformation lies within. It is not what happens to me in Life that determines who I am; it's how I react to it. I create my personal melodramas and then become the leading lady. As the True Self emerges and the client realizes that his mind is creating the life he is seeking, he will undergo a redefinition of Self that can be both exhilarating and frightening. He is discovering his power! He will look at the ways he's been defining himself with new understanding.... the I AM statements he's been making that have been *literally* creating his reality: "I can never do this...." "I am never like that...." "I am always such and such...." "Sorry, that's just how I am." All such statements are viewed by *you* as limiting concepts, identifications that are keeping him *down,* structuring his reality. And he now begins practicing their opposites: "I am free to change how I am," etc.

LETTING GO OF LIMITATION

Dealing with the pain and fear that result in letting go of the past and opening to the present is the crux of the therapeutic process. Your skill at listening, empathizing, encouraging, softening, and staying truthful will be your instruments of healing for this client.

In more detail, here is what is happening: As your client begins to affirm what she believes she can achieve, or even what she desires to achieve, remnants left over from the past dwelling in the subconscious recesses pop up and unbalance her. Fears she thought she'd left behind reappear, doubts that seem elementary pervade her awareness. Even new fears she didn't even know she had come to the surface and must be observed and equilibrated.

But as Jesus said: "Get thee behind me, Satan (limitation)!" We do not give our fears power over us; we just acknowledge them and allow them to pass on by. We don't identify with it; we just say "Well, there goes *that* one!" They are only there because we've allowed them to exist. Blocked energy is limitation — the fear of releasing something we do not understand. And since we won't bring it out and look at it, it remains misunderstood and consequently, very powerful. Once the fearsome thing is seen and comprehended for what it really is, limitation vanishes. Neutralized through understanding, the fears are transcended. They become the force behind the positive quality hidden underneath the limitation. Negativity is merely the opposite of a positive potential, unrealized because the negative has held us under its spell.

Once examined, my jealousy of other women turns out to be a misconception of my own power and beauty. My fear of rejection is merely an inability to know my own Self-sufficiency, to recognize my ability *to validate myself.* I forgot that I am part of you and you, me. I thought I was separate and alone.

Level Three consciousness is where we learn to analyze fragments of Reality, making sense of the pieces of Life. Level Five consciousness is contemplating and understanding the whole concept in question. The unenlightened scientific mind operates at Level Three; the enlightened one at Level Five. For example, at Level Three, an investigator might become preoccupied with measuring the number of eyeblinks that correlate with certain levels of anxiety. She might even spend her entire career focusing on this subject, and argue that her findings *define* anxiety in human personality. Sometimes you might browse through the indexes in a psychology department library and look at the myriad research topics that have preoccupied our behavioral scientific minds. You will come away feeling that if you added it all up together, it still would not make a whole human being! And you'd be right!

Without Level Five's comprehensive, intuitive understanding of the whole picture, Level Three consciousness becomes a string of irrelevant data. Level Five transcends limitation, placing the data gathered at Level Three within the context of the nature, meaning and purpose of anxiety in the Personality, the uniqueness of the person experiencing the anxiety, and the conditions within which this Personality is functioning in time and space. When we become preoccupied with fragments, we lose sight of the whole. Level Three is logical, analytical thinking (left-brained dominance); Level Five is creative, intuitive thinking (right-brained). The two working in cooperation with one another provide a science based on Truth. (Please refer to Note #4.)

Intelligent persons stuck at Level Three often become chemically addicted due to the frustration and outright despair of trying to figure out the world based on fragments of unrelated data. Three books on the subject you might find useful are *Zen and the Art of Motorcycle Maintenance, The Crack in the Cosmic Egg* and *The Tao of Physics.* (See Bibliography)

⋆ ⋆ ⋆ ⋆

A NOTE ABOUT MENTALIZATION

We've spent most of our time focusing on the individual's evolutionary path. Just to keep our perspective, it might be helpful here to point out that humanity as a whole is also evolving.

Once upon a time the human being was naturally controlled by raw instinct. And then passion became the master. Cannibalism, cavemen dragging their women by the hair, fury and viciousness have all been a natural part of human history. But now we are becoming mental beings, capable of discussing rationally the state of things and deciding with precision, insight and logic how to live in peace.... at least, this is how we are supposed to be. Persons still stuck at the instinctual and emotional levels of functioning are dragging behind in their evolutionary journey, and consequently, are holding us *all* back. The energy drain that results from infantile emotionalism has been experienced by all of us at some time or another. Balancing our emotions is tied specifically to the ability to use our minds positively and realistically, thus enabling us to create our lives based on Truth.

Clients who are stuck in their emotions need to be taught and encouraged to use their minds. During the humanistic era of psychology, we were given an injunction against over-intellectualizing (one of the hazards of learning to use the mind). Fritz Perls even developed the term "Mind Fucking," which became a by-word during the encounter group period. "Lose your mind and come to your senses," another Perls maxim, stresses the over-emphasis on the intellectual mode. It is as though when we first began mentalizing, we overdid it.... as we seem to do with most things when we are "young." But now that we are "maturing," the pendulum is swinging in the other direction: Discrimination, will, intentionality, direction, purpose, realistic planning — all are valuable uses of the intellect that can counteract the addict's overuse of the emotions and the senses. *Thinking and feeling go together; one is not superior to the other.* As so often is the case, balance is the key.

QUESTIONS AND ANSWERS

Question: I'm a little confused about the difference between Level Three knowledge and the understanding or comprehending what happens at Level Five. Can you elaborate on this?

Answer: Third Level knowledge gathers facts from the external world with little awareness, or even interest, in what all these fragments actually mean at a deeper level. This type of knowledge is usually not grounded in the person's experience, but comes instead from stereotypic values external to the person. Third Level discriminates and makes a lot of judgments, preferring one thing over another. It is thinking based on *separating,* rather than uniting.

Fifth Level consciousness, on the other hand, sees all of Life as a "teaching" and is gathering its "data" from the inner world. Consequently, this person can sleep on the ground or on a fine silk sofa and love either experience equally. He can live in a shack or in a mansion and find Truth in each experience. He can be impartial because his main concern is the quality of experience for his Soul's sake, not the quantity of the possessions of life. Everything becomes grist for the mill for the real work of life, Self-creation. You can see that this leads to freedom from ego control. Level Three knowledge is still very egoistic; Level Five has transcended the ego. Level Five produces a comprehensive, non-judgmental understanding of the whole, an inner quality derived from a high level of being.

Question: When I am operating at Level Three, is Level Two or One still active in me as well?

Answer: Yes. Here is the model.

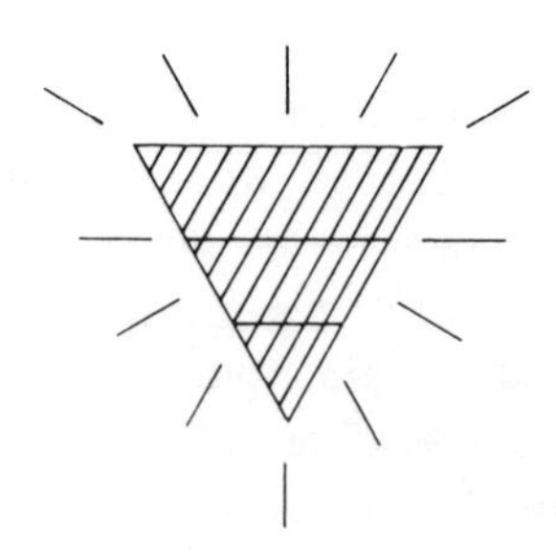

All three levels are operating. But the mind is the highest, most integrated of the three; consequently, the mental life contains the emotional and the physical/instinctual. The Level Three stage of development is designed to make us masters of life by the proper use of the intellect — what western psychologists call an integrated personality.

But we've been talking about the *traps* of the Third level without the help of Level Five consciousness — polarization. This then becomes the ego's search for its definition. But unfortunately, the ego always looks outward. This is its nemesis, for the outside world can really never define us. We are not *of this* world. "The world" is something we are *doing;* not something we *are.* We are *in* it, but we are something *other.* We are seeds sown into the Earth; some by the wayside; some on shallow ground; some amidst the thorns; and some in good soil — depending upon our willingness to know and live in Truth. (See Matthew 13: 1–23.)

Question: If the outside world is only appearances, what is the purpose of it? Does it have a purpose? Or is it all just one great big mistake?

Answer: "The world," *our* "world," provides us the context within which we experience our consciousness.... the tension we "push against." Our particular circumstances are the reality we have created by the level of consciousness we are living in. Through interaction with "our world" we learn, and we grow. Life is our teacher. Someone once said, "Circumstance is another word for God."

Question: And how does Level Four enter into this particular duality of 3/5?

Answer: When we begin operating on Level Three without a conscious shock (an idea or experience that mentally transforms us), we stagnate at this level. This is a person who has a well-defined personality containing a physical, emotional and mental component, but views external life as *the whole truth.* He is ego-dominated and hardly senses a deeper meaning in life, that "something else" we know resides within.... the life of the Spirit. Consequently, he is literally determined by whatever facts life deals him. In the parable of the Sower, referred to above, he would be a seed sown by the wayside. (Truth was offered him "and he understoodeth it not," so the fowls devoured the seed.)

If a higher Truth awakens in him, like "There really is something bigger than myself" or "Even *this* has a meaning," he will begin to use his Observer Self.... the Self who can rise above its conditions and see them clearly and completely. In so doing, Fourth Force comes into play: Harmonizing the energies of Levels Three and Five is its function here.

As we experience harmony and acceptance, we begin to have the ability to examine ourselves without judgment. Only then can we arrive at understanding. Otherwise, we still have to hide the "despicable" parts of ourselves from our own conscious awareness. Judgment separates and keeps us stuck. Often I've heard clients say, "I just can't look at that, it's too awful." Or, "I wouldn't be able to stand myself if this were seen." This fear that we are rotten at the core is the main stumbling block to Self-knowledge, *especially for alcoholics, who as a rule, are very sensitive and conscientious people.* Fourth Force dissolves judgment, creating openness and a willingness to see both sides of the pole, the positive and the negative as well. Then a thing can be accepted.... in its wholeness.

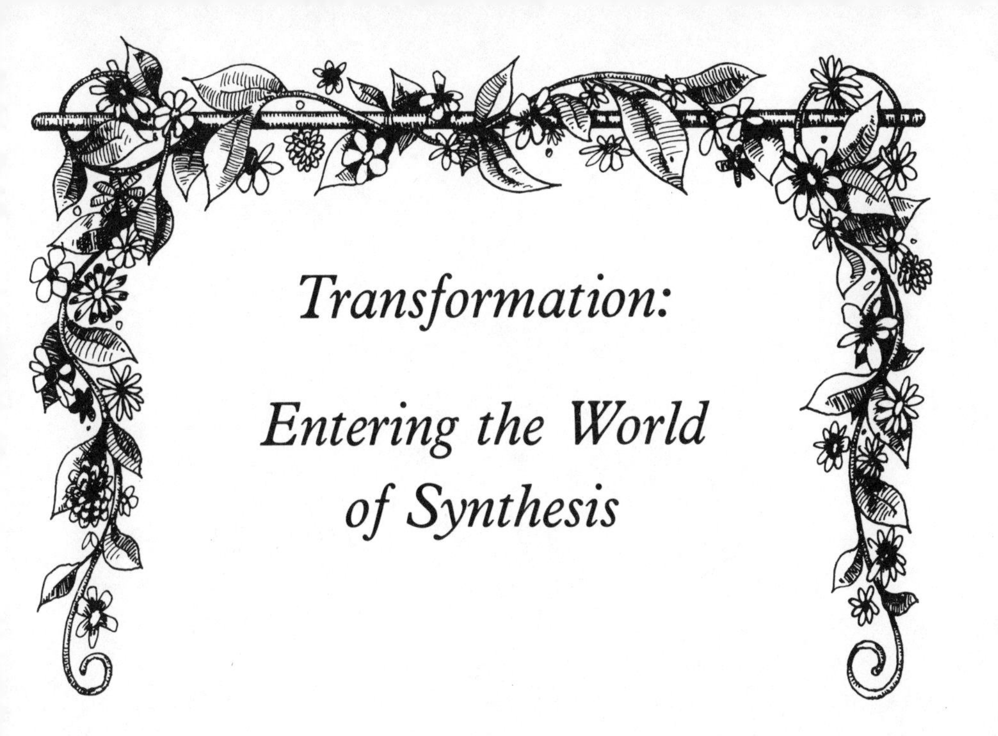

Transformation: Entering the World of Synthesis

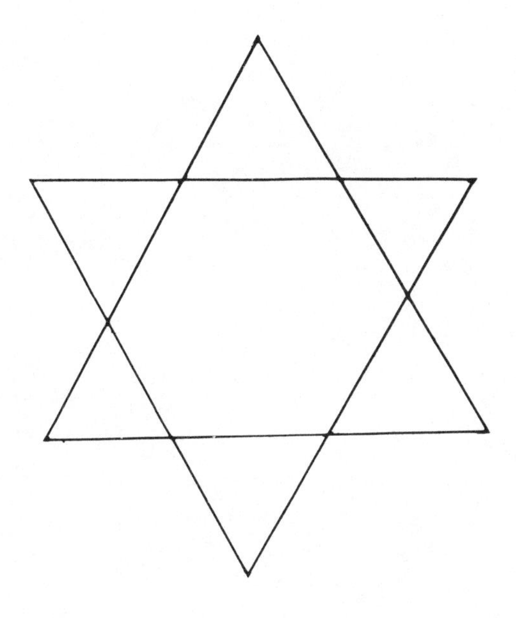

10

The Journey Beyond Addiction

In this chapter we will look at the alcoholic as the paradigm of a person caught up in a web of addiction. The alcoholic's progression through the stages of addiction are so dramatic and obvious to us, he serves as our teacher for this debilitating process and how it unfolds in the human personality.

THE ABSTINENT ALCOHOLIC

Many abstinent alcoholics show signs of stagnation, resentment, and a general unhappiness that may be related to the cessation of personal growth.

A study of the abstinent alcoholic conducted by Gerard, Saenger, and Wile indicates that the majority of abstinent alcoholics are not functioning effectively in life even though they have achieved sobriety. Of those sober, 54 per cent were reported to be overtly disturbed and 24 per cent were considered to be living life inadequately. Some 12 per cent were termed "AA successes" but had achieved little or no social life or identity apart from Alcoholics Anonymous. Only the remaining 10 per cent were considered to be achieving a state of self-respecting independence, personal growth, and/or self-actualization. These 10 per cent were reported to be more alive and interesting on the basis of personal interest. Resentment and aggression, so noticeable in the other groups, were not observed among these independent successes. Thus, it appears that the recovering alcoholic often sells himself short, believing that he is *only* an alcoholic and that sobriety is all he can achieve.[48]

Abstinence from a debilitating addiction, then, may be only a beginning. But to what end? What is it we *all* hunger for as we journey along this road, separate and together, alcoholic or not? This question is a crucial one if we are to aid others in realizing their unique potential. We need to be united in a philosophy based on Truth about *human nature*, not just the facts about the *form* the addiction takes.

Each and every one of us is perfectly designed to be one-of-a-kind .... a fact many of us forget as we continually search for people to copy and to please. Realizing this one-of-a-kind potential *IS* the journey; it is the meaning and the purpose of our lives.

> "Every man should know that since creation no other man ever was like him. Had there been such another, there would be no need for him to be.... Each is called to perfect his unique qualities...."[49]
>
> — *THE TORAH (GENESIS)*

THE THREE DIMENSIONS OF GROWTH

Looking more closely, this journey beyond abstinence toward discovery of the True Self follows a natural progression from identification with our little ego self to identification with the Higher Self that is connected to the Source of ALL THAT IS. And the journey unfolds along three dimensions:

The Personal Dimension. We must all begin by being selfish. This focused pursuit of Self-understanding and personal goals enables us to form an increasingly well-integrated, creative personality that can enter into relationships with others in a loving manner. And as we discover, through the trials and delights of living, what we are really like, we really *do* look selfish sometimes.... preoccupied with thinking about ourselves, talking about ourselves, and often totally caught up in our own ego needs. But is this wrong, really? How else are we going to learn who we are?

Selfishness is a stepping stone to Self-ness. We cannot give to someone else something we do not ourselves possess. So we must develop a Self in order to give this Self to others. Viewed this way, maybe we can forgive ourselves and each other for times of destructive self-centeredness and move on away from the past.

The Interpersonal Dimension. This stage begins to naturally unfold as we learn to know and trust ourselves, because now we begin attracting others to us. We fall in love. Or we become conscious of our responsibility within a family or a group. And then entirely new sets of learning situations occur surrounding the area of interactional goals and aspirations. Becoming interdependent, instead of too dependent or too aloof, is the next training ground our evolving Soul encounters. Intimacy and isolation issues are dealt with, creating the "melodramas" that often require family therapy, relationship counseling or groupwork.

The Transpersonal Dimension. Once our personalities are fairly well developed (healthy body, balanced emotions and sane thoughts), and once our relationships form and flow with confidence, our consciousness is no longer so captivated by the pains and pleasures of ego. Now we begin moving beyond our idiosyncratic point of view into a larger realm of consciousness: identification with humankind. For the first time, gratifying our needs becomes secondary to the desire to serve others. We yearn to express our unique talents in the world *for another's good,* not just for personal acclaim. This ushers in a stream of energy from the superconscious mind, the Higher Self that seeks completion of the True Self, spiritual experiences, and creative Self-expression.

Most recovering alcoholics I've known have a strong sense of the superconscious, or The Higher Power. Many have experienced "peak experiences"[50] where the Self feels uplifted by an overwhelming sense of meaning, purpose and gratitude.... moments of bliss when we realize we really *are* connected to ALL THAT IS. Psychic or "religious" experiences accompany this stage, because these phenomena *are* of this world, a natural part of our humanness. Our awareness expands now to a more universal viewpoint, and this feels good because we stop taking our little ego selves so seriously. Our attitude becomes one of forgiveness and compassion for ourselves and others, as we begin to realize that our circumstances are merely the trials our Soul deliberately seeks out for its own development. Our circumstances, in others words, are the Teacher we must and *will* attract in order to overcome our illusions and our fears.

In the transpersonal dimension we seek more than anything else clarity of vision and the sense of freedom and harmony which come from transcending our ego's limited point of view. Attachment to addictions becomes painful and just plain boring! Our addictions are now experienced as distractions from our important purpose in life. This is the dimension of growth that enhances our life with purpose and meaning, a more certain direction and lots of creative expression of the True Self. It just feels so good!

ALCOHOLICS ANONYMOUS

Anyone familiar with the program of AA recognizes immediately that it contains this progression from surrender of the little self to identification with the Higher Self, moving through stages of personal and interpersonal work toward service to fellow alcoholics. What a gift! Here is a natural Path that leads to freedom from addiction and a sense of purpose in life.

It is no secret, however, that many recovering from alcoholism only intellectualize the twelve-step program, rather than committing to the real work of facing and transcending the Lower Self. These people are *controlling* their addiction rather than transforming it. The energy will still be stuck in focusing on the addiction (alcohol), even though the person is now abstinent. They will have blocked at the third step, thinking they have indeed "turned their lives over to God as they understand Him" but they truly still lack faith — so much so, they have not been able to trust they can really let go and take a good long, honest look at themselves, which is what naturally happens when one enters upon the work of the fourth and fifth steps. In AA, these people are referred to as "dry drunks." They still have the same personality structure as they did before they quit drinking — still the same defenses, the same way of viewing life and themselves. The only difference is they no longer drink alcohol.

There are many abstinent alcoholics, however, who get bored with this way of living. They can see other possibilities and are willing to take the risk required for further growth, even though they may not realize yet just how to do this.

Let's take a deeper look at the transformation process a recovering alcoholic undergoes when this man or this woman truly commits to the path of inner development. It can serve as a model for all people struggling with addictions.

Prerequisites. There is a certain mental preparation that precedes entering upon The Path to Self-knowledge and Self-creation. Like preparing the soil for a bountiful crop, this work happens naturally, as a result of knowing (sometimes we don't know *how* we know, but we know) what must be done before something can come to its complete fruition. Sometimes this "knowing" comes from having become healthy enough to begin following the intuition. Attending workshops and lectures or reading books is another way we sometimes "prepare the soil." But for whatever reason, the people who venture beyond abstinence have prepared their minds in the following manner:

They realize they are merely controlling their addictions, still focusing on the disease, rather than learning the conditions of health that are its opposite. Alcoholics still focusing on the disease are continuing to live in the past. And though they are feeling good about maintaining their abstinence, they are still not learning how to live a life based on the principles of health. Consequently, what's really happening is they are no longer sick, but they are not yet well: they are in a never-never land in between illness and health, that quite frankly, feels dull and uninteresting. There is a lot of grief and depression that comes from having given up all one's ways to "kick up one's heels" in life. This is the basic problem of the "dry drunk." He's no longer having fun: living has become a *sobering* experience.

So we begin our transformation work with recovering alcoholics by helping them wake up to who they really are, *beyond just being sober.* The first realization that must come is one that serves the purpose of relieving guilt:

> ALL MY EXPERIENCES, INCLUDING MY YEARS OF DRUNKENNESS, HAVE BEEN PERFECT: THEY HAVE AFFORDED ME THE GROUNDING FOR UNDERSTANDING HUMAN SUFFERING. NOW I AM PREPARED FOR A LIFE OF SERVICE ON THE PATH OF THE HEART.

In other words, this first Realization is a *healer.* It enables your clients to realize they have done their homework!

After this Seed Thought sinks in, here are the beliefs they must now acknowledge before the total Twelve-Step process can unfold:

1. That there is something higher (or wiser) than ego residing *within me.*
2. That we are all evolving toward more and more completion.
3. Others have gone before who can serve as guides.

4. We can do it, too.
5. That this path is predictable in *principle,* only varied in form.
6. That we are co-creators with the Higher Power; we have *our part* to do.
7. And, finally, that surrender to a Higher Power happens from *within.* (We go inside our Selves to find the wise, all-knowing Power; it is no longer a looking *outward* for "the answer.")

From these beliefs, the soil is now prepared for the next Realization.

> I AM CREATING MY FUTURE RIGHT NOW BY THE CHOICES I AM MAKING. AND I HAVE A WISE SELF WITHIN THAT WILL GUIDE ME TO THE NEXT RIGHT STEP, IF I WILL BE STILL AND LISTEN.

So now, your client will begin to see he always has, *in the moment,* two choices — a higher one and a lower one. He can opt for the life-producing choice or the death-producing one, in the now.

And next, we realize something very simple: THE HIGHER CHOICE WILL ALWAYS BE A POSITIVE ONE! The Higher Self cannot work with negatives! So now we move through the Twelve Steps, seeking the positive choice every step of the way.

THE 12 STEPS OF ALCOHOLICS ANONYMOUS AS A SPIRITUAL PATH: A GUIDE FOR THE TRANSFORMER

Paradoxically, when we succeed in turning our lives over to a Higher Power, the first realization that comes is that WE, ALONE, CONTROL OUR PERSONAL DESTINY! As Seekers of the Truth, we discover we are existing within the Universal Mind of God, the Source of All Things manifest and unmanifest; we will draw into our own personal reality as much of this giant, limitless Mind *as we can conceive.* So now, rather than passively turning ourselves over to a "power in the sky" separate and apart from us, we realize this process of surrender is an active, powerful, *positive* statement about our Self,

1. WE ADMITTED WE WERE POWERLESS OVER OUR EMOTIONS — THAT OUR LIVES HAD BECOME UNMANAGEABLE.

STAGE 1 SURRENDER

2. CAME TO BELIEVE THAT A POWER GREATER THAN OURSELVES COULD RESTORE US TO SANITY.

3. MADE A DECISION TO TURN OUR WILL AND OUR LIVES OVER TO THE CARE OF GOD, AS WE UNDERSTOOD HIM.

STAGE 2 PURIFICATION

4. MADE A SEARCHING AND FEARLESS MORAL INVENTORY OF OURSELVES.

STAGE 3 RIGHT RELATIONSHIP

5. ADMITTED TO GOD, TO OURSELVES AND TO ANOTHER HUMAN BEING THE EXACT NATURE OF OUR WRONGS.

6. WERE ENTIRELY READY TO HAVE GOD REMOVE ALL THESE DEFECTS OF CHARACTER.

STAGE 4 HERE & NOW

7. HUMBLY ASKED HIM TO REMOVE OUR SHORTCOMINGS.

8. MADE A LIST OF ALL PERSONS WE HAD HARMED, AND BECAME WILLING TO MAKE AMENDS TO THEM ALL.

STAGE 5 COMPREHENSION

9. MADE DIRECT AMENDS TO SUCH PEOPLE WHEREVER POSSIBLE, EXCEPT WHEN TO DO SO WOULD INJURE THEM OR OTHERS.

10. CONTINUED TO TAKE PERSONAL INVENTORY AND WHEN WE WERE WRONG, PROMPTLY ADMITTED IT.

STAGE 6 LIVING & LOVING WISELY

11. SOUGHT THROUGH PRAYER AND MEDITATION TO IMPROVE OUR CONSCIOUS CONTACT WITH GOD, AS WE UNDERSTOOD HIM, PRAYING ONLY FOR KNOWLEDGE OF HIS WILL FOR US AND THE POWER TO CARRY THAT OUT.

STAGE 7 AUTHENTIC BEING

12. HAVING HAD A SPIRITUAL AWAKENING AS THE RESULT OF THESE STEPS, WE TRIED TO CARRY THIS MESSAGE TO OTHERS, AND TO PRACTICE THESE PRINCIPLES IN ALL OUR AFFAIRS.

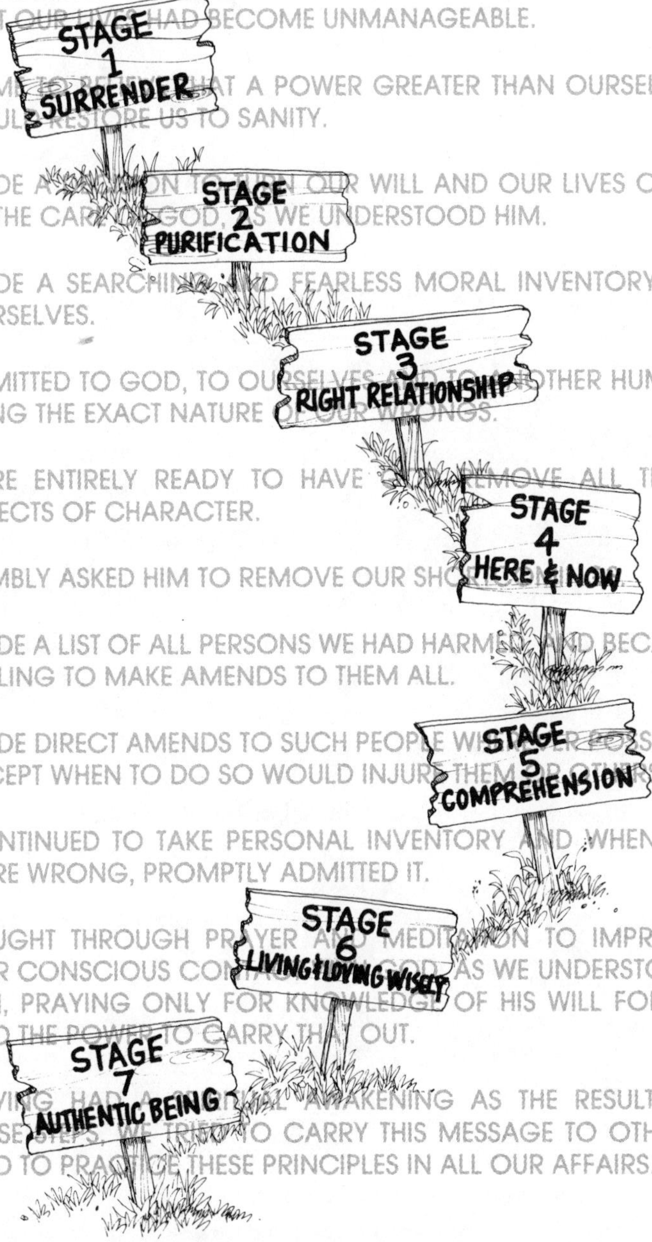

rather than a weak, pitiful one. We know now that we are creators-in-miniature, and we are turning our little limited ego self over to the greater Self *that resides within us,* the Self that is connected to The Source of All Things.

Consequently, the first stage on any path of Self-realization is *SURRENDER,* correctly understood.

(1) "Admitted we (our egos)* were powerless over alcohol — that our lives had become unmanageable" (under the control of the ego).

(2) "Came to believe that a Power greater than ourselves (greater than our ego) could restore us to sanity." (This is the correct use of the Power of Mind — utilizing a belief that is transforming: that a Power greater than our ego resides *within us.*)

(3) "Made a decision (again the Power of Mind) to turn our will and our lives over to the care of God as we understand Him."

The first three steps can be restated to say: "In the past I've allowed an addicted partial self to rule me, and it *cannot* control its use of alcohol. *I* am now putting a stop to this dictatorship and will allow the more integrated Self within me to take over. This Self, my essence, is identical to God's essence, and is really my *True* and rightful *Self.* So, I am not giving away my power, but *accepting* it by becoming identified with who I *really* am."

Each one of us today is the result of how we've made use of our minds either consciously or unconsciously. We are *now* what we've thought; and the answer to what we will be in the future is contained in how we are thinking and what we are believing in the present.

We now realize that when we operate from our True Self, our authentic identity, ALL IS ONE. Consequently, we are aligning ourselves with Universal Law.

The second stage of the Path of Self-realization will always be concerned with *PURIFICATION.* Now that we are thinking correctly (Right Thought), we have created an inner environment of malleable, fertile soil ready to bear healthy fruit. We now realize LIFE MUST FLOW HARMONIOUSLY FROM EXPERIENCE TO EXPERIENCE. All experiences are connected and valuable, even the negative ones. Consequently, we will be required to undergo an internal and

*All parenthetical comments are those of the author.

external catharsis. No more evasion of personal responsibility for our life. As Socrates said, "The place to study is where you are."

(4) We "made a searching and fearless moral inventory of ourselves." (Clearing out the past, redefining our actions and reactions toward self and others according to Right Thinking, and releasing any pent-up emotion that is blocking our progress, which will include forgiveness of self and significant others.)

(5) "Admitted to God, to ourselves, and to another human being the exact nature of our wrongs," which enables us to take full responsibility for ourselves. It is extremely difficult to continue self-defeating patterns when we've confessed these problems to others. The very act of externalizing these realizations through verbalization *in itself* is healing, for it clarifies, concretizes and focuses us on Truth, enabling us to move beyond irrational thoughts, what AA calls "stinking thinking."

(6) "We're entirely ready to have God remove all these defects of character." Again, this is a statement of the power of the Self, not a passive giving in to some Super Energy Source separate and apart from us. It is choosing consciously to purge ourselves of our *wrong thinking, feeling, and acting,* putting our True Self in charge, for it is aligned with the Higher Power. When we commit to this inner movement of purification, the Higher Self *descends* and cleans out anything negative that cannot be contained within its brilliance, drawing its energy from the Higher Power. Therefore, we can expect this to be a very painful stage on The Path, but *permanently* rewarding.

It might be wise to point out here that what we are seeking is *not* drastic extreme measures of discipline, but gentle, effective ways of eliminating vices and faults. The discipline should be *effortless.* Extremes revert to their opposites. Self-violence and fads should be avoided at all costs. Again, to quote Socrates, "In all things, not too much." Moderation is the desired quality seeking expression.

First comes the body. A healthy, balanced diet, exercise and quiet times of prayer/meditation will be sought. The diet should contain the nutrients that the body is deficient in from the former lifestyle of addiction. Live foods like fresh vegetables, herbs, vitamins and minerals must replenish the body's depleted energies. Sugars, white flour, cigarettes, caffeine and heavy carbohydrate junk foods must be curtailed, *with love....* gently....[51]

Physical exercise should be natural and *fun,* but practiced daily. Violent and unaccustomed exercise programs exhaust you and hurt you, and should be avoided for they are an act of intemperance. Someone once asked a Greek philosopher to go to see a famous athlete who could swim like a fish, jump like a deer and run like a hare, to which he declined, saying: "I do not wish to imitate the animals; but if you know of someone I could see who thinks like a God, I will go." The use of exercise for the Seeker on The Path is not to become a famous athlete, but to enter upon a pleasant routine of aesthetic expression.

And finally, the body needs peace and quiet. The ex-addict is learning to live with his energies comfortably. He is tired of the swings from high to low; he needs *contact* with his Higher Power, not just a realization of It. Instead of looking to the outside world for excitement, he now desires peace, courage, security, a sense of purpose, loving relationships and altruistic quests.

As he reworks his past and discovers the defeating patterns of interpersonal relating he's been involving in unconsciously, he seeks a new way of belonging to a group. The Seeker does not become "a joiner;" he maintains his individuality, thinking his own thoughts and feeling personally responsible for building his own life. But he does benefit greatly from a support group of Seekers like himself to bolster mutual courage. In this way, he can begin to work out his emotional and mental levels of relating with truthfulness and practice in a selfless sharing of himself with others.

(7) As his courage mounts he will truly be ready to "humbly ask God to remove all his shortcomings," a painful and dangerous move to make if one is not prepared for the havoc this wreaks when this purifying Higher Power begins to move through us. But if we are sincere in our desire to become an advanced member of the human race, and if we are somewhat prepared for what this request actually entails, we will welcome the opportunity to work on ourselves that this stage on The Path brings.

And now we will be entering the interpersonal area of growth, the area of *RIGHT RELATIONSHIP,* where we learn to face up to the responsibility of human sharing in the here and now. We are training to become Co-workers in the Master Plan for Humanity by first getting our own relationships in order.

(8) "We made a list of all persons we've harmed and became willing to make amends." Making amends does not mean a superficial "I'm sorry." It means *transforming our ordinary mode of involvement with another.* First, we will redefine our relationships realistically, letting go of the ones that cannot work for us, and committing to the ones that matter. Then we will begin the arduous task of learning to communicate.

(9) "Making direct amends to such people wherever possible, except when to do so would injure them or others." Discrimination is another virtue that must now be refined. We don't just walk about venting and sharing our past with others *for our sake.* Every interpersonal situation contains a *whole gestalt,* an entire perspective that must be acknowledged. We learn to be sensitive to the entire group we might affect by an indiscriminate need to confess or cathart. Some people cannot deal with our past mistakes and weaknesses, *for they are not ready to deal with their own* — and maybe for a good reason. Sometimes we must do this work alone, even though it involves another.

(10) "Continued to take personal inventory and when we were wrong promptly admitted it." Now we are shifting the emphasis to *LIVING IN THE HERE AND NOW.* Self-analysis, Emotional Clearing and Right Thinking have now brought us to the place where we can begin living our life consciously moment by moment, *as we experience it.* We can reprogram our minds with character traits we wish to develop. We can draw to us the personal qualities we've sought: perseverance, lovingness, tranquility, poise, detachment from results, sense of humor, personal harmony, mastery over unhealthy appetites, ways to go beyond worry and fear, enthusiasm, and the development of any artistic endeavor we wish to pursue.

Now, in all our comings and goings, our Observer Self is operative. It will guide us to the Truth Point in any experience, in any condition in which we find ourselves. *We will find the Truth and live by it.*

The next stage on The Path will be concerned with learning to listen to our Higher Self, our contact with the Higher Power. We must now develop our ability to discover *experientially* "that which cannot be written about." In the midst of our active, daily lives we must learn to listen for the Truth, which will enter into our consciousness quietly when we are open to receive it. SINCE THE HERE AND NOW IS "THE VANISHING POINT" IN TIME, WE ARE MERELY GOING WITH THE FLOW.

(11) We "sought through prayer and meditation to improve our conscious contact with God as we understand Him, praying only for knowledge of His will for us and the power to carry that out."

This deep serenity arises from a deep wholistic understanding of Universal Truth, of the *rightness* of Life and the laws that govern it. This is the stage of *COMPREHENSION.* No one is a victim of his conditions! Everything is unfolding as it should. Happiness comes from within, for it is the result of spiritual unfoldment. And there is no blame: Everyone gets exactly what he earns, the "good" with the "bad." There is no way we can live in avoidance of our just deserts. At this stage on our journey we learn to understand the Law of Karma — the immutable balancing Law of Cause and Effect. And by proper study and discipline, we can master our personal chain of cause and effect events by the practice of *Harmlessness.*[52] By refusing to think, feel or act in any manner that produces harm to our Self or another, we begin to live rightly. Staying constantly in tune with an inner voice that quietly guides us (the voice of our intuition), and making note of the "comments" of our Observer Self, we begin to master our life.

Patience will become an active ingredient in the personality — an attitude that recognizes that in the fullness of time everything works according to Law. Another virtue that develops during this stage is the ability to conserve all one's energy for the purpose of living life consciously. The Seeker learns to do the tasks of life by the simplest, most direct means, to live by the simplest codes, and does not get caught up in negative emotions or situations that deflect her peace of mind and sense of direction. She learns to discriminate between necessary and unnecessary action, feelings and thoughts, and we begin to notice in her a quality of poise and loving non-attachment. At this stage on The Path, the addictive lifestyle has been transcended. The voice of the Higher Self is now easily discerned, for she has become an attentive listener to the Voice within. She is developing the advanced skill of *LIVING AND LOVING WISELY.*

At this point on The Path another paradox occurs: The Seeker's personality becomes subservient to the rule of the Higher Self. The inner life dominates. And though inward she goes, it is an *outward* urge toward service to others that draws her. Now the ego cannot be boss, for it is not expansive enough to live within the transpersonal consciousness — beyond the personal. By its very definition, the ego lives for the personal. Those who pursue The Path beyond this point are searching for the mystery of the inner life and can only use the higher levels of consciousness in their acting, feeling and thinking. The ordinary *personal* mind will now be of very little service, the Lower Self emotions of very little value. The Observer Self watches these lower drives, acknowledges them, and allows them to pass on by.... *giving them no energy.* "Ah, yes, and there goes *that* one." (Dis-identification.)

People who have gone past the personal difficulties of the addictive life by having done the work at the personal and interpersonal levels will tell you they have discovered that the search for personal gratification is not enough; that living solely for ego pleasure is a base and shallow experience. They come to the realization that our mortal actions, feelings and ideas produce an outer world of calculating minds, politics, and institutions that, in the long run, become meaningless symbols for the building of false personality — more and more ego difficulties! More pitting oneself against others in useless competition, more frustration, more power needs, more demands made upon the self, more comparisons, more duality, more addiction. ON THE PATH TO SELF-CREATION THE EGO MUST BE TRANSCENDED. BUT IT CAN ONLY BE TRANSCENDED BY WORKING THROUGH ITS NEEDS AT THE PERSONAL AND INTERPERSONAL LEVELS — *NOT* BY DENIAL OR ATTEMPTING TO BYPASS THEM. We will find ourselves, again and again, at the very same place of personal work we failed to complete until we work through it to a point of understanding and acceptance. This is the Law of Transcendence.

But when one has truly earned the right to live in the transpersonal realm, he becomes a valuable server of humanity. The Transpersonal Dimension is nothing exotic or unusual; it is the natural result of Right Action, Right Feeling and Right Thought. It is the *overflowing* of a full and rich consciousness, of needs fulfilled and transcended, of satisfaction, contentment and wisdom — total acceptance of the human condition — and a realization that *the Self is larger than its conditions.*

(12) "Having had a spiritual awakening as the result of these steps, we tried to carry this message to alcoholics, and *to practice these principles* in all our affairs." (Italics mine). And practicing the princi-

ples is the key; serving others is the natural by-product. The Seeker is now a model of *AUTHENTIC BEING,* no longer governed by subpersonalities struggling incessantly to meet conflicting ego needs. There is an intrinsic validity in all that the person does. Energy that was used to gain personal gratification becomes re-directed toward serving the good of others. Persons living at the transpersonal level vary in their area of service. Some are qualified to serve individuals or small groups of fellow travellers — such as counselors, group leaders, householders, or organizers of small, purposeful establishments. Some are designed for larger work — serving humanity on a national or planetary level. The area of service depends upon the person's natural abilities, latent talents and desires. One area is just as important as the other, only different in scale. At this level there is no comparison or rating-sheet mentality: Each one of us operates from his own unique and rightful expression, authentically. And sacrifice is no longer a negative word.

THE TRANSMUTATIONS

"Controlling is holding on; transforming is release!"

Transmutations are not controls. They are literally "turning the other cheek," looking in the direction of the positive side of a previously-held negative quality. As stated earlier, the Higher Self can only work with the positive. It only sees Truth. To it, the negative quality is now and always was an illusion. In other words, to your Higher Self, the negative never even existed!

Consequently, when one's energy is no longer being dissipated in negativity, activities (outer or inner) that block or distort the authentic activities of the True Self, the positive quality just naturally emerges and begins expressing itself.

Some of the signs that one is truly being guided by the Higher Power, rather than merely verbalizing it, are the following observable changes:

Fear is transmuted into courage. Fear is an ego defense based on illusion. Once we look our fears squarely in the face, we find that they are simply negative expressions of positive traits trying to express themselves. When we understand the nature of these fears and clear up the wrong thinking they represent, we will begin risking new action and opting for innovative choices. For instance, I fear you because I think you are more important than I (illusion); transmuted, this becomes the courage to express my own equal importance. I fear a situation because I believe I'm a bad person if I fail (illusion); transmuted, this is the opportunity to accept my weaknesses and my strengths realistically and to follow my own path, not someone else's idea of it. Or, I'm afraid to look at a part of myself, because if I acknowledge it I will have to see myself as "bad" (illusion); transmuted, this becomes the chance to see myself as I really am — partially unawakened and still needing more experiences to become enlightened. Once we really get the picture of who we *truly* are, self-doubt diminishes and fear becomes an irrelevant concept. When Life comes in on us, we go inward and find the key.

Self-pity and blame are transmuted into personal responsibility. Seeing ourselves as "victims" of our situations is a debilitating point of view based on illusion rather than Truth. We are *totally* responsible for our personal circumstances and for the people we attract to us! These external forces in our lives are merely reflections of our inner state of mind and our current level of understanding. Learning to say "I chose to do this, given the options I felt I had," or "Here's how I set this one up" means *freedom.*

Can you see how this works? Because we have created our past by our moment-by-moment choices, it follows logically that we are also creating our future by the choices we make NOW. There is a direct relationship between Cause and Effect, and *we,* not someone else, are setting the chain in motion with our every thought, feeling and action. And there is no blame! If we hadn't needed the experience, we wouldn't have chosen it.

Conscious action (personal choice) rather than unconscious *re*action (putting ourselves to sleep and allowing "fate" to choose for us), is the key to freedom. Blessed relief from the shackles of victimhood!

Powerlessness is transmuted into Self-mastery. As we begin to experience ourselves as having chosen our lives, realizing we are perfectly free to make any changes we really *want* to make.... in our thinking, our feelings, or in our actions.... depression cannot be maintained. Our Spiritual Will becomes operative, directing us now toward Self-mastery. A sense of joy and fascination replace feelings of impotence and fear. We now begin directing our lives toward events that lead to purpose and meaning, moving further and further away from dominance by the little ego self ("selves"). Feelings of isolation fade as we "lose ourselves" in the whole of community.

Passion is transmuted into Compassion. When one becomes involved in the art of Self-creating, passions become our teachers. They lead us to the outside world where we've been looking for something we cannot find. Passion gets caught up in diversity, absolutizing every little experience it involves in, thinking each is essential. Now we realize there is another way. We can turn inward. When we do, we begin seeing ourselves through the eyes of acceptance rather than the voice of judgment. And love is there. We can understand, as we look deeper and deeper, how we've gotten where we are, and we can comprehend the hardness of our life, the sadness of our mistakes. We develop compassion.... the place where emotion and realization merge.

As we develop this for ourselves, it begins spilling out to others. We love and see others as we love and see ourselves. Compassion is feeling, but it is not ego-involved feeling. It stands on the sidelines and weeps for humankind. Then it moves in and acts where it can, but for others, rather than emotional "highs" aimed at our own gratification. It draws diversity back into itself, realizing the unity behind it all.

Self-preoccupation is transmuted into Aspiration to Serve Humanity. And now we have the tools for serving others. We feel for ourselves and we feel for Life. But we've learned that gratification comes from within, not from all the various and sundry objects and people in the outside world. We've tried that already, hardly leaving a stone unturned. It simply doesn't work. Perhaps it is originally in self-defense that we turn to serving others for our means of true gratification. But it is a kind of work that eventually leads us beyond ourselves, and we learn a Truth: I am only truly joyful when I am experiencing myself connecting with my brothers and sisters through mutual sharing, love and purpose. Giving myself away seems to give me back to myself tenfold.

Exaggerated Mood Swings are transmuted into Serenity. And now I can work with the Law of Polarity and neutralize its energetic force. I can use it rather than it using me. Before, I was a victim of my moods, going from depression to elation, depending upon what the outside world brought into my consciousness. Now *I* am in the driver's seat. I can use my moods, my feelings, my highs or my lows for experiencing the full gamut of my humanness. And when I start going too low, I can remember who I really am and get outside my absurd preoccupation with self. I can serve. I can be still. I can pull toward the center. When I feel elated, I can enjoy it fully, not needing it to last, but appreciating the moment for what it has to offer.

My faith is now in the process of life itself: I know other true moments of joy will occur; I don't have to hang on to this one. And I feel serene. All of it is okay — even the hard times. They are taking me exactly where I need to be, showing me what I need to know.

Fragmented Knowledge is transmuted into Wholistic Truth. While we are still dominated by our little egos, we fall in love with our ideas and our ability to become an "expert" in various segments of reality. I may recount to you great academic victories in the art of loving.... without knowing the slightest about the nature of love or of the human being experiencing it!

Fragments of truth teach us half-truths, or no truth at all. Learning to see the whole picture of the nature and purpose of something within the life context of a human being can lead to great leaps of wisdom. It is the difference between the scientist and the wise man. A scientist *can* be a wise man; but a wise man is never *merely* an objective investigator of facts.

Role-Playing is transmuted into expressing one's authentic nature. Until we know who we are, we play roles, trying on first this one, then that. And often, we discover we are filling our lives with meaningless pap, involving in events that have nothing to do with the development of our true Essence.

Once we are on The Path, we begin showing the world who we really are, even if this True Self looks different from others. We develop the courage to be who we are.

Desire for external "things" is transmuted into seeking Self-knowledge. And this, of course, is the transformation. Once we truly begin seeking Truth, our teachers appear in varied forms, and since Self-knowledge is *by its nature* transforming, we are on our way. No longer is our energy so tied up in searching for things to gratify our sense of identity; we are finding our *true* identity.... the most exhilarating safari we will ever take, the journey into Self!

IMPLICATIONS FOR TREATMENT PROGRAMS

Clients who are on The Path, being guided by their Higher Power, do not benefit from programs, even AA groups, who are still focusing on the negative. They must avoid being stuck in talking about the past, their fears, mistakes, diseases, etc. and instead focus on programs that teach about the Self, how to go within, and how to live positively and healthily in the world. Recovery programs become *dis*covery programs! Seekers are no longer working on staying sober; the energy has gone out of the desire to take drugs. They are searching for Truth, and determined to find it!

A non-Seeker cannot recognize a Seeker. But Seekers *can* recognize each other. Seekers must be strong enough to resist the criticisms of non-Seekers (for they *do* appear "different" and are often misunderstood by non-Seekers). They must accept this reality and search out persons of like mind for support.

Seekers are Transformers.

A Message to Transformers

We see now that the journey of Self-creation provides the ability to live in the now with fascination and hope — a life turned on to continuing new possibilities and abstinent from debilitating addictions. Who needs them?

Seeing our predicaments as "mistakes" becomes an irrelevant concept and guilt is no longer necessary in our lives. We view our own Self-made choices as serving a positive purpose in our development. If we have harmed others by our choices, we make amends, forgive ourselves, and let go. God forgives, why shouldn't we? Our only responsibility is to stay conscious, to *stay awake,* so that we will understand the significance of our choices and the purpose they are serving.... not repeating ad infinitum situations that lead nowhere.

Realization of the Self is an attitude which views Life as a teacher and ourselves as co-creators of this Life.... co-creators with an Energy so grand, so immensely wondrous, it defies description! And yet, we are a part of this amazing Energy.... designed in Its image!

Self-realization is complete understanding and acceptance of the human experience. And for the addicted, awareness and a willingness to work on oneself provide the springboard for this inward, upward journey that takes us first *into* ourselves and finally beyond ourselves in service to others.

A true people-helper is a Transformer, a guide to this natural process of unfoldment.... not a preacher, not a judge, but a guide. Real helpers are fellow travellers, who invite others to discover the meaning of their suffering, relieve suffering wherever they can, but who resist interfering with another's free will. This means viewing abstinence from an addiction as the client's responsibility.... and only the beginning of a very exciting journey.

If we go through life caught in addictions, stuck in the first three levels of consciousness based on fear, passion and desire for status, we find we are living up our life force.... *using* it up.... depleting this precious energy designed for the creation of our very Self. Once we transcend these levels, by drawing to ourselves the creative energies from the higher centers, no longer polarizing earth and heaven, form and essence, we move beyond ego-dominance to become aligned with our Soul's purpose. Our addicted "selves," the mechanistic fragments of our personality, increasingly give way to this more integrated Self as our knowledge and conscious experiencing expands and unfolds.

Once we release in us this powerful energy source, we are being who we truly are! Then, the question becomes one of having the courage to continue living according to *our* grain instead of someone else's idea of it. And if we opt for this grand experience, we discover the greatest "high" of all. We truly begin to live.

Transformers never fear working on themselves, for it is through their own trials of balancing the higher forces with the lower, earthy self that they have grounded their knowledge of the human endeavor in Truth. Their deepest yearning is the urge toward Self-creation.

> I challenge you to a deeper life, and for the sake of your clients to seek a stronger bond with your own Soul so that you will continually bring new Truths to light and help fit others for the living and understanding of these Truths.
>
> —*A TIBETAN MASTER*

Epilogue

UNITY

Words are symbols and can merely imply the majesty of Man in his highest form. We have attempted to unveil the mystery of the twofold nature of our consciousness, the Higher Self and the Lower. When we turn within to find the amazing spiritual powers of the mind, the heart, and the body, we must become wordless. Our dualistic mortal mind really cannot define the unitary immortal Self. To understand this is the beginning of true knowledge.

The theoretical portions of this book have presented a dualistic model of man in the mode of the third level of consciousness. In order to understand the Outer World of Experience we dissect Life, studying it piece by piece — for it is in so doing that we, the "scientist," discover the atom. By going down, down, involving in Life, we use logic, making finer and finer distinctions, separating, analyzing, so as to know what is what. This is the specialty of the clever intellect, and the intellect belongs to the outer world.

But the strangest paradox exists in doing this separating — this dissecting of everything. The sages tell us to "leave the outer, and come to the inner." And at the same time, they tell us to let go of duality. Well, in speaking of an "outer" and an "inner," we are still caught up in duality, obviously, as they are polar opposites. If, however, we do elect to drop the outer, *the inner automatically falls away!* If the "outer" no longer exists, how can there be an "inner," for the two define each other. Now we have become One. And this is a very great secret.

All the great Masters have taught that "I and my Father are one," that ordinary, day-to-day life is holy. The Zen masters teach that everything is perfect exactly as it is — nothing has to be changed! God is not off out there somewhere else; He is right here, now. He is that Grand Entity "within which we live and move and have our being" (Acts 17:28). We are in and of God. Creativity is God-nature.

Going down into diversity, studying the "many" piece by piece is the work of the intellect — the logical left brain, which belongs to the Outer World of Experience. Reaching for the unity, the oneness that has no boundaries, beyond dissection, is the work of the higher mind, the intuition — the fifth level of consciousness belonging to the Inner World of Wisdom. This is the function of the right brain — the relational mind, the one that "thinks" in wholes.

And if we reflect for a minute about how our life *really* works, we will see immediately that the wholistic mode fits our experiences more accurately than does the dissecting separate mode. When I fall in love, can I tell you exactly *when* in time it happened? Was it Wednesday at 2:10? Can I tell you the distinct steps I followed to make this occur? And do I love him for his bone structure, his eye color, the shape of his nose or feet? Or do I love him for that "certain quality" that defies description? When I feel joyous or depressed, can I pinpoint in time and space the exact event that created this state of mind? Did joyousness strike me at 4:03 a.m.? Of course not. We don't experience our lives in discrete units. I go from feeling happy to feeling unhappy, but I cannot say exactly when the changeover took place — because *they are not two things — they are one.* They gradually merge into one another, with no clear-cut boundaries.

> "And Jesus said to them: When you make the two one, and when you make the inner as the outer, and the outer as the inner, and the above as the below.... then shall you enter the Kingdom."
>
> — *THE GOSPEL ACCORDING TO ST. THOMAS*

Unless we realize this unity, reaching for the Oneness *behind* the polarities, we are still misunderstanding. And we will continue to live in misery.... going from extreme to extreme, loving the one and hating the other, searching for the answer. But the minute we find it, it will switch to its opposite, and off we will go again.... searching once more for the Truth.... again, stuck in the discomfort of duality — for each of us intuitively knows that "the two must eventually become one."

The most important matters in life cannot be dissected and made distinct. This separative mode of thinking may be utilitarian, but it is *not* the truth. The truth defies analysis. Duality is a myth. The wise person drops judgmentalness; he drops distinctions and lives like a little child — in a relational world with no boundaries.... and this is the promise of the future.

"In the ancient temple of Serapis at Alexandria stood a gigantic image of the weeping god. His body was fashioned out of the twigs and branches of trees; his hair was grass and grain; his eyes were precious stones; his garments were made of metal; and his body was over-cloaked in the skins of animals. He was crowned with the feathers of birds; flowers bloomed in his hands; and insects gathered honey from his mantle. This weeping god upon whose head light shone down through the open roof of the temple, is man himself, the symbol of all nature, who bears within him all questions and all answers."

".... He is, of all creatures, the most mysterious...."[53]

—*MANLY P. HALL*

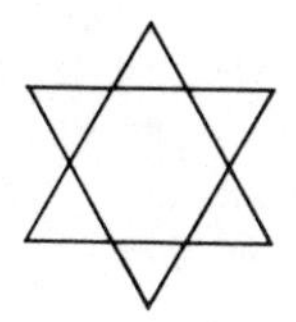

ARROWS OF LIGHT

There's a power we all know
It pulls the string and bends the bow
It hurls us spinning into empty space
    to find the place
Where we belong

We're all arrows of light
Shot from bows shining so bright
Were we aimed....
    or do we find our own course?
Yes we're all arrows of light
Shot into shadows of fright
Is the target the heart of the source?

And there's a mystery in us all
And we must answer when it calls
For there is so much more that we
    could be
If only we would try

We're all arrows of light
Shot from bows shining so bright
Were we aimed....
    or do we find our own course?
Yes we're all arrows of light
Shot into shadows of fright
Is the target the heart of the source?

There's a spirit we all share
We're tied together everywhere
Because we share a unique purpose here
    — to strike the fear
That we are alone

We're all arrows of light
Shot from bows shining so bright
Were we aimed....
    or do we find our own course?
Yes we're all arrows of light
Shot from bows shining so bright
Is the target the heart of the source?

— *BOBBY BRIDGER*[54]

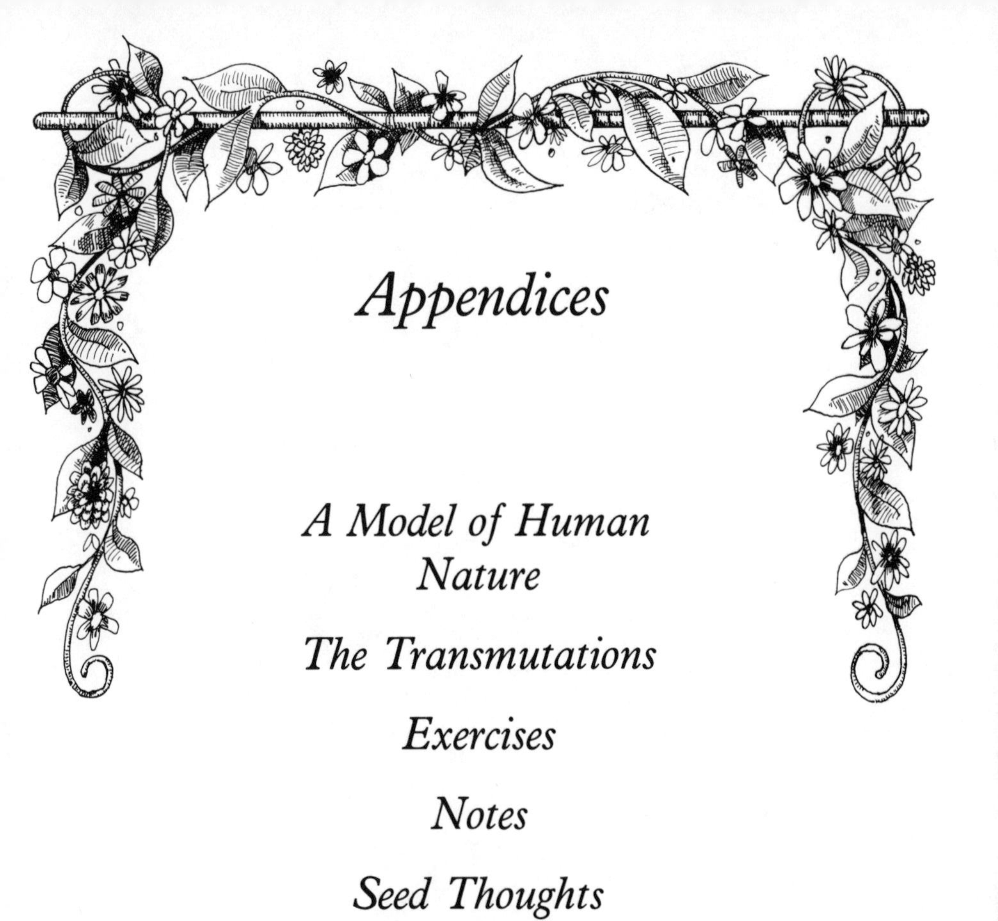

Appendices

A Model of Human Nature

The Transmutations

Exercises

Notes

Seed Thoughts

Bibliography

Appendix 1

Table 1
A MODEL OF HUMAN NATURE

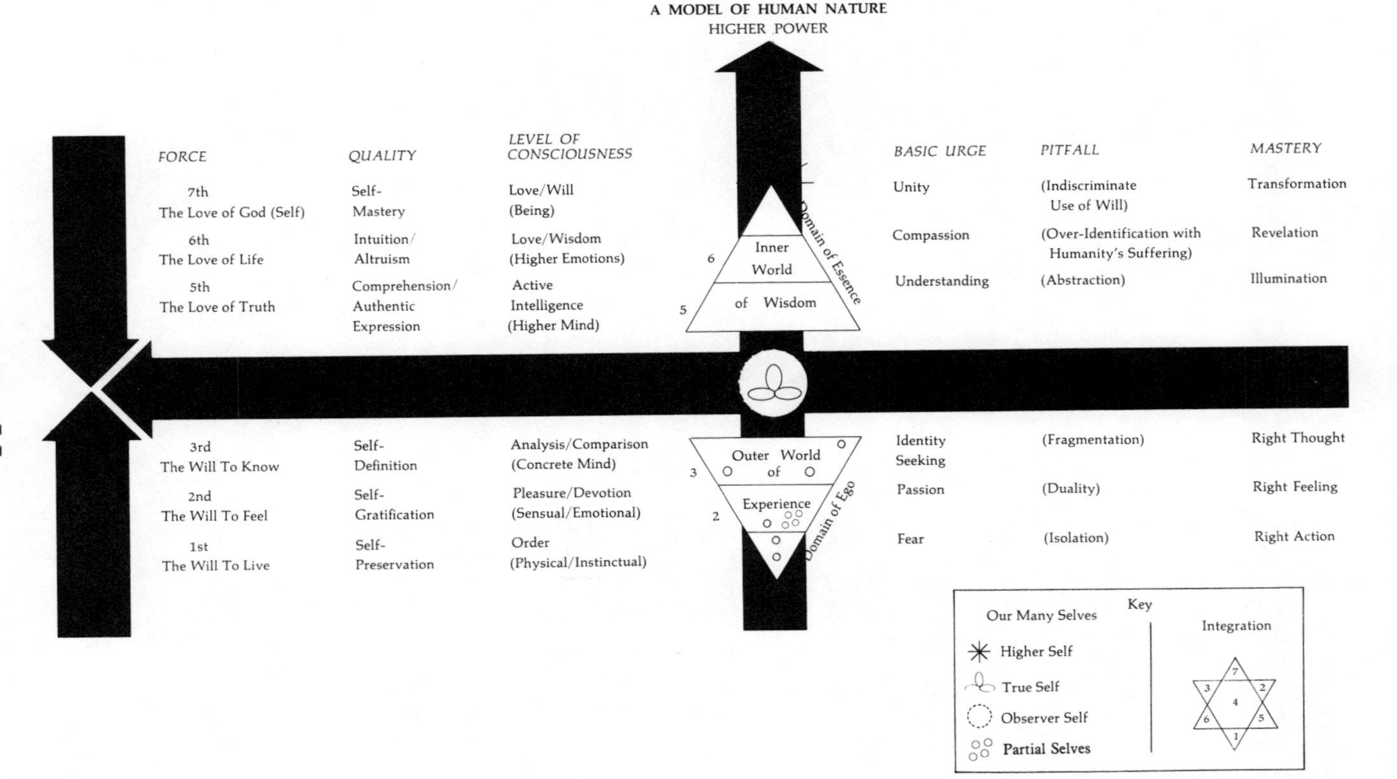

FORCE	QUALITY	LEVEL OF CONSCIOUSNESS	BASIC URGE	PITFALL	MASTERY
7th The Love of God (Self)	Self-Mastery	Love/Will (Being)	Unity	(Indiscriminate Use of Will)	Transformation
6th The Love of Life	Intuition/Altruism	Love/Wisdom (Higher Emotions)	Compassion	(Over-Identification with Humanity's Suffering)	Revelation
5th The Love of Truth	Comprehension/Authentic Expression	Active Intelligence (Higher Mind)	Understanding	(Abstraction)	Illumination
3rd The Will To Know	Self-Definition	Analysis/Comparison (Concrete Mind)	Identity Seeking	(Fragmentation)	Right Thought
2nd The Will To Feel	Self-Gratification	Pleasure/Devotion (Sensual/Emotional)	Passion	(Duality)	Right Feeling
1st The Will To Live	Self-Preservation	Order (Physical/Instinctual)	Fear	(Isolation)	Right Action

Appendix 2

THE TRANSMUTATIONS
(Working With the Polarities)

Table II
THE TRANSMUTATIONS
(Working With The Polarities)

BEING
Love/Will Merge:
Courage To Be; Unity;
Personal Responsibility;
Self-Mastery;
The Love of God (Self)

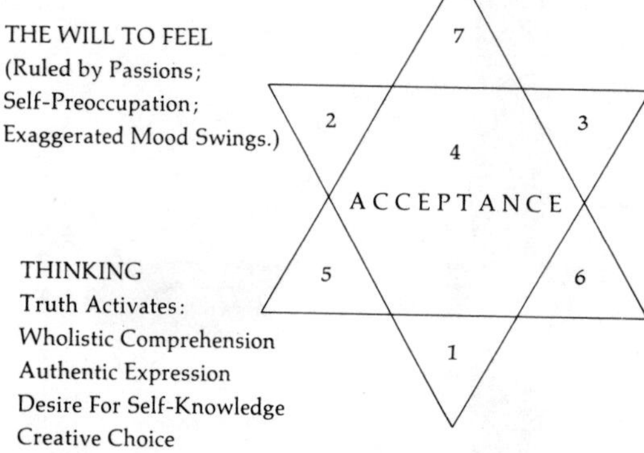

THE WILL TO KNOW
(Mind Ruled By Fragmented Half-Truths; Role Playing; Desire For Status/"Things.")

FEELING
Love/Wisdom Merge:
Compassion; Aspiration To Serve Others; Serenity; Intuition Supersedes Intellect; The Love of Life

THE WILL TO LIVE
(Fear; Isolation;
Self-Pity and
Blame;
Powerlessness.)

Appendix 3 — Exercises

A NOTE ABOUT WORKING WITH THE UNCONSCIOUS

Following are several exercises that will aid you in your work in transformation. Some of them are guided imagery, working with the active imagination, and tapping into the depths of the unconscious. Here are a few suggestions that will help to make this work a useful, positive experience.

1. If you have never done guided imagery or work with the active imagination, please experience these techniques with a friend or therapist yourself before you attempt using them with others. This will enrich your experience with your clients and give you the key to using your own imagination and intuition in guiding them. Otherwise, the exercises will come across as superficial, or you may get into difficulty with them.

2. Any imagery of *ascension,* going upward, will take the client into the Superconscious realm. And, conversely, any symbolism of *descending* will move the client into the Subconscious. The Superconscious is seldom scary and usually produces very beautiful, high experiences. But the Subconscious can be extremely dark and sometimes frightening, and the client may show resistance in viewing whatever is trying to emerge from the dark recesses of his mind. In his imagery provide him with a tool of protection.... a light, a cord to pull to bring him up, a suit of armor to wear, a sword, whatever he feels he needs.... and you may overcome the resistance. If not, do not push it. If the issue is an important one, you can be sure another time will come when the client will be more ready to work on this particular problem.

3. Always end trips into the Lower Unconscious (Subconscious) with a positive experience.... surrounding the "evil" with love or light; telling it you are going to try to understand it and grant it its wishes in an appropriate way; allowing it to run away, or your client to run away from it. If it gets really uncomfortable, surround your client with love and light.... these are examples of what I mean. NEVER LEAVE YOUR CLIENT DOWN IN THE SUBCONSCIOUS IN THE MIDST OF A NEGATIVE EXPERIENCE.

4. In the Guiding Instructions of the exercises to follow, all dots (....) represent a five to ten second pause, unless otherwise specified.

5. Symbols are carriers of *meaning* and *energy.* They show us the *causative* level of the issue they represent. For this reason they are agents of transformation — extremely potent. Working at the symbolic level of a problem often produces amazingly rapid results. You must be prepared for this and trust the process. Symbols have personal meaning to each individual, depending on his or her own unique life history. Therefore, please avoid interpreting your client's symbolic relationships. This should be a non-directive process, asking the client to tell you what it means to him.

6. I have been doing this work for years, and I, too, began as a novice. To my knowledge, I have never seen any harm come from working with the unconscious, only powerful, positive growth. But, I've always followed these guidelines I am sharing with you. Also, I am basically a supportive therapist who easily sees the positive in my clients. One can seldom get into trouble when feeling sincere love and empathy for others. The rule I use for myself is: "All the work I do is designed to lead to a furthering of truth, goodness and beauty."

Please study each exercise in its *entirety* and familiarize yourself with the steps to follow before you guide a client through one of these experiences. The instructions to your client should not impede the meditative process of each exercise.

* * * *

EXERCISE NO. 1

Getting a Message from the Higher Self

Purpose: This exercise is used when a client needs to get an answer to a problem from his higher unconscious mind, because he has been unsuccessful problem-solving at the conscious level.

Instructions to Guide: Begin by helping your client phrase his question properly and have him write it down. Tell him that in a minute you will be guiding him through a meditative process that will enable him to get a message from his Higher Self. The message will be coming in the form of a symbol and he must wait with a certain attitude — one of being a moviegoer awaiting the picture to come on the screen — expectantly, but with no anxiety. Tell him he is *not* the projectionist! It will not be his responsibility to make the picture come on the screen. Now, guide your client in the following manner:

Guided Imagery Exercise: "Close your eyes and become aware of your breathing. Begin letting go of the tension in your body and feel yourself relaxing.... letting go. Allow your breathing to become balanced and calm.... realize that gravity will hold you up.... let go.... relax....

"Focus on your body and notice any physical sensations you are having.... Now, ask your body to become perfectly relaxed and still....

"Focus on your emotions and notice any movement you are feeling.... especially in the heart or the solar plexus.... Now, ask your emotions to become calm.... like a lake with no ripples.

"Focus on your mind and notice any thoughts you are having. Just be aware of your thoughts for a while.... Now, ask your active mind to be quiet.... Experience the stillness.... the silence....

"Now imagine yourself sitting here inside a warm, beautiful bubble of rose-colored light. Just feel the pleasant, safe warmth. And above your head, at the top of the bubble, picture a brilliant star.... shining its radiance down upon you.... This star is your Higher Self. Know that your Higher Self wants to communicate with you. It is the voice of your very Soul! But it can only speak in symbols, and you must be willing to receive its messages.... Experience this beautiful star for a moment, and tell it you are open to receive its message.... Now, ask your Higher Self whatever question you wish to ask it. Phrase it carefully so that you can understand the answer you will receive....

"Now sit still and wait for the answer. When the symbol comes, take whatever it is as your message, and then thank your Higher Self for this meaningful gift."

(Note: If the client balks and does not seem to be receiving an answer after a minute or so,, say to him, "Take whatever comes when you hear my hand clap," and clap loudly. Then say, "Now, what did you get?")

Processing: When the client tells you the symbol, have him work with it in this way: Write or draw it on a piece of paper and *immediately* write down any descriptive words or sentences that he associates with this particular symbol. The client is not to be concerned at this point with the question he asked; he is just working now with the interpretation of the symbol — what it means *to him,* not to anyone else.

When your client has run out of things to write about his symbol, have him take a look at what he has written and now go back and apply this knowledge to the question that he asked his Higher Self. He will probably see his answer clearly.

Ponder together the answer your client received. If the symbolism was too obtuse, he can go back to his Higher Self and ask for a clarification symbol or he can ask to be shown a picture of how he would be acting in his daily life if he were *doing* the answer to his question. Use your own imagination and intuition in processing this exercise with your client. Be sure he understands how his answer applies to his daily life.

Note: Since the Higher Self does not work in the dimension of time, the client needs to be aware that he must use practical discrimination about when and how to apply the solution he has received, such as putting off a decision until an appropriate time, making arrangements for persons dependent upon himself, gathering more material resources before following such guidance, etc. Messages from the Higher Self are answers at a higher level than *living in the world.* And, since we *do* live in the world, we must always use our practical nature along with our Higher nature in determining our life's decisions.

EXERCISE NO. 2

Centering

Anytime we feel "caught up" in a situation where our emotions are beginning to rock around, we will notice a strange shift in consciousness has occurred: Our consciousness has left us and gone over and attached itself to the someone or something that is upsetting us. We have literally lost ourselves for the time being, and have given away our power! Consequently, we cannot think straight; we cannot control our emotions; and our body even feels out of hand (like a stabbing pain hitting our stomach, or our heart is beginning to pound.) Before we can resolve this intolerable situation, we must GET AHOLD OF OURSELF AGAIN.... bring our consciousness back into our own body, in the *center* where it belongs, attached to the True Self.

Here's a way to do this — Example: You are having lunch with your boss and he is telling you he is removing you from the project you've been working on and putting you in charge of something else.... but you are hearing a threat: Your consciousness runs off and "sees" a perfect, ideal person replacing you and the project working better without you, and you are off somewhere in a corner no longer being noticed, making less money, being told you are not needed anymore, etc., etc., etc. The whole time your boss is talking to you, you are "not at home": you're off out there in your imagination.

When a situation such as this is happening, this exercise can be used.

Guiding Instructions: "Close your eyes for a moment and picture yourself being out there in the other person or thing.... literally! *See* your consciousness over there IN the other or scurrying around the scene that is upsetting you....

"Now gradually, in your mind's eye picture yourself (the You who is aware of this predicament just now; i.e., your Observer Self) tossing a rope out to your consciousness over there and lassoing it.... very slowly now, bring it back in toward the center of your body, putting it in its rightful place within you. *Feel this happening as you do it.*"

Processing: If your client is successful, she will experience a calming down, a settling in.... a lightening up and a letting go of anxiety and fear. She will be "home" again.

Once this happens, have her check out her body, her emotions, and her mental attitude, and if this process has worked, she will discover that she is feeling fine and thinking sanely. *Now,* you can deal with the issue realistically as the two of you process this together. Your client will know exactly what to do, and her response will match the reality of the situation.

EXERCISE NO. 3

Following the Drink

"The man takes a drink
The drink takes a drink
The drink takes the man...."

Purpose: Most alcoholics, when recovering from their addiction, experience times of craving, or building toward a "slip." When these times occur, it is helpful to have the client talk about them and make the cravings explicit. Often they are ashamed of these desires and are hesitant to discuss them, so they may need prompting. Give them permission to experience the craving *in their mind.* Something experienced on the symbolic level (in the mind, in dreams, etc.) is truly a way of experiencing, and it will often keep the behavior from manifesting on the physical plane.... the symbolic experience discharges the pent-up energy that is getting built up around the subject of returning to the addicted behavior. Here is an exercise that will aid this process of experiencing symbolically.

Instructions to Guide: After discussing with your client his craving, or his fantasizing about returning to the addicted behavior, ask him to close his eyes, relax, and begin to see himself in his mind's eye in the scene he wishes to be in (a bar, a party, etc.), and have him begin to describe it in flowery detail.... let the imagination run wild.... and *live it through.* Have him exaggerate the "high," the "delights" that he imagines, etc.

(Example: "I'm in this bar having two double scotches.... one right after the other.... and I look great! I'm dressed to the hilt, my hair is perfect, I'm really grand. A gorgeous lady comes over and joins me, and we begin to kid around, really getting high on each other! I order another drink, and we dance awhile.... etc.... then we leave together...." Have him continue his fantasy on through the entire evening. And on into the waking up the next morning.... the hangover.... the remorse.... the rest of the next day.... etc. DON'T ALLOW THE FANTASY TO END UNTIL THE CONSEQUENCES OF THE DRINKING HAVE ALSO BEEN EXPERIENCED. FOLLOW IT COMPLETELY THROUGH. If the client wants to "kid himself" by trying to stop while it's all still pleasant, prod him on into the day after.... or as long as you need to until he experiences his compulsive, slave-like addictive behavior returning on him. Then process this experience extensively, drawing him out about *all* his feelings, ideas, plans, etc.)

Processing: Make a realistic plan for the next several days to ensure a support system for your client, if you sense he is really about to slip. Do not act alarmed or judgmental. Be light, pleasant, and supportive of the progress he has made and how natural it is to have fantasies about returning to the addictive behavior.

Note: Your client may need to grieve about giving up the addiction. Sometimes the fantasizing is a way of getting in touch with the pain of the loss. *Be very sensitive to this.* That bottle may have been his best friend.

EXERCISE NO. 4
(For use in groups)

Observer Self

Purpose: This exercise is designed to help your clients learn they have a consciousness level that can rise above their predicaments and see things comprehensively and clearly. This is a very profound exercise that leads to a practical use of the emotions and the Observer Self Consciousness in sticky situations where confrontations or negative experiences are occurring.

Instructions to Guide: Have group members each choose a partner, and decide who will be A and who will be B. Now, give the following instructions:

(1) "All who are A, I would like for you to think of a situation that has occurred in your life recently that you still have some energy in that made you mad or hurt your feelings.... some kind of negative experience you felt you had to really process or deal with."

(2) "Now, tell this story to your partner as vividly as you can recall it. It's okay to get back into the feelings.... in fact, it's even advisable. And partners, all you have to do is listen and empathize, those of you who are B's.... as if you are simply a sympathetic friend."

(Allow five minutes for this.... or go a little longer if your intuition says to.)

(3) "Now, stop wherever you are in your story. Just cut it off for now. And those of you who are B, if you will, please tell a story that has happened to you lately that made you upset, and A's listen to them in the way you've just been listened to."

(Allow another five minutes or so.)

(4) "Now, stop again, wherever you are in your story.... just stop for now. And, all A's, those of you who shared your story first, I want you to go back now and tell your *same* story again while B

listens. Only this time, you must tell it in the *third person,* using your first name, and the pronoun he or she, as though you are watching the scene on *As the World Turns.* You may not use the word 'I,' and partners, please monitor this.... if they say 'I' they are getting re-identified, so move in and stop them. It will sound like this: 'Well, Jacquie was in the supermarket the other day and she was minding her own business, when she noticed an old friend standing nearby, and she....' Just tell the story, purely and simply in the third person."

(Allow four minutes. It shouldn't take as long because there will be less justifying and less emotional involvement.)

(5) "Stop, please, wherever you are in your story. And now, A's, you listen while B's tell their story in the third person. Remember, don't allow them to use the word 'I.' "

(Again, allow four minutes or so.)

(6) "Please stop now, and let me have your attention. Take a minute or two to appreciate your partner. Then come out of your pairs and let's all process this together."

Processing: Group leader, use blackboard now that is divided into two columns:

PERSONAL SELF (Ego)	IMPERSONAL SELF (Observer)

From the group, draw out the descriptions from each state, "I" and "He/She," from the experience they just had with their partner. Allow them to volunteer this information by raising their hands: "Who is willing to share how that was for them? What differences did you notice when you told your story in "I" language versus how you were when you told it in third person?"

(Example: Some types of answers will be — "In, 'I,' I was very emotional, very angry. In the third person, it seemed rather humorous that I got so hot over something so ridiculous." On the board under "PERSONAL SELF" write "emotionally upset," under "IMPERSONAL SELF" write "humor" and "unemotional" or "less emotional." Another example might be: "In 'I' self I felt intensely concerned about proving my point. In 'he/she,' it didn't matter so much."

And you write in first column "need to justify or prove point" and in second column "less intensity in proving point." Use your imagination to draw these dualistic states of consciousness for comparison, but be sure and stick to the facts of what they are reporting. The idea is for them to see that the Personal Self is stuck in ego needs and cannot see the larger picture and that it comes from a fragment of truth while the Impersonal Self is the Higher Self, and can see the situation wholistically and without ego involvement. The Higher Self, as Observer, is *in* the situation but is also above it; while the Lower Self (ego) is totally caught up in its own perspective.)

Point to be made: Emotional over-reactions are a clue that we are stuck in our ego and we need to stop at a time like that and analyze what is going on with us, because it will show us something about our personality structure that is being offered a chance to grow beyond a weakness. Perhaps I need to have the power. Maybe I have to be the boss. Perhaps I'm protecting an image of myself I am addicted to, etc.

Note: Sometimes someone will report a Higher Self emotional reaction, like reacting to a child being beaten or an animal being abused, etc. Remind the group that the Higher Self reacts to injustice, but it still does not *over*-react. *Over*-reaction is the key (Would *everybody* have felt rejected or hurt by that? If not, then it is probably an ego need rather than an inhuman act.).

EXERCISE NO. 5
(For use with individuals)

Observer Self

Purpose: There are times when you feel it is important for the client to get outside her emotional reaction to a situation and see it from a wider point of view (from the standpoint of Reality rather than from the personal reality.) When this occurs, the following will aid you in achieving this aim:

Instructions to Guide: Ask your client to close her eyes and picture herself totally involved in the scene where the problem is manifesting strongly. After she has gone inward and become silent and you sense she is picturing the scene, guide her with these types of statements, spoken quietly and unobtrusively:

Guided Imagery Exercise: "Be aware of how you are feeling as you involve in this scene.... Notice the look on your face and on the faces of those involved with you.... Be aware of the kind of energy that is in the air as you involve in this.... Notice your body movements.... Be aware of the intentions of yourself and others involved.... the message you're trying to get across to the other(s).... Now, just *feel* for a moment the very *essence* of this experience, as though it's happening right now.... just be with that for awhile...." (PUT ON SOME QUIET MEDITATIVE MUSIC AT THIS POINT, IF POSSIBLE.)

"Now, from above, look down on the scene you left behind and see it in its entirety.... Notice what you are doing.... Notice how the other(s) is reacting to you.... Be aware of the *context* within which this scene is occurring.... the role you and others are playing out, the place it's happening.... this particular time in history.... In the city where you live.... In this country you are in.... this culture.... this age....

"Now, very slowly allow yourself to descend back into the scene you've been witnessing.... Now re-enter your body and begin acting out this scene based on what you saw from above.... Notice any changes you are making in how you are relating to this situation.... Notice any changes in others.... Be aware of how your body now looks and feels.... Be aware of any insights into the situation you are now having.... Be especially aware of the needs the other(s) has, or what is motivating his behavior, and notice your reactions to him now that you have this awareness....

"Now allow this scene to come to an end in whatever way you wish to resolve the matter for now....

"Now, slowly open your eyes and come back here to this room with me."

Processing: In processing this experience, pay special attention to the difference in how the client felt from above as from being totally involved down below. Point out that the uninvolved (Higher) Self had the most loving responses. (Often we confuse passionate emotional involvement with love.)

EXERCISE NO. 6

I Am Aware

Purpose: Some clients are very unconscious of how they are using their awareness continuum to select what they do and do not attend to in life. Sometime spend a whole session with your client exploring her continuum of awareness.

Instructions to Guide: First of all, teach her that we can only be aware of (1) inner states or feelings, (2) outer objects contacted by our senses, or (3) mind activity. And we can only be aware of one thing at a time. (If I am focusing on an inner feeling, I will be oblivious to an outside noise or color or smell.... unless, of course, it becomes so overwhelming it shifts my awareness to it.... in which case I will no longer be aware of my inner feelings.)

Guided Exercise: Ask your client to close her eyes, and give her some time to relax.

"Notice your breath as it goes in and out of your body.... Now, gently begin to balance out your breathing.... feel yourself letting go.... calming down.... centering."

"Follow the awareness. Stay with it.... What's happening now?" (Keep client in her awareness and just follow it for awhile.)

"Now, I want you to become aware of any sounds you hear. Just notice for awhile." (Allow client to report out loud what she is hearing....) "Now, shift to any smell you are experiencing.... any light you are aware of.... color.... how it feels to be touching something...." (Your client can open her eyes during this part, as she is using her external awareness continuum.) "Just follow your awareness for awhile and report to me what your senses are picking up....

"Now, close your eyes, and go up into your mind and become aware of any thoughts you are having.... any activity in your mind.... and report to me. Such as 'I'm aware I am worrying about tomorrow..., or, 'I'm wondering if I'm doing this right...', or, 'I'm remembering a conversation I had yesterday with my husband...', or, 'I'm aware my mind is jumping all around, won't stay focused.' Now, just be with your mind activity for awhile. Watch the content of your mind ...." (When observing mind activity, notice that the activities all end with *ing*.... recalling, worrying, planning, thinking.... as they are all here and now activities. Point this out to your client.)

"Now, slowly open your eyes and come back here with me.... and let's talk about what you learned about your awareness."

Processing: Allow client to discuss this experience fully with you. Emphasize any new learning about herself that she discovered, such as how much she uses one kind of awareness almost exclusively, etc.

Homework assignment: Ask your client to spend 10 minutes each day for a week following her awareness, as she did in this exercise, then write in her journal what she discovers.

EXERCISE NO. 7

Reverberation!

(An Exercise in Empathy)

Purpose: To use with a client in a session where clarity on some pressing issue is needed.

Instructions to Guide: Sit, face to face, with your client, closely, so that you can hold hands. Now, say to him: "Let's each close our eyes for a few moments and focus on allowing the highest good from this session together."

Now, both of you close your eyes and go into this meditative state together. (Counselor focuses on being an instrument for client's highest good. After a few moments, counselor breaks the meditative state by slowly withdrawing hands and opening eyes.)

Quietly invite the client now to begin telling you the problem in all its ramifications. As the client shares, you remain silent.... *completely* silent.... except for spontaneous, simple statements that keep the client speaking, like "I understand" or "please elaborate." *Non-verbal* empathy or warmth is permissable, and even desirable, such as head nods, smiles and warm facial expressions, etc.

When your client has stated the problem completely, ask him to sit quietly for awhile and write down his own analysis and solution to the problem. While he is doing this, you write down your impressions of the client's situation and possible solutions. Tell the client to use *whatever* impressions come in while doing this written assignment. *Anything* that comes through the senses or the intuition should be put on paper. This is very important because we want the intuition to work! For example, a feeling of repulsion or excitement might occur as the client is stating something, or an image, a picture or a symbol might come into the mind. Or a flash of insight might hit, with a creative solution to the situation. An old memory might emerge, or an old association. Anything can be used. But it is important that each does his own written impressions silently, with no feedback from the other.

Now, when each is finished, have the client share what he has written, and elaborate.

Processing: When he is completely finished, share what you have written, and the two of you process this together.

Now, the session progresses as usual, using the material which has surfaced from this exercise as the content of the session.

(Note: You will find that the non-verbal contact with the client with instruction to focus on the highest good, and the silent period that comes while writing down what is coming through the consciousness will give each of you a profound contact with your Higher Self.)

EXERCISE NO. 8

Transforming Resentments[55]

Purpose: To be used to release energy tied up in past resentments and repressed anger. Use after rapport is established and the client is fully ready to work on herself. Study this exercise in its entirety and practice it with a friend before attempting it with a client.

Instructions to Client: "Close your eyes and take a few deep breaths.

"In your mind's eye, reflect rapidly back over your life of relationships and situations, and become aware of any angry, hurt or resentful feelings that you have toward particular people or places.

"Now, begin telling me (or listener) who or what you feel resentment toward. List them out loud." (Listener, take notes, enough to describe each specific situation for recall later.)

"Open your eyes, and one by one we are going to put these people here in this empty chair and begin telling them *specifically* what we resent, or what feels unfinished that is painful to you."

Steps in the Process:

To the client:

1. "See person clearly in the chair. Describe to me what he/she is wearing, the look on their face, the attitude they are projecting, etc. See them clearly.

2. "As I call out each specific event you recalled, please begin telling them what you resent; just spell them out one at a time. Don't worry if you are not being rational about it, or feeling justified. Feelings are feelings. Just express them.

3. "Now begin telling them what you would rather have had from them.... what you wished they had done, been, etc. It's okay to feel sadness or regret. Just tell them.

4. "When you feel done with this, close your eyes and begin breathing evenly, slowly relaxing yourself." (Therapist put music on with low volume, as background music. Allow silence to pervade the room except for the music. The music needs to be meditative and melodic, very quiet and not disruptive. Ron Dexter's *Golden Voyage,* Volume One, Two or Three; Georgia Kelly's harp music, any of it; or *Pachabel's Canon in D* are examples of the type of sound that works best.[56]

5. As music plays and relaxation occurs, tell your client to picture herself and the one she is resenting sitting together surrounded in rose-colored light. "Just be in that space together for a minute or two. Now, when it feels right begin telling the person you resent that you release him with love and you surround him with light.... that you surround the *two* of you in the light of compassion, together.... that you are ready to let go of the past and be with this person in whatever way the Universe sees fit....

6. "Now, gently tell him anything about him that you appreciate."

7. Wait quietly with your client until you sense an inner change of mood occurs. If forgiveness and letting go clearly happens, your client will sigh, feel lighter, smile, or weep quietly with a kind of joyfulness. If forgiveness does not occur, you will sense nothing is happening, in which case you invite your client to go back to Step 2 and bring up other resentments or feelings that have not yet been shared, then proceed through the steps again.

Note: *Do not use music until Step 4,* because the earlier steps are to come from the Personal Self, with ego energy.... not from the Transpersonal Self.

EXERCISE NO. 9

Focusing on a Feeling

Purpose: This exercise allows clients to become aware of their feelings in their physical body, and to connect the feeling with its meaning.

Instructions to Guide: When your client is expressing something you sense must have feeling accompanying it, ask him if he is experiencing a feeling somewhere in his body as he talks. If he says no, then just continue listening to him. If he says yes, have him point to where the feeling is located. Then ask him to close his eyes and go to the feeling, focusing his entire attention there. Have him watch the feeling and see what happens, reporting to you as he notices changes. Stay with him, following the feeling wherever it wants to go. Often the feeling will dissolve when noticed, and you can share this insight with your client: "It only wanted you to notice it. Now it can go away." Or, sometimes the feeling will become intensified. If so, have him focus on the feeling, *stay with it.* If he tries to leave, bring him back. Keep bringing him back. As it intensifies, allow the feeling to speak. *Not* the intellect, the feeling. The feeling has a voice. "Let it talk to you." As the feeling speaks its mind, help your client cathart the feeling — cry, moan, yell, whatever is asking to be expressed. If there is no catharsis, have your client ask the feeling what it needs in order to release itself and then follow the feeling's instructions. Example: The feeling might say "I need to be alone with you to experience this." Or, "I need for you to express this directly to your father." Or, "I need permission to express myself."

Processing: Once the feeling is out, go back and make sure there is only relief and serenity left. If there is something else remaining that needs to be dealt with, go for it in the same manner as you did the first one.

Note: When a feeling is willing to dialogue with the client, you might find it useful to have it tell its body what it needs from it, and its mind what it needs from it. Often we gain insight when we see how our three bodies are working or not working together. For example, my emotions once told my mind to quit giving them so much data to process! My emotions felt they had to block off a lot of feeling because they couldn't handle all the thoughts that came in. And my emotions told my body they wanted to color my body some beautiful colors! Because my body was too devoid of feeling sometimes, too aligned with my mental life. This insight has helped me greatly in aligning my physical, emotional and mental selves.

Eugene Gendlin's book, *Focusing* is an excellent source for this process. (See Bibliography.)

EXERCISE NO. 10

Going into the Silence

An exercise in mindfulness.

"Sit in a quiet place, pleasant and warm. Close your eyes and begin feeling yourself relax.... Let go of the tension in your body.... Realize that gravity will hold you up.... Just sit.... just be.

"Take a few quiet, even breaths. (Long pause)

"In your mind's eye, imagine you are going inward toward the center of your being. Deeper and deeper.... inward.... inward.... down into the center.... where all Truth resides....

"Everything is totally still.... stillness.... complete silence.... silent stillness (Long pause)

"Be here now.... absorb the silence.... feel its weight...."

(Allow two minutes to pass with no sound.)

In a low, calm, quiet voice, say the following:

"Now allow the Silence to speak.... to show you who you are.... what you need to know...."

(Allow another two minutes to pass.... or however long your intuition says your client needs. Do not allow your own anxiety or impatience to rule you. Stay tuned in to your client's experience, and you will know exactly when to speak.)

"Now, slowly allow yourself to ascend back out to the surface of yourself.... Slowly come back here with me...."

Processing: When the client is back and her eyes are open, ask her to tell you what she learned, and process it together.

Note: You can use this exercise with no particular goal in mind, or you can use it to have the client gain understanding of a specific difficulty, or to get a sense of Level Five consciousness.

EXERCISE NO. 11

Becoming a Being of Light

Purpose: This imagery will aid your clients in experiencing a moment of enlightenment.... all the way into the cellular level of their beings.

Instructions to Guide: Ask your client to stand quietly, closing her eyes for awhile, and begin to breathe with balanced breath.... *in* to the count of 4, *out* to the count of 4.... to feel herself relaxing and letting go.

Guided Imagery Experience: "Realize that gravity will hold you up. Spread your feet apart about 14 inches and feel your weight balancing between your legs, bending your knees a little so that you can sway as a tree in a gentle wind.

"Now become aware of your body, standing here so gracefully, and realize it is a vessel of a supreme beauty and bliss, casting the beauty of the light of the spirit as a lamp reflects the luminosity of its indwelling flame. Realize that your expression is the workings of the gods.... the Joy of Life channels through you into a world that needs your light. Be this God-self. Be this bliss.... this joy.... this consciousness.... Feel yourself to be Light, transparent and filled with the flow of universal love and confidence.... A Being of Light. (Long pause)

"Now, open your eyes and walk around in this new-found state of consciousness.... Being truly who you are at the highest possible level. Stay very close to your experience, and *realize* this Truth...."

Processing: After a few minutes of this, have your client share with you what this experience was like.... what insights were gained, what feelings were experienced.

EXERCISE NO. 12

Enlightening

Purpose: For clearing emotional energy or physical pain that is stuck in the body. Use quiet, meditative music, such as Ron Dexter's *Golden Voyage.*[56]

Instructions to Guide: Ask your client to close his eyes and begin relaxing, noticing his breath as he breathes in and out. Then have him begin balancing his breath.... breathe in to the count of 4, breathe out to the count of 4. "Notice any tension or pain anywhere in your body.... Gradually breathe your breath into these tense parts, breathing out the tension.... Feel yourself letting go.... Allow gravity to hold you up."

(As you feel your client is really inward, continue:)

"Now, in your imagination, see yourself standing there at the top of a staircase looking down at seven steps. You are going to descend to the bottom, knowing that there you will be completely relaxed. Now you are going down: 1....2....3....4....5....6....7...." (NOTE: WHEN COUNTING, KEEP THE VOICE EVEN, WITH SAME AMOUNT OF TIME BETWEEN EACH COUNT.)

"Now you are at the bottom and you see yourself standing there with the Lantern of Consciousness in your hand. You are going to go down into your emotional space. Please point for me where that is in your body.... the place where you feel the emotion." (Client will point, probably to the solar plexus or the chest). "Okay, now in your right hand is your Lantern of Consciousness, shining its clear light. And in your left hand is a cord you can pull anytime you wish to be lifted up out of the emotional place you are going to. So you are safe and protected, and everything is fine. Now you are going into the emotional place.... See in there.... and tell me what your emotion looks like.... What is it? (Client will report a thing, or a symbol).... Now, ask your symbol (Call it by the name client gave it) what it needs and tell me what it says."

(As client is reporting what the emotion needs, ask him if he is experiencing any feeling right now? If yes, have him express the feeling.... tears, anger, whatever. If the client is *not* feeling anything, continue with the exercise.) "Who does (*name of emotion*) need this from?.... And how can (*name of emotion*) get it?"

Follow your client's train of thought and experience and logically lead him on to conclusion, getting as much data from the emotion as you can, and getting out as much feeling as the client is in touch with. When you sense all has been brought into the light and seen clearly, have your client picture the emotion standing there with the full light of consciousness shining its light upon it, feeling its warmth, and surrounding it with love and appreciation. Then have him ascend back up the seven steps to the top, counting slowly from 7 to 1, and end the experience any way he wishes. Then have him come back to the room with you by experiencing his body on the floor (or in the chair) and slowly opening his eyes.

Processing: Process this experience with your client, writing down any significant insights that occurred.

NOTE: You can use this same exercise to go to a place in the body where a physical problem is occurring. For example, tightness in the neck, a nervous stomach, etc. The point is to have the client *personify* the feeling, or physical ailment, experience it, and have a conversation with it in order to understand it.

Always end by shining the Light of Consciousness on it, encircling it with love and appreciation. This work is occurring on the symbolic level, which is *the causative level.* It will have far-reaching effects on the consciousness of your client, even though sometimes he cannot verbalize completely what happened.

You can trust the process.

EXERCISE NO. 13

Seeing Yourself Completely

Purpose: For aiding clients in achieving 4th level consciousness.... loving acceptance of themselves *as they are.*

Instructions to Guide: Use background music, soft, meditative.

Guided Imagery Exercise: "Stand quietly, erect, centered. Close your eyes and breathe deeply a few times to relax. Experience yourself in an egg-shaped bubble of soft rose-colored light. Above your head, about 18 inches, resides your Higher Self (your Soul-star). Picture it as a shining star, pouring its warmth and brilliance down upon you.

"Now, begin reflecting on your past. Just let it float by you as if on ticker tape. See it without judgment.... just warmth.... Now, ask yourself if there is anything *about yourself* you've gained from your past that you would like to keep.... say them out loud...." (Therapist, record them.)

"Realize now, with eyes still closed, still reflective, that your past has determined your present.... likewise, your present is determining your future....

"Is there anything about you in your present you would like to keep?.... Say them out loud." (Therapist, record them).

"Now, see yourself in the future at whatever time you choose as manifesting these qualities you wish to keep and this life-style you dream of.... See yourself doing it and being it in all its clarity....

"When you are ready, come back here to this room with me."

Processing: Process this experience with your client, attributing patterns, meaning or dealing with any unfinished emotion. If something emerges that is too much to work on in one session, make a note of it for a later emphasis.

EXERCISE NO. 14

Nature of Resistance

Transformers do not abruptly press clients past a point of resistance. They view resistance as a gift to be respected. They do believe, however, that it is their obligation to assist the client in discovering where the resistance is coming from. Consequently, when they sense resistance, they begin by pointing out to the client that they are perceiving their objections as resistance and ask the client what it feels like. If the client affirms that it is indeed some sort of blockage to a particular aspect of personal work, the Transformer then asks the client if they would like to explore where the resistance is coming from. Then explain that it can be a message from their Lower Self, having its basis in fear; or it can be a message from their Higher Self, as a way to step down their energy which the Higher Self senses is moving too rapidly. In order to determine from which unconscious mind the block is being constructed (the subconscious or the Superconscious), the Transformer asks the client to close his eyes, breathe a while (to relax the body), and when the therapist feels the client is somewhat relaxed, she says:

> "Now, very spontaneously allow an image to come into your mind that symbolizes your resistance...."

When the client says he has a symbol, the therapist asks him to describe it in detail. If the symbol is representative of anything that is down, heavy, dark, or thick, it will be from the subconscious (fear-based). Examples: a dark wall with no windows, black mud covering the entrance to something, heavy weights bolting a door, a "No Exit" sign beside one spelling "Danger," etc. Or sometimes the subconscious images will be shadows, murkiness, thick, dark clouds, or other amorphous substances that block one's vision.

If, on the other hand, the image is one from the Higher Self, it will be one of a Master, a teacher, guide or Christ figure, usually robed in white, or beautiful or aged (representing strength, purity or wisdom). Or often it will be a symbol of a cross, a rose, a serpent encircling a staff, a crown, a field of green grass, a brilliant light, or some type of religious symbol — white, golden, yellow, shades of blue or violet. All of these are symbols from the Superconscious Mind, the home of the Higher Self.

If the Subconscious is blocking, ask the client if they would be willing to talk about their fear, and see what "guarantees" they would need for safety or comfort in order to proceed with the therapeutic task. If they still resist, let it go. (If the pattern is significant, you can bet the subject will return for another chance to be worked through!)

If the Superconscious is blocking, tell the client to respect his Higher Self's wishes and follow Its guidance. It knows more about what's better for him than you do! If your client asks you why your Higher Self would be blocking a piece of personal work, you can share with him the knowledge that his Higher Self (for some reason) knows he is not ready yet to deal with this particular issue in Life — perhaps it would require certain moves in the client's circumstances that would adversely affect innocent persons, or give the client too much to deal with right now, which might produce discouragement on The Path.

The point is: When resistance is present in the therapy session, work *with* the resistance, not against it. And drop the content of the personal work that created the resistance until you are clear on what the resistance is.

EXERCISE NO. 15

Evoking an Ideal Model

Purpose: This exercise can be used to get your client in touch with his Higher Self, or some other ideal model he needs to use to help integrate his personality or achieve a desired behavior.

Instructions to Guide: Take some time to put your client in a quiet, relaxed state. Then have him begin visualizing himself walking down a corridor of a museum, slowly approaching a statue that is emerging in the distance.

"As you are approaching this statue, you are beginning to see its form emerge, and you realize this is your Higher Self! (If it is another ideal model you want him to identify with, such as your Playful Self or your Responsible Self, substitute here). Be aware of what this Higher Self looks like, its stance.... the expression on its face.... its attire.... let yourself experience its essence for a moment.... discover how you feel in its presence. Now, just allow yourself to be there in the presence of this statue for a moment and experience a relationship. Now slowly move toward this glorious statue, allowing yourself to come closer and closer, staying in touch with how you feel.... and merge with this Self, come down off your pedestal and move around as this Self.... just do this for a while now.... discover how it feels to be walking in its feet, moving its arms, breathing its breath.... just being this Self."

"Now imagine you as your Higher Self are returning back to your pedestal to take your stance once again, and slowly experience yourself as you are now stepping out of its form and stand in front of it once again. Your Higher Self is now giving you a gift to use whenever you need it for strength, courage or loving action. See the gift being handed to you, accept it.... and in your own way thank your Higher Self for this wondrous gift and take a few moments in silence to assimilate this experience. (Long pause)

"Now, slowly return to the room here with me by experiencing yourself sitting in the chair, becoming aware of your body.... now, slowly open your eyes when you feel ready."

Processing: Take a few minutes to process this experience with your client. Make sure you ask questions about the main points you have covered in this imagery. The main purpose is to be sure your client emerges with a clear picture of this Self, in detail, the *essence* of this Self, and a clear understanding of what the gift means for him in his everyday life.

EXERCISE NO. 16

Evoking a Positive Quality[57]

Purpose: To be used when a client seems stuck in a negative characteristic way of behaving, feeling or thinking, and is willing to really work on opening to a new possibility.

Instructions for the Guide: The first task will be to clearly define the negative quality the client seeks to transform. Let's say for example that it is Extravagance. The client, then, will need to contemplate what its opposite would be *for him.* After careful thought and discussion with you, he chooses the quality "Simplicity" as the desired trait he feels would counteract his wasteful extravagance.

The essence of Simplicity must now be planted in his consciousness and prepared to manifest. Once the preparation is properly instigated, it will manifest naturally, with absolutely no effort. Here are some suggested ways to do this (and you may think of others just as valid):

1. Have your client meditate on the word "Simplicity" and discover for himself its nature. He should do this for perhaps a week, writing down the insights and feelings he has concerning the concept.

2. Tell your client to ask his Higher Self for a symbol for this quality. The symbol, then, will provide more information on the essence of Simplicity. He can evoke the symbol, as well as the word, in his consciousness several times a day.

3. In his everyday life, your client can begin talking about the quality to his friends, declaring his intention to develop it in his character. This grounds the thought in Reality, giving the unconscious mind a chance to believe it and to *cause* it to happen.

4. Your client can begin acting "as if" he possesses this quality.... doing things that are representative of Simplicity's nature. You do not need to suggest what these actions might be; it is better to allow his own creativity to work on it. He will find that he does things he wouldn't have dreamed of as this quality comes alive in him! It will feel like magic!

5. He can write the word several times a day, or make cards or artistic renditions of it and place them around his room or his office.

For your aid in teaching clients to evoke positive qualities, here is a listing of the qualities that have emerged most often from persons using this technique:

> acceptance, appreciation, aspiration, authenticity, beauty, Being, belongingness, calmness, centeredness, child-like, compassion, comradeship, concreteness, courage, creativity, curiosity, daring, decisiveness, detachment, determination, discipline, discretion, discrimination, ease, empathy, endurance, enthusiasm, faith, freedom, friendliness, generosity, genuineness, good-heartedness, grace, harmlessness, harmony, humility, humor, initiative, integration, integrity, leadership, Light, love, mutuality, non-attachment, order, patience, peacefulness, persistence, position, positiveness, power, purity, reality, responsibility, serenity, service, significance, silence, simplicity, stability, synthesis, thoughtfulness, tolerance, trust, Truth, understanding, unity, vitality, wholeness, will, wisdom, wonder.

Appendix 4 — Notes

1. Maslow, A. H. *The Farther Reaches of Human Nature.* New York: The Viking Press, 1971. pp. 281–282.
2. Ornstein, Robert. *The Psychology of Consciousness.* 2nd Edition, New York: Harcourt, Brace & Jovanovich, 1977.
3. Ferguson, Marilyn. *The Aquarian Conspiracy: Personal & Social Transformation in the 80's,* Los Angeles: JP Tarcher, 1980.
4. Capra, Fritjof. *The Tao of Physics.* Boulder: Shambhala Press, 1975.
   ______. *The Turning Point.* New York: Simon & Schuster, 1982.
5. Houston, Jean. *The Possible Human: A Course in Extending your Physical, Mental and Creative Abilities.* Los Angeles: JP Tarcher, 1982. p. 217.
6. Selzer, Richard. *Mortal Lessons.* New York: Simon & Schuster, 1976.
7. English, Jane. "Science and Transformation: Levels of Reality in Science and in Consciousness." Unpublished paper — 867 Arlington Ave., Berkeley, CA 94707.
8. Hoeller, Stephen A. *The Gnostic Jung and the Seven Sermons to the Dead.* Wheaton: Theosophical Publishing House, 1982.
9. Maslow, A. H. *Toward a Psychology of Being.* Princeton, NJ: Van Nostrand Co., 1962.

10. A special appreciation is extended to Harper and Row Publishers, Inc. for granting permission to quote extensively from Satprem's, *Sri Aurobindo or the Adventure of Consciousness,* 1968.
11. Research on human brain functioning has led to the discovery that we have basically two modes of thinking available to us, emanating from two distinct hemispheres of the brain, one that processes ordinary sensory data in a logical, lineal fashion, and the other that intuitively transforms ordinary data into new creations — one that "analyzes over time"; the other that "synthesizes over space" (J. Levy, Cal. Tech. researcher).

    The left brain is our computer. It reasons, organizes incoming data, using speech and concrete, materialized facts for its explanation of reality. This verbal brain dominates most of us most of the time, not because it is the best, but because it has been granted the seat of honor in most institutions of learning. It is the *valued* mode of thinking in the West.

The right brain has been devalued, for it is non-rational. It "sees" in wholes. Something "feels" right or wrong, and it cannot explain it. It thinks all-at-once, has flashes of insight based on intuition, and creatively involves with life through meditation, movement, creative inspiration and intuition. It has been equated with negativity, femininity, emotionalism, the dark, and the moon. Whereas, the left brain has been equated with masculinity, positiveness, the sun, rationality, and being conscious — as though it is "right" and the right-brain "wrong."

The left brain controls the right side of the body, and the right brain, the left side of the body.

Following are some of the common parallels that are made of left-brain and right-brain functioning that will familiarize you with these two modes of knowing.

RIGHT-BRAIN	**LEFT-BRAIN**
emotes	reasons
intuition	intellect
Yin	Yang
abstract	concrete
dark	light
feminine	masculine
free-associates	directed thought
divergent	convergent
simultaneous	successive
relational	analytic
nonlineal	lineal
subjective	objective
multiple	sequential
night	day

For those of you wishing to pursue the study of split-brain research, I recommend the following:

Ornstein, Robert. *The Psychology of Consciousness.* 2nd ed., rev., New York: Harcourt, Brace & Jovanovich, 1977.

Dimond, S. J. and Beaumont, J. G. *Hemisphere Function in the Human Brain.* New York: John Wiley & Sons, 1974.

The works of R. W. Sperry, California Institute of Technology, Dept. of Psychobiology.

Gazzaniga, M. "The Split Brain in Man" in *Perception: Mechanisms and Models.* Held, R. and Richards, W., ed., San Francisco: W. H. Freeman, 1972.

Jaynes, J. *The Origin of Consciousness in the Breakdown of the Bicameral Mind.* Boston: Houghton Mifflin, 1976.

12. For a comprehensive study of this quiet, though dramatic social transformation, read *The Aquarian Conspiracy: Personal and Social Transformation in the 1980's* by Marilyn Ferguson. (J. P. Tracher, Inc.: Los Angeles, 1980.

13. Maslow, A. H. *The Farther Reaches of Human Nature.* New York: The Viking Press, 1971.

14. Edwards, Alexis. "Guidelines," a Findhorn publication, 1971. This quotation was slightly altered by its author in 1979.

15. Adapted from Assagioli, R. *Psychosynthesis.* New York: Penguin Books, 1976.

16. Jampolsky, G. *Love Is Letting Go of Fear.* New York: Bantam Books, 1979.

17. Bobby Bridger, personal friend, poet and epic balladeer wrote these words to his song "Heal in the Wisdom" from his album of the same name. The song has become the theme song for the Texas Annual Music Festival held each year in Kerrville, Texas. His work captures the essence of the coming Age. For a copy of his record album, *Heal in the Wisdom,* write: Golden Egg Records, P.O. Box 12602, Austin, Texas 78711. ($8.50 postpaid). Reproduced by permission of the author © 1981 Stareyes, ASCAP.

18. The following is a synopsis of Carl Jung's thoughts about the Self as described in Stephen Hoeller's book, *The Gnostic Jung and the Seven Sermons to the Dead.* (See Footnote number 8).

19. Guillaumont, A., Puech, H.–CH., Quispel, G., trls. *The Gospel According to Thomas.* New York: Harper & Row Publishers, Inc., 1959. Logion 45.

20. Naimy, M. *The book of Mirdad.* New York: Penguin Books, 1962.

21. Golas, Thaddeus. *The Lazy Man's Guide to Enlightenment.* New York: Bantam Books, 1972.

22. See *New Pathways in Psychology: Maslow and the Post-Freudian Revolution* by Colin Wilson (Taplinger, 1972), for an expansion of this idea.

23. This quote and analogy of the oyster is taken from *Sermons and Prayers of Peter Marshall,* edited by Catherine Marshall, in the sermon entitled, "Mr. Jones Meets the Master" (Fleming H. Revell Co., 1949, 1950).

24. Suggested readings:

    Freud, Sigmund. *The Standard Edition of the Complete Psychological Works of Sigmund Freud,* Vol. 19, "The Ego and the Id," James Strachey, ed. London: Hogarth Press, 1953–1964.

    Horney, K. *The Neurotic Personality of Our Time.* New York: Norton, 1968.

    Jung, Carl. *The Collected Works of C. G. Jung,* Vol. 9, Part 1, "The Archetypes and the Collective Unconscious," Bollingen Series XX, Princeton, N.J.: Princeton University Press.

    Sullivan, H. S. *The Interpersonal Theory of Psychiatry.* New York: Norton, 1953.

25. Wilber, Ken. "Psychologie Perennis: The Spectrum of Consciousness." *Journal of Transpersonal Psychology,* 1975, Vol. 7, No. 2: 121.

26. Maslow, A.H. *The Farther Reaches of Human Nature.* New York: Viking Press, 1971. pp. 280–295.

27. Karmic Balancing — In Hindu philosophy, the Law of Karma is the Law of Retribution which balances out everything in the universe, based on the Law of Energy. Everything must finally come to the zero point, where no energy remains in an event, either positive or negative. This Law has been interpreted in the Judeo-Christian religion in a judgmental manner, "an eye for an eye"

and "as ye sow, so shall ye reap." But the Law of Karma was never intended to be construed as punishment. It has nothing to do with morality; it is a fact of nature, as evidenced in the law of physics that states "for every force, there is an equal and opposite force that counteracts it."

Hindu philosophy teaches that we reincarnate in order to balance experiences and relationships that still contain energy, either positive or negative. One will return to make positive an unfinished negative experience — or to complete a positive experience to which the person is still attached. According to this Law, if one dies addicted to something (cigarettes, alcohol, etc.), the Soul will seek ways to re-embody in order to complete the addiction. Some say the Soul becomes earthbound, literally "hanging around" persons who are addicted to a particular attachment. Or it will choose another lifetime addicted to the same substance.

"Karmic balancing" explains why we are sometimes receiving a negative or positive experience in this life that we feel we do not deserve. If we were able to view the whole picture of our Soul's entire evolutionary process we would be able to observe the balancing that is presently occurring.

28. In Eastern philosophy, the three aspects of the Higher Nature are called Satchitananda — "sat" means Truth, "chit" means consciousness, and "ananda" means bliss.

29. Rama, Swami, Ballantine, R. and Ajaya, Swami. *Yoga and Psychotherapy, the Evolution of Consciousness.* Glenview, Illinois: Himalayan Institute, 1976. p. 222.

30. As quoted on page 54 of the above work. The original research referred to is the following: Waters, Frank. *The Book of Hopi.* New York: Ballentine Books, 1963. pp. 10–11.

31. Nicoll, Maurice. *The Mark.* London & Dulverton: Watkins, 1981. p. 20.

32. Haich, Elisabeth. *Initiation.* Palo Alto, Calif.: Seed Center, 1974. p. 366.

33. Small, Jacquelyn. *Becoming Naturally Therapeutic,* rev. ed., Austin, Texas: Eupsychian Press, 950 Roadrunner Road, Austin, TX 78746. To order: send $5.95 plus $1.00 postage/handling. (Special discounts for quantity orders given — write publisher).

34. My special thanks to Dr. John Enright for helping me to conceptualize this.

35. As told in *Emotion to Enlightenment* by Swami Rama and Swami Ajaya. Honesdale, Pa.: Himalayan Institute, 1976.

36. Besant, Annie. *The Seven Principles in Man.* Wheaton, Ill.: The Theosophical Publishing House, 1972. pg. 30.

37. My thanks to Anne Hubbell Maiden, who gave us this Govinda quote in a Psychosynthesis workshop in California in 1980. In our group's study of resistance, many of the Seed Thoughts given in this book were clarified.

38. Haich, Elisabeth. *Initiation.* Palo Alto, CA: Seed Center, 1974. p. 366.

39. Prem, Sri Krishna and Ashish, Sri Madhava. *Man, the Measure of All Things.* Wheaton, Ill.: The Theosophical Publishing House, 1969, p. 23.

40. Pfeiffer, Franz. *Meister Eckhart,* Vol. 1 and 2. Gordon Press, 1977.

41. My special thanks to my friend and occasional co-leader, Dr. Art Brownell, for this concept.

42. See the book *Frogs Into Princes: Neuro Linguistic Programming* by Robert Bandler and John Grinder (Real People Press, Moab, Utah, 1979) for an excellent introduction to neuro-linguistic programming.

43. Those of you wishing to become familiar with the scientific exploration of the Doctrine of Rebirth will be interested in reading *Reincarnation, an East-West Anthology,* Joseph Head and S. L. Cranston, eds. (Wheaton, Ill.: The Theosophical Publishing House, 1968). Especially of interest will be pages 285–304, "Scientists and Psychologists on Reincarnation."

44. Paulos, Jean, Ph.D. and Stoddard, Donald, Ph.D. "Sugar to Booze to Blues." *Journal of Health Sciences,* Nov., 1980. Vol. 1, No. 1: 34–37.

45. See *Ego, Hunger and Aggression: The Beginning of Gestalt Therapy,* by Fritz Perls, for a comprehensive study of the philosophy of Gestalt Therapy.

46. Thera, Nyanoponika. *The Power of Mindfulness.* San Francisco, Ca.; Unity Press, 1972.

47. Read *Narcissus and Goldmund* by Hermann Hesse (New York: Bantam Books, 1971) for a profound statement about following the Path of the Senses as a way toward Truth.

48. Gerard, D. L., Saenger, G., and Wile, R. "The Abstinent Alcoholic." *Archives of General Psychiatry,* 1962. 6: 99–111.

    Small, J. and Wolf, S. "Beyond Abstinence." *Alcohol Health and Research World,* NIAAA, 1978, Vol. 2, No. 3: 32–36.

49. Quote from the Jewish Mystic, Baal Shem Tov., in *The Torah, Genesis, A Modern Commentary,* by W. Gunther Plaut. (New York: Union of American Hebrew Congregations, 1974.)

50. Maslow, A. H. *Religion, Values and Peak Experiences.* New York: Viking Press, 1970. pp. 59–68.

51. Natural food grocery stores offer a variety of coffee and sugar substitute products that are delicious *and* nutritious. Also, several herbal tea companies offer rich, full-bodied tea blends that taste good with cream which satisfies one's craving for coffee. Food shopping patterns can change and offer an exciting new adventure. An excellent resource for a general and wholistic view of nutrition and diet is *Diet and Nutrition* by Rudolph Ballentine. (Honesdale, Pa.: The Himalayan Institute). Also *Laurel's Kitchen* by Laurel Robertson, Carol Flinders & Bronwen Godfrey is a wonderful reference for wholesome and nutritious recipes while also being an excellent handbook on nutrition. (Berkeley, Ca.: Nilgiri Press, 1976).

52. The practice of harmlessness is a self-discipline, practiced moment by moment by not allowing ourselves to say, think, or do any actions that produce harm to any living creature. You can see how this will dissolve karmic predicaments, because it sets up no new negative causes.

53. Hall, Manly P. *Self-Unfoldment by Disciplines of Self-Realization.* Los Angeles: The Philosophical Research Society, Inc., 1942. p. 113.

54. More beautiful lyrics by Bobby Bridger from his record album, *Heal in the Wisdom,* reproduced by permission. © 1981 Stareyes, ASCAP.

55. My special thanks to Dr. Edith Stauffer, who has served as one of my teachers, for her loving understanding of forgiveness and in helping me to formulate the *specificity* with which we must work on this task.

56. There is an increasing number of selections of music for relaxation, meditation and guided imagery. A large selection of these tapes and records is available from Book People, 503 W. 17th Street, Austin, Texas 78701. (512) 476-0116. The following are especially good for use in guided imagery and relaxation: Ron Dexter's *Golden Voyage, Vol I–111* (sold separately), Pachabel's *Canon in D,* Marcus Allen's *Breathe* and *Petals.* Each of these mentioned is available in record and cassette tape.

57. Adapted from Roberto Assagioli's *Psychosynthesis.* (See Bibliography).

Appendix 5 — Seed Thoughts

Our inner state of mind determines our outer life, not the other way around. (p. 5)

A seed thought is an idea whose time has come that takes hold and changes our reality. (p. 21)

Transformation does not occur from changes in the world outside us; *we* create the miracle.... from within! (p. 21)

When we decide to let go of the addiction, by the act of surrender to the Higher Power — an action willed by the True Self — we draw from within ourselves that quality of the True Self that the addiction was masking. Now we are ready to manifest it. (p. 23)

Transformation is not trying to be another way, pushing for the answer.... it is being the answer. Be *now* who you want to be.... even if you "think" you can't! (p. 24)

All suffering is the result of infringement of universal principles. (p. 25)

Conditions that seem opposed to our highest good are merely chances to test out the truth principle we are currently being exposed to in order to expand our consciousness. (p. 34)

No one comes into my pathway by accident. (p. 40)

Love points the way for us to express our human nature; Truth makes these ways possible. (p. 43)

We can recognize an addiction by its lack of life-giving qualities. It drains us of our prime energy, the energy to Self-create. (p. 46)

In personality we are many, in Essence we are one. (p. 52)

When the natural drive at each level of consciousness is allowed to express itself, we move gracefully and with ease toward personality integration. If these urges are thwarted, dis-ease sets in. (p. 55)

The ego will continually draw us backwards, toward the level where the unmet need exists, *until the need is met.* (p. 60)

Victimhood is a myth that only leads to powerlessness. (p. 61)

Being stuck in the past is just another form illusion can take. The message seems to be: Complete, with honesty, whatever is bothering you, and then.... stop looking back. (p. 62)

The highest part of us can only exist when there is energy to move it, and this energy is the overflowing from the lower levels of our experiencing. (p. 66–67)

Addiction is non-growth.... a way of being stuck in the past. If a natural urge has been thwarted, addictions set in. Therefore, addiction can be viewed as blocked creative energy. (p. 70).

The Lower Self operates in the world of strife consciousness. (p. 77)

If I die to the dictates of my ego and surrender to the Higher Self, the Self I really am, I will be reborn into Truth. (p. 83)

Transferring energy from outer-dominance to inner-dominance, from ego to Essence, is the work of transformation. (p. 111)

When we *realize* a total concept of something *as we are experiencing it,* we are for that moment perfect. (p. 117)

Our life is the outcome of the images we weave in our mind based on the illusory stuff of the ego. As it seeks to gratify itself in its self-made reality, it opts for dependence on outside things that it thinks it needs. (p. 129)

Because we can change our thinking, we can change our lives. Heaven and Hell are nothing but states of consciousness. (p. 136)

One does not have to be fully enlightened to work from the enlightenment model consciousness. (p. 140)

Transforming is effortless because there is nothing to be done; there is only someone to *be.* (p. 144)

You have forgotten yourself, and that is your only fault. (p. 147)

Self-knowledge is knowledge of the Spirit and does not belong to any sect or religious group. (p. 150)

My problem is a teacher to me — a vital contact with my past that I am to attend to and make conscious. It has surfaced so I can know it. (p. 156)

The body knows and the soul knows: only our minds can lie! (p. 669)

Emotion follows thought. (p. 175)

The Self is greater than its conditions. (p. 182)

We can only leave behind us what we have mastered, balanced or outgrown. (p. 188)

Whatever we feed into our minds and then nurture will grow! (p. 194)

All my experiences, including my years of drunkenness, have been perfect: They have afforded me the grounding for understanding human suffering. Now I am prepared for a life of service on The Path of the Heart. (p. 207)

I am creating my future right now by the choices I am making. And I have a wise self within that will guide me to the next right step, if I will be still and listen. (p. 208)

The higher choice will always be a positive one! (p. 208)

We, alone, control our personal destiny. (p. 208)

Life must flow harmoniously from experience to experience. (p. 210)

Since the here and now is "the vanishing point" in time, we are always merely going with the flow. (p. 214)

On the path to Self-creation, the ego must be transcended. But it can only be transcended by working through its needs at the personal and interpersonal levels — *not* by denial or attempting to bypass them. (p. 215)

Bibliography
(AND SUGGESTED READINGS)

Alcyone (Krishnamurti), *At the Feet of the Master,* Wheaton, Ill.: Theosophical Publishing House, 1970.

Anonymous, *The Initiate: Some Impressions of a Great Soul,* N.Y.: Samuel Weiser, 1977.

Assagioli, Roberto, *The Act of Will,* New York: Penguin Books, 1974.

______, *Psychosynthesis,* New York: Penguin Books, 1976.

Bailey, Alice A., *Education in the New Age,* New York: Lucis Press, Ltd., 1954.

Ballentine, Rudolph, *Diet and Nutrition,* Honesdale, Pa.: Himalayan International Institute, 1972.

Besant, Annie, *The Seven Principles of Man,* Wheaton, Ill.: Theosophical Publishing House, 1972.

Capra, F., *The Tao of Physics,* Boulder, Co.: Shambhala Press, 1975.

______, *The Turning Point,* New York, Simon & Schuster, 1982.

Dass, Ram, *The Only Dance There Is,* New York: Doubleday & Co., 1974.

Dass, Ram and Levine, Stephen, *Grist for the Mill,* Unity Press, 1977.

DeRopp, Robert, *The Master Game,* New York: Dell, 1968.

Dimond, S. J. and Beaumont, J. G., *Hemisphere Function in the Human Brain,* New York: John Wiley and Sons, 1974.

Eastcott, Michael, *"I," the Story of the Self,* Wheaton, Ill.: Theosophical Publishing House, 1979.

English, Jane, "Science and Transformation: Levels of Reality in Science and in Consciousness." Unpublished paper, Berkeley, CA.

Ferguson, Marilyn, *The Aquarian Conspiracy: Personal & Social Transformation in the '80's,* Los Angeles: J. P. Tarcher, 1980.

Freud, S., *The Standard Edition of the Complete Psychological Works of Sigmund Freud,* Vol. 19, "The Ego and the Id" (James Strachey, ed.) London: Hogarth Press, 1953–1964.

Gawain, Shakti, *Creative Visualization,* N.Y., Bantam Books, 1982.

Gazzaniga, M., "The Split Brain in Man" in *Perception: Mechanisms and Models,* (Held, R. and Richards, W., ed.) San Francisco, Ca.: W. H. Freeman, 1972.

Gendlin, Eugene, *Focusing,* New York: Everest House, 1978.

Gerard, D. L., Saenger, G., and Wile, R., "The Abstinent Alcoholic" in *Archives of General Psychiatry,* 1962, 6: 99–111.

Golas, Thaddeus, *The Lazy Man's Guide to Enlightenment,* New York: Bantam Books, 1972.

Green, Elmer and Alyce, *Beyond Biofeedback,* Delacorte, 1977.

Guillaumont, Al, Puech, H.-CH., Quispel, G., trls., *The Gospel According to Thomas,* New York: Harper and Row Publishers, Inc., 1959.

Haich, Elisabeth, *Initiation,* Palo Alto, Ca.: The Seed Center, 1974.

Hall, Manly P., *Self-Unfoldment by Disciplines of Self-Realization,* Los Angeles, Ca.: Philosophical Research Society, Inc., 1942.

Head, J. and Cranston, S. L., eds., *Reincarnation, An East-West Anthology,* Wheaton, Ill.: The Theosophical Publishing House, 1968.

Hesse, Herman, *Narcissus and Goldmund,* New York: Bantam Books, 1971.

————, *Siddhartha,* New York: Farrar, Straus and Giroux, 1975.

Hoeller, Stephen. *The Gnostic Jung and the Seven Sermons to the Dead.* Wheaton, Ill.: Theosophical Publishing House, 1982.

Horney, Karen, *The Neurotic Personality of Our Time,* New York: Norton, 1968.

Houston, Jean, *The Possible Human: A Course in Extending Your Physical, Mental and Creative Abilities.* Los Angeles: J. P. Tarcher, 1982.

Jampolsky, Gerald, *Love Is Letting Go of Fear,* New York: Bantam Books, 1979.

Jaynes, J., *The Origin of Consciousness in the Breakdown of the Bicameral Mind,* Boston: Houghton Mifflin, 1976.

Joy, W. Brugh, *Joy's Way,* St. Martin Press, 1979.

Jung, Carl, *The Collected Works of C. G. Jung,* Vol. 9, Part 1, "The Archetypes and the Collective Unconscious," Bollingen Series XX, Princeton: Princeton University Press.

Karagulla, Shafica, *Breakthrough to Creativity,* Marina del Rey, Ca., DeVorss & Co., 1967.

Keyes, Ken, Jr., *Handbook to Higher Consciousness,* Coos Bay, Oregon: Living Love Publications, 1972.

Kitselman, A. L., *E-Therapy,* New York: Institute of Integration.

Koile, Earl A., *Listening As a Way of Becoming,* Waco, Tx.: Word Books, 1977.

Mascaro, Juan, tr., *The Bhagavad Gita,* New York: Viking Penguin, 1962.

Maslow, A. H., *The Farther Reaches of Human Nature,* New York: Viking Press, 1970.

______, *Motivation and Personality,* New York: Harper & Row, 1970.

______, *Religions, Values and Peak Experiences,* New York: Viking Press, 1970.

______, *Toward a Psychology of Being,* Princeton, New Jersey: Van Nostrand Reinhold, 1968.

Nicoll, Maurice, *Psychological Commentaries* (on the teachings of G. I. Gurdjieff and P. D. Ouspensky), London: Watkins, 1975, Vol. 1–5.

Ornstein, Robert, *The Psychology of Consciousness,* New York: Harcourt, Brace and Jovanovich, 1977.

Oyle, Irving, *The New American Medicine Show: Discovering the Healing Connection,* Unity Press, 1979.

Paulos, Jean and Stoddard, Donald, "Sugar to Booze to Blues," in *Journal of Health Sciences,* Vol. 1, No. 1, 1980.

Pearce, Joseph C., *The Crack in the Cosmic Egg,* New York: Simon & Schuster, 1971.

Perls, Fritz, *Ego, Hunger and Aggression: The Beginning of Gestalt Therapy,* New York: Random House, 1969.

Pfeiffer, Franz, *Meister Eckhart,* Vol. 1 and 2, Gordon Press, 1977.

Pirsig, Robert, *Zen and the Art of Motorcycle Maintenance: An Inquiry into Values,* New York: Bantam Books, 1976.

Prem, Sri Krishna and Ashish, Sri Madhava, *Man, the Measure of All Things,* Wheaton, Ill.: Theosophical Publishing House, 1969.

Rajneesh, Bhagwan Shree, *The Psychology of the Esoteric,* New York: Harper and Row, 1978.

Rama, Swami and Ajaya, Swami (Allen Weinstock, Ph.D.), *Emotion to Enlightenment,* Honesdale, Pa.: Himalayan International Institute, 1976.

Rama, Swami, Ajaya, Swami and Ballantine, R., *Yoga and Psychotherapy: The Evolution of Consciousness,* Honesdale, Pa.: Himalayan International Institute, 1976.

Satprem, *Sri Aurobindo, or the Adventure of Consciousness,* Harper & Row, 1968.

Selzer, Richard, *Mortal Lessons,* New York: Simon and Schuster, 1976.

Silverstein, Lee, *Consider the Alternative,* CompCare, 1977.

Small, Jacquelyn, *Becoming Naturally Therapeutic,* Revised ed., Austin, Tx.: The Eupsychian Press, 1981.

Small, Jacquelyn and Wolf, Sidney, "Beyond Abstinence," *Alcohol, Health and Research World,* Vol. 2, No. 3, Washington DC: NIAAA, 1978, p. 34–37.

Speeth, Kathleen Riordan, *The Gurdjieff Work,* Berkeley, Ca.: And/Or Press, 1976.

Stewart, Rosemarie, ed., *East Meets West: The Transpersonal Approach,* Wheaton, Ill, Theosophical Publishing House, 1981.

Sullivan, H. S., *The Interpersonal Theory of Psychiatry,* New York: Norton, 1953.

Tart, Charles, ed., *Transpersonal Psychologies,* New York: Harper and Row, 1977.

Taylor, Gordon Rattray, *The Natural History of the Mind,* New York: Penguin Books, 1981.

Thera, Nyanoponika, *The Power of Mindfulness,* San Francisco, Ca.; Unity Press, 1972.

Trungpa, Chogyam, *Cutting Through Spiritual Materialism,* Boulder, Co.: Shambhala Press, 1973.

Waters, Frank, *The Book of Hopi,* New York: Ballantine Books, 1963.

Watts, Alan W., *The Wisdom of Insecurity,* New York: Random House, 1968.

Weil, Andrew, *The Natural Mind, a New Way of Looking at Drugs and the Higher Consciousness,* New York: Houghton Mifflin, 1972.

Wilber, Ken, "Psychologie Perennis: The Spectrum of Consciousness" in *Journal of Transpersonal Psychology,* Vol. 7, No. 2, 1975, p. 121.

Wilson, Colin, *New Pathways in Psychology: Maslow and the Post-Freudian Revolution,* Taplinger Press, 1972.